Jonathan & Lynn Sixsmith

— the pen is still mightier than the sword!

Much love

18 December 2006

Articles of Faith

Articles of Faith

The Story of British Intellectual Journalism

Neil Berry

First published in 2002 by

THE WAYWISER PRESS

9 Woodstock Road, London N4 3ET, UK

T: +44 (0)20 8374 5526
F: +44 (0)20 8374 5736

waywiserpress@aol.com
www.waywiser-press.com

Editor
Philip Hoy

A CIP catalogue record for this book is available from the British Library

ISBN 1-904130-08-9

Printed and Bound by
T.J. International Ltd., Padstow, Cornwall PL28 8RW, UK

For my daughter, Emily,

and in memory of my mother and father,

Doris and Ernest Berry

‘For he that writes may be considered as a sort of general challenger whom everyone has a right to attack, since he quits the common ranks of life, steps forward beyond the common lists and offers his merits to public judgement. To commence author is to claim praise, and no man can justly aspire to honour but at the hazard of disgrace.’

Dr Johnson, *The Rambler*, No. 93, 5 February 1751

Contents

Illustrations

Acknowledgements

This book owes more than a little to conversations formal and informal which the author has enjoyed with Karl Miller over a period of more than twenty years.

It also owes much to another metropolitan man of letters, Alan Ross, who edited the *London Magazine* from 1961 until his death in February 2001, and who published early versions of the chapters, 'The Reviewer Triumphant', 'Ideologues of Destiny' and 'Miller's Millennium', helping to sustain me in what seemed to some to be a madly specialised enterprise. A poet who was also a cricket enthusiast and devotee of the turf, Alan could seem like the last amateur. But his biographer may well conclude that his steadfast efforts as a nurturer of writers and artists were bound up with an antediluvian sense of public service.

At various stages in the book's gestation, I derived stimulus from interviews with the following people: Norman MacKenzie, John Freeman, Clive James, Dan Jacobson, Stuart Hood, Frank Kermode, George Steiner, the late Isaiah Berlin, Anthony Howard, John Gross, the late Stephen Spender and his wife, Natasha Spender, Francis Wyndham, the late Noel Annan, the late Janet Adam Smith, Conor Cruise O'Brien, Paul Johnson, Peregrine Worsthorne, Claire Tomalin, Jonathan Miller, Richard Wollheim, D.A.N. Jones, Neal Ascherson and the late Ian Hamilton.

At all stages in the writing of *Articles of Faith*, I have been a beneficiary of the London Library, its obliging staff and its superlative collection of periodicals. Situated in St James's Square, adjacent to the gentlemen's clubs of Pall Mall, the Library was a favourite resort of Kingsley Martin and other intellectual journalists who figure in the following pages; indeed, this essentially

Victorian repository of polite learning in a way belongs to the story which I set out to tell.

Another library that proved of great use to me was Sussex University's. I am indebted to Elizabeth Inglis for having kindly given me access to Martin's papers, which are held in the library's Special Collections section.

In less specific terms, I am also indebted to: Letty Blyth, Zo Sinclair, Tony Rowlands, Gill Shephard and Peter Loizos, Harvey, Luke and Nathan Rendell, Nick Rankin and Maggie Gee, Richard West and Elizabeth Cain, Jenny Shaw, Richard Lafferty, Bill and Linda Katz, Steve Williams, Lucy Browne, Raymond and Maureen Berry, John Bradley, Dave Ball and Dave Eames.

Separate thanks are due to the editors of the *Times Literary Supplement* for printing an extract from my chapter 'The Chief', and to Grace Eckley, editor of the journal *NewsStead*, for publishing a draft of the chapter, 'The Distinguished Functionary'.

Finally, I should like to thank Peter Dale for having reading the book in manuscript and making many useful suggestions.

Introduction

Throughout the nineteenth century, and for much of the twentieth, it was the patrician class that set the British cultural tone. And nowhere was the mind-set of that class more manifest than in the pages of Britain's voluminous periodical press. During the Victorian era, political and literary periodicals like the *Edinburgh Review* and the *Quarterly Review* made the culture of patrician Britain familiar to the rest of the world. In the twentieth century, such journalism perhaps found most telling expression in the form of highbrow weeklies, foremost among them the *New Statesman*, once a paper of world-wide renown. In common with the great Victorian Reviews, the *New Statesman* brimmed with that peculiarly British patrician quality: high-mindedness. In common with them, too, it was in many ways a creature of empire, a weekly paper which – even as it argued the case for de-colonisation – projected the moral authority of a nation steeped in the exercise of imperial power.

Arguably a British invention, intellectual journalism is a field to which Britain has not only made a major historic contribution but to which it makes a significant contribution still. Founded in 1902, the *Times Literary Supplement* remains a British Review of international standing. And since it began publication in 1979, the *London Review of Books* has come to enjoy comparable prestige. Minority status notwithstanding, these polished, erudite, cosmopolitan periodicals are probably more widely and attentively read outside Britain than any of the country's mass circulation newspapers. Well-wrought discussion is a universal currency.

Asked for his opinion of Western civilisation, Mahatma Gandhi tartly remarked that it would be a good idea. Yet it was precisely for 'civilization' that exponents of Britain's 'higher journalism' believed themselves to stand, and many, especially perhaps in India, where the *New Statesman* used to elicit reverence, seemed ready to accept them at their own valuation. Indeed, British intellectual periodicals did more than a little to nourish the phenomenon of Anglophilia – or 'Anglomania', to borrow the subtitle of Ian Buruma's book, *Voltaire's Coconuts* (1999), which sets out to explain the cachet that has attached to British upper-crust mores in the eyes of foreign (chiefly European) observers. Much that anglophiles in France and Germany and elsewhere envied about Britain went into the making of the 'higher journalism', qualities long taken to be synonymous with that fabled British creation, the gentleman, such as poise, urbanity and fair-mindedness. That there was an old and intimate connection between the gentleman and the journalism in question needs no underlining.

My own introduction to highbrow Reviews took place in the late 1960s. For me, a print-addicted Liverpool teenager, discovering papers like the *New Statesman* and the *Listener* (the BBC weekly which closed down in 1991) was a formative experience. Here, in contrast to much of the rest of the press, was journalism which conjured up a world where bookishness, wit and choice phraseology were the stuff of human intercourse. Of course, I was by no means the first person to have felt that Reviews were instruments of self-improvement. The propagation of enlightenment was central to the historic *raison d'être* of such publications, and there had always been individuals, especially among sections of society bereft of formal education, whose eyes they helped to open. Consider the case of the Scottish poet and man of letters, Edwin Muir. In the early years of the twentieth century, friendless, poor and desperate to better himself, Muir frequented a Glasgow public library and studied the well-thumbed volumes of Victorian Reviews held there for hour after hour. Reviews were Muir's salvation, and like many a Scot before and since he went on to become an assiduous reviewer himself.

Kingsley Amis's novel, *Take a Girl Like You* (1960), features a character who is scoffed at as a 'stooge' on account of his penchant for keeping old copies of the *New Statesman* and arranging them in chronological order. Yet at the height of its fame, a byword for brilliant prose and mental provocation, the *New Statesman* really was a periodical around which many people's lives more or less revolved. Amis was a great *New Statesman* aficionado himself. Along with its rival, the *Spectator*, the paper occupied a special place in his surly affections. In the fullness of time, this literary John Bull was to edit an anthology of writings on the 1960s wholly made up of *New Statesman* and *Spectator* articles, declaring in his introduction to the book that for bracing breadth and challenging intelligence these venerable national institutions were without parallel in the English-speaking world.

Not without setbacks, the *New Statesman* and the *Spectator*, the latter of the Right, the former of the Left, have kept going. Monuments to the British periodical press of yore, they may outlast us all. Nevertheless, the 1960s – heralding as they did the emergence of today's hectic, multi-media communications industry – marked a watershed in the history of old-style Reviews. It was the sense that the heyday of the 'higher journalism' was over that piqued my curiosity about its genealogy. Here, it seemed, was a fertile field of inquiry – territory into which few had hitherto ventured. As a postgraduate student at University College London, in the early 1980s, I applied myself to researching a thesis on the *Edinburgh Review* as edited by Francis Jeffrey at the beginning of the nineteenth century. By common consent, this was an episode which inaugurated modern reviewing practice, establishing in the process stringent new standards of public discussion.

Research is a solitary business. But those who embark on it are obliged to report from time to time to an academic supervisor. In Karl Miller, a veteran literary journalist turned university professor, I was lucky to find a supervisor who needed no persuading that mine was a subject crying out for scholarly investigation; what is more, he could even be seen as part of that subject in his own person. The fact was that Miller, whose own roots were in Edinburgh, had formerly worked as literary editor of both the *Spectator* and the *New Statesman* and as editor of the *Listener.* That he was now consumingly busy not just as a professor but also as the editor of the intellectually exacting new journal, the *London Review of Books*, suggested to me that the career of this severe Scotsman and the legacy of the *Edinburgh Review* were all of a piece. Albeit dimly, I could already see the potential for a book which began with the Scotch reviewers of Jeffrey's day and ended with the multifarious literary activities of Miller himself.

Slumped in his office on a *chaise longue* and looking full of years, the Karl Miller with whom I grew familiar was much given to issuing news bulletins on the war of attrition that he was waging against insomnia and ill-health. Wintry wit spiced the talk of a middle-aged literary man appalled by the anti-intellectual government of Margaret Thatcher and apt to seem like an old king living in reduced circumstances. Yet even when he showed signs of being about to subside once and for all, Miller's mental energy remained formidable – and so did his pedagogic demands: here, it seemed, was a flesh-and-blood exemplar of that *perfervidum ingenium* long ago identified as an archetypal Scotch attribute. Much dogged, apparently thankless submitting of draft chapters on my part went on before he at length conceded that there had been a 'gain in penetration of the material'. Miller's approbation, it will be gathered, was nothing if not hard-won. Despite, or perhaps because of this, journalists and students alike spared no efforts in trying to impress him.

Just how fit a place University College was for studying the *Edinburgh Review* I did not at first grasp. It was not immediately apparent to me, either, how appropriate it was that Miller the Scotch reviewer should have become a London Professor of English Literature. For the creation of a university in London owed a lot to Scotsmen and Scottish intellectual pressure. It was thanks in some measure to *Edinburgh Review* polemicizing orchestrated by Jeffrey that the university took shape in the mid-1820s as a modern metropolitan alternative to Oxford and Cambridge, free from the eccesiastical restrictions and the academic and social exclusiveness of those medieval foundations. Moreover, in the background of reviewers and university alike, lay the Scottish Enlightenment, the eighteenth century cultural awakening that spawned a seminal body of Scotch writing concerned with the evolution of civil society and much biased towards the proposition that intellectual enquiry is at once democratic work and a contribution to the common good.

Like a number of Scottish literati of previous times, Miller acted on the assumption that teaching students and publishing reviews were simply different aspects of the same enterprise. The present book – a selective but wide-ranging study of the 'higher journalism' in Britain which culminates in an appraisal of Miller's journalistic career – explores the historic significance of Scotch reviewers and their role in championing what has been termed the 'democratic intellect'. But the book is not concerned solely with the part played in the development of the periodical press by Scotland, by the culture of Calvinism – sizeable though that has undeniably been. Designed to shed light on the remarkable tradition of politico-cultural journalism that sprang from the *Edinburgh Review*, it also attempts to anatomize that self-styled presidential figure, the intellectual editor, and encompasses such guiding spirits of Victorian reviewing as John Morley, W.T. Stead and James Knowles, Englishmen all three, as well as that English eminence among modern intellectual editors, Kingsley Martin, who, in common with Morley and Stead, was a cradle Puritan soaked in the influence of Nonconformism. It includes, too, a chapter on the American Jewish ideologues, Melvin Lasky prominent among them, whose lives became inseparable from the Anglo-American magazine, *Encounter*, founded in London in 1953 and fashioned after the great political and literary Reviews of the nineteenth century.

With the CIA as their secret patrons, *Encounter*'s executives were Cold War conservatives, votaries of the Right. But where they and the higher journalism's left/liberal exponents were akin was in the more or less religious zeal that they brought to their labours. What now seems remarkable is how often the luminaries of the intellectual press have been Puritans or Jews by birth with a sense of themselves as members of the Elect, and a quasi-Biblical belief in the primacy of the word and the inescapability of judgement. It may be that the great Reviews of the past were conduits of 'spilt religion', of displaced proselytising, and that the articles enshrined in them were articles of faith.

If the energies poured into British Reviews derived from secularised religiosity, they were also bound up with a sense of national, not to say racial, destiny. Contributors to British intellectual periodicals could be said to have been caught up in an epoch-making corporate endeavour to bring to fruition a mature society, a 'rational' and 'enlightened' Britain that could serve as a beacon of progress to the rest of the world. Throughout the period when imperial Britain's writ ran far and wide, and even afterwards, British reviewers seldom seem to have doubted the global import of all things British, or their right to set themselves up as mentors of mankind. Something of this anglocentric sense of the special authority vested in British reviewing was, I believe, still being nursed by Karl Miller in recent times. In many ways the heir of the self-consciously 'British' *Edinburgh* reviewers of the nineteenth century, this Scottish editor of London-based Reviews was much at home in the role of metropolitan bringer of light.

Described by W.T. Stead as the 'forum of civilisation', the periodical press was an enduring influence on British 'official' thinking and did much to shape the 'civilised' Britain that emerged in the course of the twentieth century, with its Welfare State, public service broadcasting corporation and vaunted commitment to raising general educational standards. There was a time when an intimate rapport obtained between high political circles and the 'higher journalism'. Aside from reaching swelling numbers of ordinary readers, the copious articles published in Reviews were once the routine reading matter of the British political élite; indeed, it was far from unusual for ministers of state to compose such articles themselves. During this high season of the Review, intellectual editors were heeded figures, consciences of the nation who upheld the principle that public and private conduct is best based on knowledge and reflection – as crystallised by a well-written contribution to their magisterial pages.

The 'higher journalism' may be said to have reached its historic zenith when Kingsley Martin was presiding over the *New Statesman* during the middle decades of the twentieth century. The last great highbrow editor of the pre-television era (today he seems like a Victorian manqué), Martin was committed to creating the definitive Review, a publication that no intelligent human being could possibly be without. His success was phenomenal; the weekly paper edited by him engrossed the attention of thinking people everywhere, challenging them and irritating them in equal measure. A believer in social planning who was himself a cranky individualist, Martin personified the humanist optimism of the eighteenth century, together with the do-gooding impulse, the ethic of *noblesse oblige* long characteristic of the British gentry. It was Kingsley Martin's example, I argue in this book, that Karl Miller sought to emulate – at a time when the old periodical press was becoming a marginalised medium, when the very culture that nurtured it was slipping into history.

I

Francis Jeffrey and the Birth of the 'Higher Journalism'

> 'There is a northern junto of periodical writers, who have rendered themselves extremely formidable to us poor authors, and to whom such of us, as have viands at our command, offer them as Indians do their oblations to the devil; while they, who know we do not incense them out of love but fear, receive our knee-worship with indifference and despise us for our meanness.'
>
> Richard Cumberland,
> *The Memoirs of Richard Cumberland*, 1807

Francis Jeffrey

1. The Reviewer Triumphant

The prime of the *Edinburgh Review* was a chastening time for authors. Thanks to the sprightly example of Francis Jeffrey, the journal's editor from 1802 till 1829, reviewing assumed a formidable new eminence at the beginning of the nineteenth century, and writing books came close to being robbed of all dignity. An Edinburgh barrister by profession, who did his editing and reviewing in his spare time, Jeffrey was a scourge of literary 'delinquents' and 'blockheads'. It was, he fervently believed, the reviewer's duty to subject overweening authors to the 'wholesome discipline of derision'. With a mixture of high-mindedness, glee and no little superciliousness, he conducted himself like a literary policeman, brusquely rebuffing unworthy aspirants to the republic of letters. Among the victims of his critical severity were Wordsworth, Coleridge and Southey, poets comprising what Jeffrey christened the 'Lake School'. Wordsworth was regularly pilloried in the *Edinburgh Review*'s punitive, keenly read, pages. As a reformist Scottish Whig, Jeffrey objected to Wordsworth as a simple-minded enthusiast for the French Revolution, depicting him as a bucolic buffoon, much given to mouthing 'babyisms'. No one could have guessed that in private Jeffrey was capable of being moved to tears by Wordsworth's verse. But that is another story.

Scathing reviews often make their victims' blood boil, and it is perhaps surprising that this merciless critic never met with physical retribution. He came close enough. Persecuted almost beyond endurance, and nothing if not thin-skinned, Wordsworth itched for the chance to kick his Scotch tormentor in his breech. Another poet, the Irishman, Tom Moore, stung by the *Edinburgh Review*'s censorious treatment of his latest volume of amorous verse, wasted no time in challenging Jeffrey to a duel. One summer morning in 1806, the two men of letters, both of diminutive stature, met at Chalk Farm, north London, armed with pistols and apparently ready to open fire on one another. The encounter might have resulted in bloodshed, or worse, but for the timely intervention of the Bow Street Runners, who placed the ridiculous pair under arrest. In a rum sequel to the affair, Jeffrey and Moore became good friends; and Moore, likewise a staunch Whig, later made his own début as a slashing *Edinburgh* reviewer, flaying hapless authors quite as hard as Jeffrey ever did.

'Tis strange the mind, that very fiery particle / Should let itself be snuffed out by an article': Byron's sally (prompted by Keats, who was acidly reviewed and who, shortly afterwards, died) was no mere joke. Against the background of a burgeoning reading public, reviewers in the early nineteenth century discovered a new power to terrorise authors. Indeed, Jeffrey had successors – like Keats's foes, the swaggering young hotheads of *Blackwood's Edinburgh Magazine,* founded in 1817 – who carried vituperative reviewing to ugly extremes. (Some years after the confrontation between Moore and Jeffrey, another Scottish editor, John Scott, was shot dead in a duel inspired by *Blackwood's* 'brutalities'.) By comparison, Jeffrey's reviews, always argued with cogency, were models of restraint, and ultimately he repented (or at least affected to repent) his own youthful 'vivacities'. Nevertheless, the rampancy attained by reviewing during his own lifetime was a matter to which the editor of the *Edinburgh Review* remained proud to be party. 'Judex damnatur cum nocens absolvitur' ran the *Review*'s admonitory motto – the critic stands condemned when the felon is acquitted. And both early and late, the attitude towards books adopted by Jeffrey and his fellow reviewers was: guilty until proved definitely innocent. Revered for its cleverness and wit, the *Edinburgh Review* issued an uncompromising challenge, a warning to authors that they and their works were henceforth to be the occasion of far more searching scrutiny than hitherto. It was an approach that heralded a new era in literary journalism.

Jeffrey stood for editorial independence, something hardly known in former times. Eighteenth-century Reviews were owned and manipulated by booksellers, and it was long taken for granted that their personnel were denizens of that notorious London locality, Grub Street, and that when not 'puffing' their employer's books they were plying poison pens to discredit the wares of his rivals. Recent research, however, has revealed that by no means all their contributors fell into this category. The *Monthly Review,* best-known of the early Reviews, published writings by eminent scholars; and before assuming the editorship of the *Edinburgh Review,* Jeffrey himself wrote for it – as did the costive Scotch literatus, Sir James Mackintosh, later to be among Jeffrey's leading reviewers. Moreover, in the remarkable figure of William Taylor of Norwich, the *Monthly Review,* according to Hazlitt, could boast a writer who patented the 'philosophical' or discursive style of reviewing that became the *Edinburgh Review*'s hallmark. It is true that Ralph Griffiths (1720-1803), who ran the Whiggish *Monthly Review* for half a century, had once published a version of *Fanny Hill,* brazenly puffing the novel in his own journal. But in later years, Griffiths appears to have behaved conscientiously enough, and the *Monthly,* like its Tory rival, the *Critical Review,* drew Dr Johnson's qualified approbation. (Johnson esteemed the *Critical* reviewers for knowing how to 'lay about a topic', even if they did not always 'read the books through'; in his opinion, this placed them above the *Monthly* reviewers, 'duller men' who were 'glad to read the books through'.) Equally esteemed among the *Edinburgh Review*'s precursors was the short-lived *Analytical Review,* run by the Doctor's namesake, Joseph Johnson, a sober-minded Dissenter and laudable champion of the victimised – Jews, women and maltreated animals among them.

Yet the authorship of a lot of the material in the early reviews remains unidentified, and the suspicion cannot be entirely dispelled that there had indeed gathered round them a literary underclass of underpaid and embittered hacks, like the wretches caricatured by Smollett in *Humphrey Clinker* (1771). This was certainly the view of Jeffrey and his fastidious Edinburgh colleagues, who were anxious to project themselves as a new and superior species of reviewer. The fact was that eighteenth-century reviewing involved much work for relatively little pay. It may be felt, too, that something very like drudgery was inherent in the whole enterprise, for the old reviews stuck rigidly to the traditional reviewing ideal of endeavouring to notice all new books – a policy rendered increasingly unrealistic by the ever-growing volume of new publications. Still, at best, Ralph Griffiths and his like were providing a service, satisfying the public appetite for book-news. And for the most part, it has to be said, reviewing had never aspired to do much more than this. The ancestry of the eighteenth-century Review may be traced back to the *Journal des Sçavans,* the first periodical devoted to accounts of new books, begun in Paris in 1665 and largely composed of book summaries. Reviewing before the *Edinburgh Review,* in other words, was often as much a bibliographical as a critical enterprise, and for every contribution essaying anything approximating to rigorous, independent criticism, many more could be cited which are little more than digests. Expansive, discursive criticism like William Taylor's was the exception, not the rule.

The aims of pre-*Edinburgh* reviewing were essentially modest. 'The true design of a literary journal', declared the preface to *Analytical Review* in 1788, 'is to give such an account of new publications as may enable the reader to judge for himself. Whether the writers ought to add to this their own judgement is with us a doubtful point. If their account be sufficiently full and accurate, it seems to supersede the necessity of any addition of their own.' Chiming with this wholly unassuming conception of their role was a tendency, patent throughout the eighteenth-century Reviews towards leniency. If there was a plying of poison pens, there was also much indulgence shown to new books. Indeed, since the booksellers who owned the Reviews usually purveyed other booksellers' stock as well as their own, there was naturally a common interest in eschewing critical severity and settling for a customary blandness.

At all events, just a few years later, the *Edinburgh Review*'s predecessors were recalled – by those who could be bothered to remember them at all – as more or less moribund. It was Walter Scott's view that the 'common Reviews' became 'extremely mawkish', emitting a 'dawdling, mawdlin sort of applause to everything that reached even mediocrity.' However, this was a fairly charitable verdict compared to what Scott's friend, the literary veteran, R. P. Gillies, had to say on the subject. 'Up to the year 1802,' sneered Gillies, 'what pitiful aboritions were our so-styled reviews! The object of their authors was "to give an account of the books" and the notion that upon every occasion, there could be a special drift to contend for, an opportunity caught and improved for benefiting the cause of literature, or politics, or morals, or science, by placing the subject in a new light, seemed never once to have entered the calculations of our self-complacent editors.' With the advantage of hindsight, it was felt that the old reviews had lost whatever vigour they once possessed, in the process becoming vulnerable to any form of energetic and imaginative rivalry. Only a modest amount of enterprise was required to supplant them – and from its inception in October 1802 the *Edinburgh Review,* brimming with intellectual zest and impudence, was nothing if not enterprising. 'Its effect', exulted Jeffrey's friend and pious biographer, Henry Cockburn, 'was electrical ... The old periodical opiates were extinguished at once.'

▼▲▼

Francis Jeffrey dedicated his *Contributions,* the collected *Edinburgh* reviews that he published in 1844, to his old friend Sydney Smith. Ironically, it was the Englishman Smith who projected the *Edinburgh Review,* and who thereby gave Jeffrey the chance to pursue his ambition of matching the literary fame of Adam Smith and David Hume. Destined for great celebrity as a wit, irreverent *Edinburgh* reviewer and portly *bon viveur,* the Reverend Sydney Smith had taken Holy Orders at Oxford before ending up in Edinburgh as tutor to a young aristocrat. Smith's residence in what was then known as the 'Athens of the North' lasted from only 1798 until 1802, but it profitably exposed him to Edinburgh University's strenuous debating societies and to the versatile literati who frequented them – mostly young advocates whose Whiggish sympathies conflicted with their professional prospects in a city then under rigid Tory control. Soaked in the teachings of the eighteenth century Scottish Enlightenment, they included Francis Jeffrey himself, the gifted but volatile Henry Brougham, Francis Horner, student of political economy, John Allen, budding authority on the Constitution, the lawyer John Murray, the visiting English Lord, Webb Seymour, and the Professor of Mathematics, John Playfair. It was these young men who formed the nucleus of the *Edinburgh Review* – and who, in later times, were given to remembering themselves as Whig conspirators, 'concerting' their Review in a hostile Tory city.

Sensing the potential of this talented, tight-knit group to sustain an intellectual Review far superior to the torpid Reviews of the South, Smith assured the publisher Archibald Constable that he would soon own the best Review in Europe – provided that he appoint a wholly independent editor, reward him generously and empower him to pay contributors at treble the existing rate. For Smith and everybody else connected with the Review – not least Jeffrey, who rapidly emerged as editor – the overriding concern was to avoid becoming implicated in a project smacking of book-trade venality. Jeffrey feared that to become known as the editor of a Review was to run the 'risk of degradation', and before committing himself, he sought elaborate assurances from

Constable that the conditions laid down by Smith were going to be honoured in every particular. An anonymous contemporary witness – possibly Scott – stressed what pains were taken to clear the *Edinburgh Review* of anything resembling 'mercenary drudgery', all contributors being equally and amply remunerated regardless of rank. 'If Czar Peter laboured in the trenches,' noted this Edinburgh wag, 'he drew his pay as a common soldier; and thus the degrading distinction was excluded between those whose fortune enabled them to work for nought, and the less fortunate scholar, to whom reward was in some degree an object; the pride of the latter remained unwounded and, mingled as he was among many critics of wealth and rank, it remained a secret known to none but himself, whether he was actuated by any personal motives besides the desire for literary distinction.' The writer added that news of the 'uncommon premium' that was being offered to contributors gave an éclat to the undertaking, indicating that the 'assorted critics claimed a merit and consequence beyond the ordinary class of reviewers; that their band, like the confederates of Gadshill, were no "footland-rakers, no long-staff sixpenny strikers, but nobility and tranquillity, burgomasters and great one-eyers".'

Jeffrey presided over a dramatic transformation in the status of reviewing, and by his own example may be said to have done much to take reviewing out of Grub Street and to establish professional standards in a field where beforehand they had barely existed. When he retired from editing in 1829, it pleased him to reflect that he had 'never dirtied his hands'. On the contrary, he had, he believed, confined himself to dealing 'pretty strictly' with 'gentlemen'. By that stage, the *Edinburgh Review* was an institution, acclaimed by William Hazlitt – himself perhaps only dubiously a gentleman – as the 'highest rank of modern literary society'. With its growing prestige, the *Review* became a magnet for leading writers and thinkers, publishing, in addition to the copious contributions of Brougham, Smith and Jeffrey, the work of

James Mill, Walter Scott, Samuel Taylor Coleridge, Sir James Mackintosh, Tom Moore, Payne Knight, the historian Henry Hallam, William Wilberforce, John Wilson *alias* 'Christopher North', Thomas Babington Macaulay, Thomas Carlyle, P. M. Roget (author of the *Thesaurus)* and Hazlitt himself. In his memoirs, Henry Brougham pointed out that among the *Edinburgh* reviewing corps were those who, while they might never have gone to the length of preparing a book, were yet prepared to work up substantial articles, if not treatises, for the *Edinburgh Review,* confident that their compositions were going to appear in a place of 'respectability' surrounded by 'decent' company. Nonetheless, for all its high-standing, the Review remained a uniformly anonymous publication, anonymity having long been – as it was long to remain – standard journalistic practice, and one that Jeffrey seems to have had no wish to challenge.

Whereas Ralph Griffiths fretted that his *Monthly Review* might alienate readers if it failed to notice every new book, the advertisement drawn up for the first edition of the *Edinburgh Review* spurned any attempt at comprehensiveness. Proclaiming its intention to discuss only books of moment, the advertisement, in its way a revolutionary document, declared:

> Of the books that are daily presented to the world, a very large proportion is evidently destined to obscurity, by the insignificance of the subjects, or the defects of their execution; and it seems unreasonable to expect that the Public should be interested by any account of performances which have never attracted any share of its attention . . . The very lowest order of publications are rejected, accordingly, by most of the literary publications of which the Public are already in possession. But the contributors to the *Edinburgh Review* propose to carry this principle of selection a good deal further; to decline any attempt at exhibiting a complete view of

> modern literature; and to confine their notice, in a very great degree, to works that have either attained, or deserve, a certain portion of celebrity.

This combative statement concluded with the announcement that since its value was not going to depend on the 'earliness of its intelligence', the *Edinburgh Review* would be published at quarterly, not monthly, intervals, as had hitherto been customary with Reviews. Hence, material that appeared in the *Edinburgh Review* enjoyed a much longer gestation time than had contributions to its predecessors, making possible maturer consideration of books and issues arising from them. This, according to the nameless Edinburgh critic cited earlier, was an approach that 'at once added to the merit of the work and greatly enhanced its character with the public' – just as, he felt, did the reviewers' refusal to judge books without first treating the subject at some length, and laying out the grounds of their judgement, so that they could be assented to if reasonable, and rejected if not. 'Thus', the writer sonorously concluded, 'everything in their plan bespoke the purpose of men, capable and confident in their powers, bending themselves gravely to purposes from which they had excluded all that was trifling, vulgar or insignificant.'

In reality, the temptation to pour scorn on literary trivia was one which Jeffrey and his cocksure colleagues made small effort to resist. All the same, the *Edinburgh Review*'s criticism characteristically proceeded from principle. The very first review that appeared in the journal, a review by Jeffrey of Jean-Joseph Mounier's *De L'influence attribuée aux Philosophes, aux Franc-Maçons et aux Illuminés, sur la Revolution de France,* was, in effect, a manifesto, an announcement that for the *Edinburgh Review* books were to be the subject of dispute and argument, and that the ideas enshrined in them would, whenever necessary, be questioned and discussed, not simply summarised with a few critical comments. This opening review, moreover, set the pattern of later *Edinburgh* reviewing, as both a rigorously argued essay and a declaration of faith that there exists an intimate connection between intellectual activity and social progress, between printed argument and political action. In his discussion of Mounier's book, Jeffrey jibbed at the author's materialistic account of the French Revolution, stressing that he had greatly underestimated the impact of the *philosophes*: by directing attention at the failings and corruption of the *ancien régime,* Jeffrey contended, they had 'spread very widely among the people the sentiment of their grievances and rights.'

Jeffrey's sinuous, vivacious prose dazzled his contemporaries. William Taylor of Norwich freely confessed that he was captivated by his Scottish rival's 'comprehensive knowledge', by his 'brilliant and definite expression', and by his 'subtle argumentative power'. Admittedly, such enthusiasm was not often endorsed by later commentators, who were possibly too quick to view Jeffrey in limited literary critical terms, scorning him as Wordsworth's wrong-headed critic and failing to grasp the wider significance of his career. Nor has the style of reviewing practised by Jeffrey – expansive, judicial, supremely self-assured – always won favour. In the British literary scholar, Derek Roper, the old, modest mode of reviewing epitomised by Ralph Griffiths's *Monthly Review* has found a dogged modern champion. Roper believes that the adoption of discursive, argumentative reviewing by Jeffrey and his fellow reviewers led not to a more elevated brand of criticism but to verbal flatulence and ostentatiousness – a view in which he is not alone. Still, the whole issue of what form reviewing ought properly to take is far from easily settled in point of principle, and has long occasioned controversy. Today's descendants of the *Edinburgh Review* – the *New York Review of Books* and the *London Review of Books*, for example – seem to attract adherents and detractors in equal measure, simply on account of the type of enterprise that they represent. Perhaps John Gibson Lockhart – himself a great Victorian exponent of discursive reviewing – was right to say that the 'essay-like fashion of reviewal' introduced by William Taylor was a thing of both merits and demerits, with much to be said both for and against it. By this stage it seems doubtful if a consensus on the matter is ever likely to emerge.

It is a common objection to *Edinburgh*-style reviewing that it amounts to an act of presumption for a reviewer not just to criticise an author but to use his work as an excuse for a composition of the reviewer's own, and to write in relative haste about a book which may have been years in the making. This, it is true, was a practice sometimes taken to extraordinary, not to say extravagant, lengths by the *Edinburgh* reviewers. It is nevertheless true that the *Edinburgh Review,* together with other British and American journals inspired by its success, comprised a literary medium that was to embody much of the nineteenth century's most challenging and enduring discussion. Indeed, such reviewing established itself as the prevailing mode of intellectual discourse, and in exploiting the argumentative and stylistic possibilities of the review-article, Victorian sages like Carlyle, Arnold, Ruskin and Mill could all be said to owe something to Jeffrey's example – as, for that matter, in more recent times, could T. S. Eliot, many of whose most pregnant prose writings were outstanding instances of discursive book-reviewing. What, for good or ill, Jeffrey accomplished in this field was vividly captured by the Scottish journalist, Hugh Miller. Reviewing his career in the 1850s, Miller remarked that Jeffrey was the instigator of a 'mighty revolution in letters' – a revolution which, if it had 'lessened the number of good books', had at the same time 'increased beyond all calculation the number of brilliant articles.'

▼▲▼

Eighteenth-century Reviews were hardly innocent of politics, but the *Edinburgh Review* marked the début of the journal of politics and letters in full modern dress. Got up in a cover of blue and buff – the colours favoured by the Whig grandee, Charles James Fox – the *Edinburgh Review* swiftly caught the attention of the English Whig aristocracy. Among its eager Whig readers was Fox's nephew, Lord Holland, who hailed the *Review* as the 'cleverest periodical criticism ever published' – even if, he wryly added, the reviewers evinced 'full as much of the Executioner as the judge in their composition.' In high Whig circles, Jeffrey himself was rated the 'ablest man in Scotland'; and before long, a symbiotic relationship had been formed between the *Edinburgh Review* and Lord Holland's ancestral home, Holland House, just then winning renown as the most brilliant literary and political salon of its day. (Situated in what is now Holland Park, the House, with its prodigious library, was wrecked by German bombing during the Second World War.) It was, however, not such much Lord Holland as his formidable wife who made Holland House what it was. A divorcée, who was suspected of 'freethinking', Elizabeth Holland held court in the capricious, tyrannical fashion of a salon hostess of the *ancien régime*, while loquacious Edinburgh *philosophes* and the odd refugee – like the Italian poet and novelist, Ugo Foscolo, author of a famed *Edinburgh Review* article on Dante – vied with each other for the chance to display their wit and erudition. This was a milieu which could be said to have had its twentieth-century counterpart in Garsington, the Oxfordshire mansion of Lady Ottoline Morrell and her husband, which also acquired legendary status as a retreat for writers and artists of mostly liberal hue.

By 1805, Sydney Smith was already established among the habitués of Holland House. In that year, Smith wrote to Sir James Mackintosh, then serving as Recorder of India, with news that Lady Holland had 'taken hugely' to him and other Edinburgh reviewers – above all, Horner, Brougham and Allen, who had begun to frequent her circle. Over the next four decades, Scottish reviewers dined regularly at Holland House. These ambitious, intellectually agile, bourgeois critics, none of whom started out with notable pecuniary advantages, were in effect 'taken up', their reviewing and polished table talk having served as instruments of self-advancement. And the perquisites enjoyed by them on account of this special relationship were real enough. Smith's clerical career was furthered by the Hollands, while through Smith's recommendation, John Allen, originally trained as a doctor, obtained a life-long sinecure as Lord Holland's secretary. Nominally librarian of Holland House, the atheistical Allen settled to a cosseted life of freethinking, amateur scholarship and writing and recruiting for the *Edinburgh Review.* Henry Brougham, too, though his relations with the Hollands – as with everybody else – were turbulent, benefited from Lord Holland's favours; the Whig magnate helped to speed his political progress. Later, in the mid-1820s, a notable new recruit of Jeffrey's, Macaulay, had especial reason to appreciate the *Edinburgh Review*/Holland House connection, enabling him as it did to swap obscurity for celebrity. By dint of his dazzling *Edinburgh Review* essay on Milton, he awoke one morning to find himself famous. By nobody more lionised than Lady Holland herself, the tirelessly eloquent and prolific young historian was soon enrolled as a Holland House favourite. Leslie Mitchell, historian of Holland House, has pointed out that the Hollands saw no distinction between patronising aspiring Whig writers and aspiring Whig politicians, though in the case of figures like Brougham and Macaulay there was, as it happened, no distinction to be drawn, since these were men for whom politics and letters were complementary aspects of a public career.

As a literary tyro, Byron had smarted under Jeffrey's lash, and in *English Bards and Scotch Reviewers* (1809), he vengefully depicted the *Edinburgh* reviewers as Holland House hirelings, flattering their hosts in order to guarantee their places at table. Certainly, Holland House commanded Jeffrey's deference. 'The resort of all that was distinguished and the school of all that was amiable and honourable' was how he described the place in its twilight days in the 1840s. Moreover, Jeffrey's political and literary opinions – those of a reformist Whig distrustful of radical innovation – were close enough in the main to Lord Holland's, and there was, perhaps, no part of the *Edinburgh Review*'s readership whose good opinion Jeffrey was keener to canvass. Even so, the *Edinburgh Review* was never a mere Holland House mouthpiece. Above all, Jeffrey fought shy of the Hollands' hero-worship of Napoleon (a romantic cult with a hint, perhaps, of the 'radical chic' sometimes imputed to monied fellow-travellers in recent times). The true relationship between the *Edinburgh Review* and Holland House is more accurately described as one of reciprocal benefits. If Holland House amplified the reviewers' influence and status, they brought to Holland House the fruits of Scottish intellectual enquiry of the previous century, disseminating the progressive Enlightenment ideas of Scottish thinkers like Adam Smith and John Millar and imbuing English Whiggery with new ideological dynamism and cogency.

The first of the great nineteenth-century Reviews, the *Edinburgh Review* inaugurated a new age. Its Tory rival, the *Quarterly Review,* appeared in 1809, to be followed in 1824 by the formidable *Westminster Review,* organ of the 'Philosophical Radicals'. The extended, argumentative reviews and polemics in which these journals trafficked were read with attention in political circles – sometimes occasioning speeches in Parliament, or even becoming their very substance. Hence evolved an intimate and lasting connection between the ruling élite and Reviews, between the political establishment and the 'higher journalism'. In the process, the editor – arbiter now of the great issues of the day, if not of the fate of nations – became an eminence, a figure courted by politicians, who might even enter politics on his own account. Indeed, this elevation of the Review editor can be said to have enhanced the whole stature of editorship in the periodical and daily press alike. As the Victorian era progressed, the editor of a newspaper like the *Times*, earlier held in no special esteem, became a dignitary, too. It was, however, to be many years before the editor of the *Edinburgh Review* felt obliged to yield anything in point of prestige to a mere newspaper editor, and it is instructive to note that when, in 1855, following a long association with the *Times*, Jeffrey's longest-serving Victorian successor, Henry Reeve, became the *Review*'s editor, it was with the sense that his new post represented a kind of professional apotheosis.

Not that at any stage the *Edinburgh Review*'s readership was confined to the higher political echelons. Jeffrey's journal was read all over Europe, and in America, too, where it became an example for the famous *North American Review.* Appalled by its Whig sympathies, Walter Scott was disturbed to note that, politics apart, the quality of the *Edinburgh Review*'s literary criticism was such that *no genteel family could pretend to be without it.* (In the twentieth century, right-wing critics were to voice a similar caveat about the *New Statesman,* whose stylish books pages once drew readers with no initial taste for the paper's left-wing politics.) Scott was writing at the time of the founding of the adversary *Quarterly Review* in 1808. Ten years later – if the contemporary novelist Maria Edgeworth is to be believed – even in Ireland both the *Edinburgh* and *Quarterly* Reviews were regularly taken by the country's big farming families. Among them, she reported, the contents of these and other Reviews – the critical fortunes of authors like Byron, Scott and Campbell and much else besides – were now as 'common table and tea table talk' as in any part of the 'United Empire'. The early nineteenth century was, after all, a time when the reading public was growing apace, when print was being devoured as never before and when the notion of public opinion was beginning to crystallise. It was an age which witnessed the birth of the phenomenon known as 'publicity'. Maybe all this helps to explain why being reviewed became such a charged issue, and why authors could be stung into challenging critics to duels. If the potential for fame had grown dramatically, so had the scope for public humiliation. Who could have anticipated this 'strange new era in the world of letters', marvelled a magazine writer of the time, with each new Review awakening a 'crowd of turbulent sensations' in authors and contributors and the few who yet belonged to neither of these classes?

The new power and prestige of reviewing and the 'periodical press' was endlessly discussed – nowhere more so than in the periodical press itself. To the Hollands and their circle, moreover, the literature of moment was less poetry than history and essay-writing – which, in contemporary terms, meant the work of reviewers like Jeffrey. And to the reading public at large, it was inevitably reviewers – *Edinburgh* or otherwise – who, with the signal exceptions of Byron and Scott, appeared to dominate literary life. The leading *Edinburgh* reviewers became, indeed, as well-known in Society, if not society, as if they had thrown off their masks and publicly advertised their identities. So much is plain from Byron's confident, and correct, naming of names in *English Bards and Scotch Reviewers,* composed before the poet entered the high Whig circles frequented by the reviewers. Partly this was because 'concealed' authorship could not always conceal writers so powerfully individual as Jeffrey, Smith and Brougham ('long and vigorous like the penis of a jackass' was Sydney Smith's colourful description of the latter's reviews). Partly it was because many reviewers were far from accepting that anonymous journalism bound them to silence. Nobody knew all this better than Jeffrey himself. Writing (anonymously of course) in the *Edinburgh Review,* he observed: 'There are instances in which, we suppose with the author's consent, the fact (i.e. the identity of the reviewer) is just as notorious as if his name had been subscribed to the article . . . The truth is that the writers of one half of the articles in a Review are impatient to be known, and take effectual measures to be so.'

Absence of signature was nevertheless calculated to invest

reviewing with mystery and intrigue, permitting its practitioners to enjoy the dual pleasure of being at once famous and unknown – or never known for certain. To this extent at least, the *Edinburgh* reviewers – often regarded as anti-Romantic – were partakers of the Romantic cult of secrecy and doubleness popularised by Gothic novels and Byronism. Yet it may seem a little strange that Jeffrey and his like went on maintaining their anonymity as reviewers long after their true identities had become known. Leslie Stephen, outstanding among later Victorian reviewers, considered that the dominance of authorial concealment in reviewing had much to do with the nagging, residual feeling that 'periodical literature' constituted the 'sphere of inferior taste'. This was a sentiment, Stephen believed, that lingered till approximately the mid-1850s. The *Edinburgh Review*'s high reputation notwithstanding, Jeffrey's anxiety that reviewing involved the 'risk of degradation' was evidently slow to subside altogether, while Macaulay worried that because of reviewing he might be classed as a 'hackney scribbler', and rated his own monumental contributions to the *Edinburgh Review* so much ephemera. The fact is that none of the *Edinburgh* reviewers ever publicly owned up to writing in the journal during the years when they were regular contributors to it. In Jeffrey's case, it was not until 1844 – when he published his collected reviews – that this prolific man of letters at last came before the public as Jeffrey the *Edinburgh* editor and reviewer, not just Jeffrey the advocate.

Jeffrey can hardly have missed the precedent for his action set by his late recruit, Thomas Carlyle. Carlyle – whose writing life began in the *Edinburgh Review* in 1827 – had published his scattered articles in book form in 1839, and was already embarked upon a literary career in which anonymity had no part to play. By that point, Sydney Smith, too, was in the process of bringing out his collected writings; and in 1842, Macaulay, prompted by a pirated American edition of his celebrated essays, grudgingly sanctioned British publication of material that had first appeared in the *Edinburgh Review.* To the egomaniacal Carlyle, the man of letters ranked among the heroes of the modern world, and whether or not this epithet befitted the *Edinburgh* reviewers, these publications of theirs bore witness to a remarkable literary development. Reviewers who had triumphed over mere authors, Jeffrey and his colleagues were a new breed: if their writings were occasioned by new books, they made out of them substantial books of their own – books which were themselves to be reviewed by later reviewers, who might in turn make books from their reviews. It was a pattern that was to be much imitated, and that is being imitated still.

2. A Person in Advance of His Age

Francis Jeffrey's editorship of the *Edinburgh Review* brought him fame not just in Britain and Europe but also in America, a country with which he formed intimate ties. His first wife having died prematurely, Jeffrey married the daughter of a New York banker named Charles Wilkes. In 1813 he sailed across the Atlantic to fetch his new wife back to Scotland. Henry Cockburn jokingly described this as one of the 'great achievements of love', for Jeffrey quailed at the prospect of 'watery adventures', and in pre-steamship days crossing the Atlantic took the better part of six weeks. In the course of the interminable voyage, the eminent editor's high spirits deserted him. Plagued by forebodings, Jeffrey was reduced to feeling 'substantially wretched and painfully low'. When, on 14 October, he finally caught sight of the scattering of villages, smoking chimneys and rustic churches which then comprised New York, his relief was acute. These embryonic signs of American civilisation greeted Jeffrey's 'famished eyes' like a 'glimpse of paradise'.

The so-called 'War of 1812' between England and America – precipitated by the British decision to stop and search neutral shipping as part of the war against Napoleonic France – was still in progress at this point. As a visiting British dignitary bearing letters of introduction from Lord Holland, Jeffrey met President Madison and Secretary of State, Munroe, and engaged with them in vigorous debate over British policy. However, hostilities between the two countries – perhaps more theatrical than real – did not prevent Jeffrey from enjoying his time in America. He returned to Scotland not only with an American wife but also with a keen concern about America's future, which he kept throughout his life. Sometimes suspecting that Europe would forever be at the mercy of kings and despots, Jeffrey saw the United States as the model of a modern, free society, with a constitution which enshrined the triumph of reason over prejudice. While not at all averse to publishing condescending comments on its present cultural backwardness, Jeffrey nevertheless predicted that America was destined to be one of the most powerful nations on earth.

Jeffrey was a complex figure. A creature of the Enlightenment (his transatlantic sympathies chimed with the Enlightenment's cosmopolitan outlook), he was also a fervently self–conscious Scotsman, with feelings about being Scottish that were by no means straightforward. Like many Scots before and since, he was caught between national pride and national shame. He venerated David Hume and Adam Smith, northern rivals to the thinkers of the French Enlightenment, coveting their fame as literary Scotsmen; equally, he was proud to be a compatriot of Burns and Scott, both of them favourite authors. Yet, like Hume, Jeffrey was embarrassed by the very speech of the Scots. To the young Jeffrey, training to become an Edinburgh barrister, Scottish speech was a mark of provincialism, the Scottish accent (in Cockburn's words) a 'national inconvenience', and he struggled to sound like an Englishman – albeit with less than euphonious results. 'High-keyed' and 'sharp', the accent that Jeffrey ended up with was a mongrel affair – an accent befitting a man of contradictions, pulled in different directions.

Jeffrey lived in an era when the term 'North Britain' was current – a coinage dear to Edinburgh literati in whose eyes Scotland, since the Union with England of 1707, had made a 'great leap forward'. It was in something of a North British spirit that Jeffrey edited the *Edinburgh Review*, anxious to advertise Scotland's dramatic intellectual progress. The curious thing was that Jeffrey himself often struck those he met as being neither neither Scottish nor British but – French. A 'little, lively gesticulating French kind of a man' was the verdict of the excitable Lucy Aiken, a London literary lady, who visited Edinburgh in 1804. And John

Gibson Lockhart, dubbing him the 'prince of reviewers', depicted Jeffrey as a Frenchified fop in pantaloons, who dined off 'Champaigne [sic] Moussu' and 'devilled biscuit' (the 'true reviewer's diet'), while indulging in 'babillage' with his numerous lady admirers. Later in the nineteenth century, when he wrote his *Reminiscences,* Thomas Carlyle immortalised his old friend and patron as a 'Scotch Voltaire' – an ambiguous compliment considering Carlyle's unflattering view of France's *philosophes*, but likewise evocative of a somehow Gallic figure.

Yet Jeffrey was so completely a Scotsman that he seldom ventured outside his native land without suffering homesickness. As Scotland's Lord Advocate in the early 1830s, he was charged with preparing the Scottish Reform Bill, and was obliged to spend lengthy periods in London; but unlike his ambitious Edinburgh peers, Henry Brougham and Francis Horner, Jeffrey seems to have had no inclination to make the English capital his home. His favourite resort was Craigcrook, the turreted mansion north west of Edinburgh that he bought in 1815. Retreating there on Saturdays from the legal world of Edinburgh, Jeffrey and his friends played bowls and loitered in the house's handsome gardens, before ending the day with a banquet. Henry Cockburn wrote lyrically about these occasions – occasions when the 'Duke of Craigcrook', as he was jocularly known, comported himself like a Laird, assuming an air of negligent ease. Relishing the role of eminent Scotsman, Jeffrey lived in grand style – much like his Tory friend Walter Scott, who was also by turns industrious Edinburgh lawyer and feudal Laird at his leisure. Craigcrook and Scott's castellated Border mansion, Abbotsford, were the places, Cockburn recalled, at which the 'most interesting strangers in Scotland' were to be encountered.

Jeffrey plumed himself on his Scottish education, the uncommon breadth and modernity of which were commemorated in the pages of the *Edinburgh Review*. Like Brougham and Horner he attended Edinburgh High School, a zealous and remarkably precocious pupil, who learned Latin and Greek at the hands of the Whiggish Dr Adam and who shed tears if he lost his place in class. Still only fourteen, in 1787 he proceeded to Glasgow University, where he remained for approximately two years, afterwards spending a year at Queen's College, Oxford. By the English part of his education, however, Jeffrey set little store. When a friend wrote to enquire what he was learning at Oxford, he replied with something like nationalistic haughtiness: 'You ask me to drop you some English ideas. My dear fellow, I am as much, nay more a Scotsman, than I was while an inhabitant of Scotland. My opinions, prejudices and systems are all Scotch...' The fact was that at the end of the eighteenth century, the old English universities, with their compulsorily clerical dons and their syllabuses of classics and mathematics, had yet to emerge from the Middle Ages. Like Adam Smith, who, a generation before Jeffrey, won a scholarship to Balliol, Jeffrey experienced Oxford as a place of deep intellectual torpor. To alumni of a Scottish education system that embraced the whole spectrum of modern knowledge and stood for what the Scottish historian George Davie christened the 'democratic intellect', Oxford looked incurably anachronistic. Nor were Oxford's traditional religious and social restrictions likely to appeal to a Scotch literatus like Jeffrey, native of a country where John Knox had prescribed that every parish provide instruction for all and where education had long been less exclusive than in England. Had he been born south of the Border, Jeffrey, the son of a humble legal clerk, might never have got to university at all.

Jeffrey was formed by a series of Scottish pedagogues and sages, all of whom left their mark on the *Edinburgh Review*, if not on the entire evolution of the 'higher journalism'. Appointed Rector of Glasgow University in 1820, he delivered an inaugural address which singled out for praise his old teacher, George Jardine, a junior colleague of Adam Smith's, who was Professor of Logic at Glasgow University from 1787 till 1824. This severe dominie –

Henry Cockburn called his class the 'intellectual grindstone of the college' – urged students to develop a systematic and generalising habit of mind, regularly subjecting them to a 'catechistical hour', during which they were challenged to address fellow students on a given subject. At the same time, he enjoined them to write both systematically and voluminously. As wide as it was rigorous, his syllabus included science, history, philosophy, Latin and Greek and what was termed 'general literature'. Scottish universities, unlike their English counterparts, were much influenced by Bacon, taking all knowledge as their province and valuing not just scientific enquiry but also its practical application. From Jardine, Jeffrey received a polymathic training. And in ascribing to Jardine his love of 'letters', he may be taken to mean 'letters' in the old (now unfamiliar) sense – that is to say, learning, intellectual endeavour in the broadest acceptation of the term.

According to Henry Cockburn, Scotland's 'liberal young' in the years following the French Revolution derived their 'mental food' from Smith, Millar, Hume, Montesquieu and Delolme. The second of these, John Millar, who became Professor of Law at Glasgow in 1751, and who ebulliently personified Glasgow University's anti-Oxford ethos, ranks as one of Jeffrey's chief mentors. Jeffrey twice wrote about John Millar and his work in the *Edinburgh Review*, appraising his intellectual legacy with a reverence conspicuously missing from much of the rest of his reviewing. He celebrated Millar as one who had 'no prejudices of veneration' in his nature, regarded the 'minute enquiries of great scholars' as so much 'unprofitable trifling', and was utterly indifferent to 'mere learning'. Only those who had 'made discoveries', Jeffrey pointed out, or 'combined into a system the scattered truths of speculation' ever gained Millar's hard-won approbation. This sharply discriminating, pragmatic attitude, highly characteristic of the Enlightenment, governed the *Edinburgh Review*'s whole outlook. Scorning what, from an advanced Scottish standpoint, appeared to be the intellectual bankruptcy of the old

English universities, Jeffrey's Review promulgated a concept of knowledge that was free from pedantry, methodical and modern.

One of the founders of sociology, Millar was a figure of Johnsonian pugnacity. The adolescent Jeffrey once ran into him wearing a 'furious Brutus wig', which the future editor reckoned an excellent complement to the sage's furious physiognomy. A skilled and enthusiastic boxer, Millar liked not just to teach this students but to step into the ring with them; if the physically delicate and hypochondriac Jeffrey is unlikely to have gone in for anything more than intellectual pugilism with him, still he was being daring in fraternising with the militant Millar at all, for this 'decided Whig' had, to begin with at least, welcomed an upheaval which inspired great alarm in Scotland: the French Revolution. As a result, he was widely believed to be a dangerous figure, one who preached Jacobin principles to impressionable youth and fomented unrest.

A protégé of Lord Kames and Adam Smith, neither of them advocates of radical change, Millar subscribed to the belief that everything could be accounted for from the general state of society and that history evolved according to a discernible pattern. The Scottish school posited four broad, fundamentally economic phases of development; and these phases – the hunting and fishing phase, the pastoral, the agricultural and, lastly, the commercial – were reckoned to have diffused ever greater wealth, intelligence and liberty. However, if Smith and his followers welcomed modern society, with its advantages, material, moral and intellectual, they never assumed that progress was irreversible. Their fear was that the new urban, industrial society and its accompanying division of labour might spawn a population of brutalised, potentially anarchic labourers. The answer, in Smith's view, lay in education – designed not least to inculcate the message that society is inherently hierarchical, and thereby to pre-empt the danger of violent upheaval. It was on this basis that Millar urged that 'every possible expedient' be adopted for the instruction of the lower orders. It was on much the same basis, too, that Jeffrey was to commit the *Edinburgh Review* to championing wider educational provision for the children of the poor and the establishment of Mechanics' Institutes for working men.

Propounding what has been labelled 'scientific Whiggism', the *Edinburgh Review* anticipated the steady advancement of the mercantile interest and the ultimate triumph of reason and liberal principles. Believing that he lived in 'commercial and enlightened times', Jeffrey was able to campaign for liberal measures like Catholic Emancipation and the reform of Parliament, confident that he was swimming with the historical tide. As editor of the *Edinburgh Review*, moreover, he could feel that he had a key role to play in moulding public opinion – to which print, increasing wealth and the general growth of communications seemed to be lending ever greater influence. Not that Jeffrey, with all his commitment to public instruction, was ever a democrat – any more than was John Millar, firebrand though the latter seemed to Jeffrey's anxious father and others: both men were far removed from radicals of the time like Tom Paine, Joseph Priestley and the pamphleteering, *Edinburgh Review*-hating 'people's friend', William Cobbett. 'He laughed', Jeffrey wrote of his teacher, 'at dreams of practical equality.' And these were sentiments with which Jeffrey readily concurred. Millar's goal, like his, was reform – the gradual and enlightened reform of existing institutions. It was precisely through pondering the catastrophic consequences of resisting moderate change in France that Millar became an advocate of parliamentary reform in Britain. Corrupted by patronage, too many old French families, he argued, had acquiesced in absolutism – thereby breeding popular resentment and ultimately sowing the seeds of their own destruction. To him, the danger that the French Revolution might be succeeded by a similarly self-inflicted British Revolution was all too plain – unless the franchise was judiciously widened to include a new uncorrupt element in the shape of the middling orders of society.

A cautious man, Jeffrey thought the forthright Millar 'jealous, to an excess, of the sovereign power', but, by and large, Millar's was the pre-emptive case for parliamentary reform that he himself came to promote in the *Edinburgh Review.*

It is impossible to exaggerate the impact on Jeffrey's generation of the French Revolution, imparting as it did a powerful fresh impulse to public opinion and debate. 'Everything,' Henry Cockburn categorically declared, 'everything, not just this or that thing, was soaked in this one event.' For inveterate students of society like the *Edinburgh* reviewers, the overthrow of the *ancien régime* was an episode big with significance. Indeed, it was the conviction of Jeffrey and his confederates that the Revolution epitomised the 'abridged history of many centuries'. What especially compelled their attention was that it had initially seemed like a more comprehensive application of the principles of Whiggery than was achieved by the 'Glorious Revolution' of 1689. In short, it had appeared like the very consummation of the old Whig ambition to circumscribe the power of the English crown. This was the impassioned message of *Vindiciae Gallicae*, the celebrated apologia for the French Revolution by Sir James Mackintosh, published in 1791. Mackintosh – later enlisted by Jeffrey as one of the *Edinburgh Review*'s chief political writers – sought to refute the conservative Burke's minatory *Reflections on the Revolution in France*, published in the previous year. However, Mackintosh's zeal for the French Revolution was to prove short-lived. As blood flowed and the reign of terror mounted, his revolutionary ardour evaporated, and he confessed that Burke had been right to view events in France with alarm and misgiving. Before the Irishman died, Mackintosh was received at Burke's home, Beaconsfield, thankful to be forgiven his youthful rashness of judgement. Versatile but incorrigibly languid (he became something of a byword for wasted talent), Mackintosh never saw Burke as his philosophical superior. It was Burke's intuitive wisdom that he came to admire, the wisdom that taught the virtue of curbing conjecture by attention to the actual. Mackintosh placed him among the 'great teachers of civil prudence'.

Jeffrey had been a reader of Burke since youth and prized his wisdom in much the same terms. It is true that an article appeared in the *Edinburgh Review* in 1808, the notorious 'Don Pedro Cevallos' article, which enthused about the Spanish uprising of that year and which frightened Tories like Walter Scott into thinking that Jeffrey and his colleagues were ardent for revolution. (Legend has it that the Earl of Buchan was so outraged that he threw open his front door and booted the offending issue of the *Review* into the street!) However, the Cevallos article, evidently a joint production of Jeffrey and the headstrong Henry Brougham, was not at all typical of Jeffrey's political writings, which fairly abound in Burkean warnings against ill-considered meddling with existing institutions. Jeffrey believed that the stability of the English Constitution depended on the monarchy and aristocracy, whose stability in turn was based on their having 'struck their roots deep through every stratum of the political soil and having been moulded during a long course of ages by the usages, institutions and affections of the community.' For all his commitment to reform, Jeffrey paid scarcely less homage to custom than Burke. Indeed, endless passages appeared in the *Edinburgh Review* that might have been written by Burke himself – passages of ornate rhetoric honouring what is old and established and depicting society as a delicate plant nurtured over time and easily spoiled by incautious hands. With his hostility to abstract, utopian schemes, Burke was perhaps the most significant non–Scottish influence on Jeffrey's thinking – and during his thirty-year stewardship of the *Edinburgh Review* he assisted manfully in diffusing and consolidating the Irishman's political legacy.

Jeffrey also championed the more technical arguments of the Reverend Thomas Malthus, another foe of the French Revolution and philosophical theories of human perfectability, William Godwin's above all. Alarmed by the rising numbers of urban poor,

Jeffrey was quick to endorse Malthus's ostensibly scientific and unchallengeable demonstration in 'An Essay on the Principle of Population' (1798) that population growth was rapidly outstripping the means of subsistence, that there were too many mouths to feed and that increasing numbers of human beings without the means to provide for themselves would have to be considered expendable. *The Edinburgh Review* lauded Malthus as that 'eminent philosopher' who deserved the 'rare commendation' of having added to that 'class of important truths that have only to be explained in order to command our immediate assent'. Malthus was himself persuaded by Jeffrey to make his début as an *Edinburgh* reviewer – as was the philosopher's dour (and comparatively crude) Scottish follower, the Reverend Thomas Chalmers, who ponderously reiterated his master's claim that to assist the poor was merely to entrench them in habits of idleness and fecklessness. The Jeffrey who embraced Malthus's harsh doctrines was hardly notable, it must be said, for the breadth of his social sympathies, but then his attitude towards the poor was, after all, that of much educated opinion during the early nineteenth century.

Perhaps Malthus's hardest critic was that dazzling occasional contributor to the *Edinburgh Review*, William Hazlitt, who upbraided Jeffrey for sponsoring the clergyman's views. This aberration apart, however, Hazlitt saw in Jeffrey an apostle of enlightenment, and in his sardonic collection of pen–portraits, *The Spirit of the Age* (1825), he described him as standing for 'supremacy of intellect', as the editor of a journal that struck a tone of 'manly explicitness', while building 'not a tittle of its influence on ignorance or prejudice or authority or personal malevolence'. For Hazlitt, Jeffrey was the personification of criticism and enquiry – those, in Hazlitt's eyes, characteristically 'modern' and admirable activities which, in his judgement, the *Edinburgh Review*'s reactionary Tory rival, the *Quarterly Review*, was bent on expunging. Jeffrey, observed Hazlitt, was a 'person in advance of his age' – yet 'perfectly equipped', by virtue of his intellectual attainments, to exercise a restraining influence on the age's 'rash and headlong spirit'. This verdict has been echoed in recent years by the English scholar of the Romantic period, Marilyn Butler, whose view it is that Jeffrey and his journal served as exemplars of rationality during a period when the pull of the irrational was being powerfully felt in politics and the arts (though, unlike Hazlitt, she believes that the *Quarterly Review* served this purpose as well). Certainly, Jeffrey was a rationalist, whose opinions and convictions – however debatable – were the fruit of careful argument and reflection and what he took to be a body of established knowledge. Though reputed to be a severe reviewer, extreme in his judgements, he became assiduous in cultivating a cool-headed mode of address, a style suited to his moderate message, calculated to assuage excitement. Jeffrey commended Millar for eschewing 'violence and exaggeration' in his work, and for maintaining a 'certain dignity of discussion'. To preserve such dignity figured high among Jeffrey's priorities as editor and reviewer, and this was one of the signal ways in which he set the pattern for the 'higher journalism' of later times. 'Surtout, Messieurs, point de zèle,' counselled Talleyrand. It was Jeffrey's motto, too.

Civic-minded men aspiring to live according to reason, Jeffrey and his fellow *Edinburgh* reviewers had much in common with France's *philosophes*, whose penchant for social and historical conjecture and interpretation they shared. With his comparable cultural background, Jeffrey was supremely well-equipped among British critics to tackle the comprehensive literary studies of Madame de Staël. Jeffrey jibbed at the faith in human perfectibility of this female scion of the *philosophes*, but Madame de Staël's French sense of the arts as by-products of specific historical circumstances and his own cultural assumptions were remarkably alike. It is striking what glamour was possessed for Jeffrey by French salon society, the society frequented by Diderot, d'Alembert, Baron d'Holbach and other *philosophes*, of which Madame de Staël was a late protégé. It was a subject about which he wrote with feeling. Reviewing the memoirs of Marmontel – the great chronicler of the *philosophes* – and recalling their world, Jeffrey exclaimed:

> This society was, we are willing to believe, the most refined and accomplished that probably was ever assembled on earth; and was rendered more engaging by an intimate and cordial union of the talents with all the literary graces of female elegance, and all the polish of exalted rank. The men of letters learned facility from their fair auditors, who gained taste and intelligence in return; and the persons of the highest consideration in the country, by placing a part of the glory in rank they held in such combination communicated to the whole a degree of dignity and personal consideration that has seldom fallen to the lot of talents elsewhere.

Jeffrey was bound to be conscious that the milieu in question was one in which his *Scottish* exemplars, Adam Smith and David Hume, had been fêted. In Regency Edinburgh, he himself played the part of *philosophe* to a drawing room society which had its share of 'fair auditors', and which bore at least a passing resemblance to the glittering ambience evoked by Marmontel. Jeffrey, however, was not inclined to forget that French salon society had ultimately been engulfed by the French Revolution – a fate which, he was convinced, its patrons had invited through their self-indulgence and insensitivity. 'When we recollect', he gravely concluded, 'that the desertion of all the high duties of patriots and statesmen, and the insulting and degradation of the great body of the people, were necessary conditions of the excellence of that society, we cannot hesitate in saying that its brilliancy was maintained at far too great a cost, and that the fuel that was wasted in its support, would have been infinitely better applied in diffusing a gentler light and a more genial heat through the private dwellings of the land.' In so far as Jeffrey was a *philosophe*, he was, for this reason, a chastened one, mindful of having come *après le déluge* and sharply aware of the need for responsible conduct on the part of statesmen, writers and critics. The high-spirited 'prince of reviewers' lampooned by Lockhart, who diverted Edinburgh *soirées* with *bons mots* and sparkling persiflage, was at the same time a dedicated member of the Scottish Bar, of a profession which, in post-Union Scotland, enjoyed a quasi-political function. And eventually Jeffrey was to become Lord Advocate of Scotland, before finishing his career as a judge. In his biographical study, *Cockburn's Millennium* (1975), Karl Miller describes the conscientious Henry Cockburn, also a lawyer, as a 'prisoner of the Edinburgh virtues of hard work, duty, severity and respectability.' Much the same could be said of Jeffrey, a man of parts and masks for whom the public interest (as conceived by a Scottish Whig patrician, wedded to order and stability) ultimately overshadowed all other considerations.

The *Edinburgh* reviewers were products of what Cockburn called a 'discussing age'. And where Paris had its salons, eighteenth century Edinburgh abounded in clubs and societies – not a few of which, in the aftermath of the French Revolution, were eyed by nervous Scottish Tories as cabalistic enclaves, hotbeds of revolution, atheism and democracy. The young Jeffrey honed his debating skills at the Speculative Society, founded in 1764, whose expansive agenda bore witness to the omnivorous curiosity of the Scottish Enlightenment. Jeffrey read papers to the 'Spec' on nobility, the authenticity of Ossian's poems, metrical harmony and the character of commercial nations. It was here that there first gathered the 'conspirators' who formed the nucleus of the *Edinburgh Review*, able young literati like John Allen, Thomas Thomson, Henry Brougham, Francis Horner and Jeffrey himself. The genesis of the *Edinburgh Review* had, indeed, much to do with the clubbable ethos of Scottish intellectual life. When a new Edinburgh venue for discussion called the Friday Club was established in 1803, Jeffrey declared that it 'promised to unite the scattered literature of the place more effectually and extensively than anything else', by which he appears to have meant, not just Edinburgh's *belles-lettres* but the town's scholarship, the totality of its learning. Precisely the same aim animated the *Edinburgh Review* – about whose *raison d'être* Jeffrey was to use remarkably similar language in the course of an abrasive exchange with the radical writer, John Thelwall. Incensed by a derogatory *Edinburgh* review, Thelwall accused Jeffrey of malignancy. With a sublime condescension guaranteed to madden the injured author still further, Jeffrey replied that he and his colleagues were not able to muster the same warmth in defending their publication that Thelwall brought to attacking it. The journal, he provokingly insisted, was but a 'secondary object' with all of them, founded for 'amusement' and to 'gather the scattered literature of the place'. In a sense, the *Edinburgh Review* was a public projection – a continuation by other means – of discussions held in places like the Speculative Society and the Friday Club.

As for rumours that Jeffrey and his set were atheists – these were not wholly without foundation. Religious scepticism was not unknown among Scottish men of letters. Indeed, Hume's 'infidelity', a source of horror to the God-fearing, became notorious, and exercised a powerful influence on the *Edinburgh Review* circle. Dubbed the 'least believing of Scotsmen', Jeffrey's eccentric friend, the bookish John Allen, appears to have been an atheist. And Jeffrey himself was hardly devout, even if he stopped well short of the freethinking which in France led to Diderot's arrest and imprisonment. The Reverend Sydney Smith, as jocund as he was rotund, twitted Jeffrey about his 'increasing and unprofitable scepticism', urging him to curb his destructive habits of mind. 'What's the use of virtue?' asked Smith, gleefully mimicking the Pyrrhonic Jeffrey. 'What's a guinea but a damned hollow circle? What's a chamber pot but an infernal hollow sphere?'

Smith advised Jeffrey to cultivate 'synthetical propensities'. Not that Smith, for all that he was a clergyman, seems to have been much of a believer himself. Few clerics of any calibre, Tom Moore noted with amusement, could ever have been less concerned about points of theology. In fact, when Smith wrote on religion in the *Edinburgh Review*, it was less to expound his own articles of faith (such as they were) than to mock religious zeal and enthusiasm. Methodism – according to this man of reason, a recipe for madness – was a favourite butt of his satirical pen.

Tory, high Church and bristling with anti-Whig animus, *Blackwood's Edinburgh Magazine* ('Maga' to its readers) stigmatised the *Edinburgh Review* as a 'great organ and receptacle of infidelity'. But if the *Edinburgh Review* sinned, it was more by omission than commission. The point was tellingly made by Jeffrey's cousin, the Episcopalian clergyman, Robert Morehead, in a sharp rebuke to John Wilson, alias 'Christopher North', a wild figure much given to intemperate invective and abuse. Nobody, agreed Morehead, was going to pick up the *Edinburgh Review* in anticipation of receiving from it 'religious instruction'. Yet, he went on, 'no one of sense' supposed – 'whatever slips' it might have made – that the Review's 'object and secret view' was to 'pull down Christianity' . It must be said that Jeffrey was not especially curious about theological or metaphysical questions. With the abstruse, Germanic musings of Coleridge, for instance, he had little patience. Nor had he much time for the 'philosophy of mind', as pursued by Dugald Stewart, Professor of Moral Philosophy at Edinburgh University from 1785 until 1808 and revered as a Scottish Whig and sage at a time when, foregoing the traditional European Grand Tour because of the Napoleonic Wars, English aristocratic families sent their sons to the 'Athens of the North' to finish their educations.

For years the grandiloquent Stewart laboured at establishing a 'science of the mind', endeavouring to further the work of Thomas Reid, whose philosophy of 'Common Sense' was evolved as an antidote to Hume's scepticism. It was a project about which Jeffrey, in his guise as cocksure *Edinburgh* reviewer, was scathing. Since, according to Jeffrey, the workings of the human mind could be neither observed nor subjected to experimentation, Stewart was engaged in a footling enterprise, wastefully misapplying Bacon's maxim that 'knowledge is power'. What were the achievements of Stewart's enquiries, asked Jeffrey, when set beside such modern scientific triumphs as ships and steam engines, mirrors, engravings, watches, barometers, etc? Compared with the 'stupendous increase in power' derived by man from investigating the laws of nature, Stewart's rarefied studies, Jeffrey mocked, had precious little to show.

Jeffrey was a Baconian for whom the business of philosophy was the 'relief of man's estate' and the 'effecting of all things possible' – a point of view that was to be magisterially endorsed by Macaulay in his voluminous *Edinburgh Review* essay on Bacon. The practical and modern-minded Jeffrey could at least concur with Dugald Stewart over the utility of 'political economy', the eminently Baconian academic discipline celebrated by Adam Smith's *Wealth of Nations*, which Stewart expounded to several generations of Edinburgh students. True to Smith's precepts, Jeffrey pledged the *Edinburgh Review* to promoting free trade and the amassing of both public and private wealth. In all this, he appears at first glance far removed from his great contemporary, Walter Scott, the huge popularity of whose verse and historical novels had much to do with their depiction of Scotland's past, with their romantic evocation of Highland clans and chivalry. However, Scott's passion for the past was not unqualified – any more, for that matter, than was Jeffrey's enthusiasm for the present. Similarly formed by the Scottish Enlightenment, the Tory Scott also applauded the material advances trumpeted by the *Edinburgh Review*. (Quick to equip his 'feudal' home, Abbotsford, with gas lighting, he was as eager to use modern appliances as Jeffrey was to extol them.) Conversely, the advanced, 'scientific'

Jeffrey was much subject to nostalgia, ruing the cost of progress and the mounting ennui that seemed inevitably to accompany it. If the modern world had freed men from the 'yoke of many prejudices', it had also, sighed Jeffrey, left them 'far less delighted with the universe in which they are placed'.

Nevertheless, for nearly thirty years, as editor and reviewer, Jeffrey committed himself to gathering and diffusing knowledge, to propagating enlightenment. By forbears like Adam Smith and John Millar, Jeffrey could be said to have been imbued with a sense of mission, if not destiny. Scottish intellectual culture in the late eighteenth and early nineteenth centuries was remarkable for its coherence – and for the piety which sustained that coherence. (However impatient he was with certain aspects of his philosophy, Jeffrey described Dugald Stewart as an essentially noble figure.) Jeffrey was heir to a corporate cultural endeavour, a grand, educative, liberalising project. It was as a Scottish Whig with a mission that he drew up the damning indictment of Wordsworth and Coleridge for which posterity was to punish him. The authors of the *Lyrical Ballads* struck him as revolutionaries, half-crazed votaries of an ideal of bucolic egalitarianism. To an alumnus of the Scottish Enlightenment, who set store by hierarchy and private property, such an ideal was anathema. Possessed, by his own lights at least, of a mature grasp of social evolution, Jeffrey deplored the poets' 'idle and splenetic discontent with existing institutions', pronouncing their work puerile – suitable for the nursery, perhaps, but hardly for the modern, rational, industrial society heralded by the *Edinburgh Review*.

There was another Jeffrey, however, a very different figure from the censorious, all too often prim and priggish, *Edinburgh* reviewer. This was the Jeffrey who, on first reading the *Lyrical Ballads* in 1798, confessed to being 'lost in enchantment', and who was to be glimpsed by Walter Scott weeping 'warm tears' over Wordsworth's poems, with their outcasts and unfortunates. A severe Whig advocate and critic in public, at home Jeffrey metamorphosed into a romantic, a moist-eyed man of feeling. (In later years, he was to become an effusive friend and admirer of the young Charles Dickens, sobbing over the death of 'Little Nell'.) On principle Jeffrey subscribed to two tastes – one for work, the other for enjoyment. In many respects, he was what would later become known as an 'ideological critic', editing a Review of politics and letters which stood for what Thomas de Quincey defined as 'Whiggism in its relation to literature'.

No one understood Jeffrey better than Thomas Carlyle, who, as an aspirant Scotch reviewer, was for a time Jeffrey's protégé. The two men first became acquainted in 1824, the famous editor of the *Edinburgh Review* being instantly attracted to the younger man – instantly attracted, too, flirtatious as he was, to Carlyle's handsome wife, Jane Carlyle. It was a measure of his high opinion of Carlyle that Jeffrey not only permitted him to extol German literature in the pages of his Review but also published his jeremiad 'Signs of the Times', attacking 'machinery and accumulation'. In both instances, Carlyle enjoyed the rare opportunity to flout the *Edinburgh Review*'s customary line on these issues. Perhaps it was inevitable, though, that the pair – in many respects temperamental opposites – soon began to differ. Jeffrey found Carlyle the embryonic thundering Victorian prophet too much in earnest, while the latter found Jeffrey, with his characteristic air of insouciance, by no means earnest enough. And when Jeffrey jestingly but undiplomatically likened Jane Carlyle to Titania and Carlyle himself to Bottom, the couple were anything but amused. Nevertheless, there is much fond feeling in Carlyle's writings about his old friend and patron. The chapter on Jeffrey included in Carlyle's *Reminiscences* (1881) is a portrait-in-depth, intriguing among other things for its revelation of Jeffrey's well-honed talent for mimicry – an aspect of the 'Duke of Craigcrook' barely hinted at by Henry Cockburn's formal and frigid biography. Carlyle brings Jeffrey before us as a chameleon, a brilliant actor, with something of the plasticity of mind that Keats termed 'negative capability'. In the days when their friendship was still fresh, Carlyle described him as a 'most tricksy, dainty, beautiful little spirit', adding that he had seen 'gleams on the face of the little man that let you look into another country'.

As vivacious as he was versatile, Jeffrey knew that there were more things in heaven and earth than were usually dreamed of by *Edinburgh* reviewers. Yet as the *Edinburgh Review*'s editor, Jeffrey felt obliged to pretend otherwise. For this protean man of letters had a strict part to play – a part entrusted to him by his native culture. The late Victorian writer and scholar, George Saintsbury, sensed that in his writings something always seemed to be holding Jeffrey back. That something was, perhaps, the heavy responsibility that he assumed in promulgating the intellectual legacy of the Scottish Enlightenment – a legacy that included the 'higher journalism' itself.

3. A Royal Road to Knowledge

Sydney Smith feared that Francis Jeffrey 'took politics to heart' more than anyone he knew. But there was one reason above all why, when it came to matters political, this public-spirited editor was peculiarly subject to agitation. For here was a realm of endeavour that placed him at the mercy of that most unruly of contributors, Henry Brougham. Full of the woes of editing, Jeffrey often bemoaned the 'daily and nightly roar' of his importunate authors, but Brougham outroared them all, including Carlyle, who sulked and seethed when Jeffrey pruned his luxuriant copy. Both politician and barrister, Brougham made monumental contributions to all the *Edinburgh Review*'s major campaigns, protesting against the slave trade, putting the case for Catholic Emancipation, urging the reform of parliament and advocating the education of the poor. (Set up in 1826 as a means of promoting literacy and 'sound principles' among the poor, the *Society for the Diffusion of Useful Knowledge* was his conception.) The trouble was that this prolific philanthropic polemicist was capricious in the extreme. Widely believed to be at least half mad, Brougham was forever scheming to transform Jeffrey's Review into his own personal mouthpiece, and in the process imperilling the whole enterprise. The occasions were many when Jeffrey – who likened himself to a feudal monarch beset by obstreperous barons – longed to be rid of this turbulent reviewer. Yet without Brougham's herculean support, he could hardly have sustained the *Edinburgh Review*'s manifold political crusades. In politics – as, to be sure, in much else – the *Edinburgh Review* was essentially a collaborative project.

Jeffrey would ultimately discover a biddable substitute for Brougham, though by that stage his thirty-year career as the

Review's editor was drawing to a close. In Thomas Babington Macaulay, Jeffrey recruited a contributor who was at once a prodigious reviewer and an exemplary Whig. For Brougham, Macaulay's emergence as a leading Edinburgh reviewer was an occasion for issuing threats and ultimatums; for Jeffrey, it was cause for celebration. Scarcely self-effacing, the ever-sanguine Macaulay had none of Brougham's perversity and was greatly in accord with Jeffrey on matters of politics and literature – so much so that he and his editor could be said to have formed a mutual admiration society. 'The more I think,' Jeffrey delightedly exclaimed after reading Macaulay's *Edinburgh Review* essay on Milton in 1825, 'the less I can conceive where you picked up that style.' The irony was that it was Jeffrey himself who furnished the young Macaulay with his favourite literary model. When Jeffrey was preparing his collected *Edinburgh* reviews in 1844, Macaulay confessed that for him they would 'lack the charm of novelty', since he had read and re-read them until he knew them 'by heart'. For sheer intellectual breadth, Macaulay believed, Jeffrey was without equal among his contemporaries. 'He is', he wrote, 'more nearly an universal genius than any man of his age.'

Retiring from the *Edinburgh Review* in 1829, Jeffrey was appointed Lord Advocate of Scotland, his career as editor of a Whig Review yielding to a fresh career as a politician proper, a man of measures engaged in piloting the Scottish Reform Bill through Parliament. In so suitable a pupil as Macaulay, he was bound to see an ideal successor – though editing the *Edinburgh Review* proved not to be one of the younger man's ambitions. It was to Macaulay that Jeffrey entrusted the delicate task of setting out the *Edinburgh Review*'s mature position on parliamentary reform. Warning of the danger of a new English Civil War, Macaulay preached conciliation, the judicious enfranchisement of the 'middling orders' as an antidote to social conflict: 'Reform in order to preserve', he famously urged, summarising the cautious campaign for constitutional reform fought by Jeffrey and the

Edinburgh Review over many years. Macaulay was echoing his editor, too, when he underlined the lessons to be learned from the career of the French economist and statesman, Turgot. For Whigs like Jeffrey and Macaulay, the significance of this 'philosophical minister' lay in his effort to 'secure' France's 'ancient institutions' by virtue of 'mild reforms' – reforms which, they believed, might have prevented the French Revolution, if only they had been sustained. The example of Turgot, whose attempted reforms were aborted by the *ancien régime*, can hardly have been lost on Jeffrey himself when he made his own début as a statesman . An Edinburgh *philosophe* in politics, bent on averting social upheaval with timely measures, he was anxious to succeed where his unlucky French predecessor had failed.

The climax to all of Jeffrey's efforts occurred in 1830, with the coming to power in Britain of the Whigs – the party of 'moderate' reform – after years of Tory hegemony. What is striking is how continuous practically all those efforts were. Politics and letters, statesmanship and reviewing – for Jeffrey and his fellow *Edinburgh* reviewers, these were complementary activities. When Walter Scott recoiled at the *Edinburgh Review*'s Whig excesses, accusing Jeffrey of injuring the Review's reputation as a literary publication, he received a sharp reply. The *Edinburgh Review*, Jeffrey told him, stood on two legs: one of them was literature, and the other was politics. Not that, for all its loyalty to the Whigs, the *Edinburgh Review* could be simply categorised as a journal of party. With its roots in the Enlightenment, Jeffrey's Review was essentially a medium of criticism and discussion charged with the faith in reason and commitment to human progress which had inspired the French *philosophes* From this point of view, indeed, the *Edinburgh Review*'s party was not so much the Whigs as that far grander body dear to the eighteenth century – the party of reason and humanity.

Jeffrey pledged himself to 'instructing the public mind' – a phrase of which he and his colleagues were fond. Possessed of huge confidence in the authority of periodical writing, in the power of polemics, he was an editor who little doubted what could be achieved through rational argument and persuasion. In correspondence with contributors, his faith in the efficacy of reviewing is everywhere apparent. 'The main object, I should suppose, with you, would be to do good,' he wrote to his old friend, Francis Horner, in 1809. 'And I take it to be indisputable that the greatest good that argument can do must be done by printed argument, in a work, read with some attention, by 50,000 thinking people within a month after it is printed.' By this stage, the *Edinburgh Review*'s circulation was approximately 13,000 per quarter, with each copy reckoned to be seen by several people. It was in comparably high-minded terms that Jeffrey set about cajoling his former adversary, Tom Moore, into joining the *Edinburgh Review*'s legislative ranks. He urged the poet to consider the 'gratification' that he would derive from his 'new vocation', from 'correcting' some 'prevailing error' or laying down 'some original principle of taste or reasoning'. And he reminded him that no 'prose preachers' boasted such an extensive readership as the *Edinburgh* reviewers.

Given to playing the *pococurante*, as a political editor Jeffrey was a crusader, earnestly engaged in the propagation of enlightenment. 'Prose preachers', anxious to expose social abuses and preach reform, was just what the *Edinburgh* reviewers were. And since the causes championed by Jeffrey and his colleagues triumphed in their own lifetimes, they were able to feel, looking back on their careers, that they had not preached in vain, but to tangible effect. When Sydney Smith published his collected writings in 1839, he prided himself on the fact that, before the *Edinburgh Review* began publication, a thousand evils had flourished which, thanks in no small degree to the *Review*, had since been eradicated. And Jeffrey himself – as may be judged from the preface to his *Contributions* – was no less convinced that through assiduous advocacy of 'just and enlightened opinions', he and his Review had changed the world for the better.

If these claims now smack of immodesty, it is because it has grown hard to share the *Edinburgh* reviewers' fundamental assumptions. Writing in what Cockburn called the 'morning of the reviewing day', they breathed a different air. Despite being of a nervous and pessimistic disposition, Jeffrey acted on the assumption that there was no wrong that could not be righted by an appeal to reason, by a sound written exposition of the case which assembled the relevant facts and arguments. This was precisely the postulate on which that great monument to the French Enlightenment, Diderot's *Encyclopédie,* rested. There are, to be sure, striking parallels between the *Edinburgh Review* and the *Encyclopédie*. Both were anonymous works which, though corporate enterprises, ultimately depended on the energy, inspiration and capacity for organisation of a single editor; both served as compendia of 'enlightened' views and information which challenged received opinion; and both wielded great authority during an era which saw unprecedented advances in literacy, with an attendant growth in the public appetite for news and instruction. For all its renown as a work of learning, observed the historian D.W. Brogan, Diderot's *Encyclopédie* was really a huge pamphlet. Much the same could be said of Jeffrey's Review.

John Morley characterised Diderot and the *Encyclopédistes* as a 'new teaching order', as the clergy's secular successors. Jeffrey and the *Edinburgh* reviewers – in common, perhaps, with Dr Johnson in the generation before them – were British counterparts of this historic new order. *Encyclopédiste*, *philosophe*, reviewer – the names are various for the versatile, self-consciously superior man of letters sired by the Enlightenment, who would later be known, among other things, as an intellectual. Jeffrey's own career heralded the arrival of the editor/reviewer as ultimate arbiter, a figure who laid claim to supreme critical authority, handing down lofty judicial verdicts and taking a dismissive view of most literary endeavour. Jeffrey was the first in a long line of 'higher journalists' who behaved as if the common run of books had little to offer beyond furnishing the 'philosophical' reviewer with raw material. Morley, who edited the *Fortnightly Review* in the 1870s – and who published a voluminous study of Diderot – was a later example of the type. The sublime sense of literary superiority animating the *Edinburgh Review* was spelled out with disarming candour by Henry Cockburn in his *Life of Jeffrey*. With the 'advantage of hindsight', observed Cockburn, 'the skilled reviewer' is often 'better acquainted with the matter of the book than its author, inasmuch that, in many cases, the criticism is the abler work of the two.' Perhaps he could have added that if the *Edinburgh* reviewer liked to think that he knew better, the *Review*'s editor had no hesitation in assuming that he knew best. Not only did Jeffrey prescribe topics for contributors, he also re-wrote their work liberally – often to the point where, when it appeared in print, they scarcely recognised it.

So far as can be judged, Jeffrey was inclined to value books chiefly for the utility. 'For a lover of books,' wrote Cockburn, 'and for one who had picked up a few, his collection was most wretched.' And in view of the customary scale of *Edinburgh* reviews and the time-consuming demands made on him by the law and public affairs, it seems likely enough that reviews and reviewing engrossed a bigger share of Jeffrey's attention than books themselves. Clearly he felt few, if any, misgivings on this score. It pleased him to think that reviewing was acquiring ever greater prestige and that he had played a presiding role in this development. When the *Quarterly Review* was bruited in 1809 as a rival to the *Edinburgh Review*, Jeffrey fretted about this Tory brainchild of Walter Scott as a potential rival, but he also exulted over the emergence of a periodical, the form of which was an exact, not to say, slavish imitation of his own Review. 'But I do rejoice', he told Francis Horner, 'at the prospect of this kind of literature, which seems to be attended to more than any other, and shall be glad to have set an example.'

Yet Jeffrey often affected not to be an editor at all. This, after all, was an era when to be involved with the press in any capacity was to invite the opprobrium of respectable society, and in Edinburgh he belonged to a genteel milieu where the business of plying a pen for financial gain occasioned especial unease. Professional authorship was felt to be an occupation that scarcely befitted an Edinburgh dignitary. Hence it was that Jeffrey conducted himself as one for whom literature was a diversion, the civilised pursuit of leisure hours – in so far as he acknowledged being an author at all. According to Macaulay, Jeffrey liked to be taken for a 'man of the world, an active lawyer or easy careless gentleman', rather than for a 'distinguished editor'. Visitors to his Edinburgh house were struck not by evidence of his literary exertions but by the profusion of visiting cards adorning his chimney piece. Not that, when it came to literary dissembling, Jeffrey – who, in order to write, would vanish into a 'little gilded closet' – could rival Walter Scott, Edinburgh's 'Great Unknown'. The lengths to which Scott went to conceal the scale of his literary labours were extraordinary: guests at his Border mansion, Abbotsford, never glimpsed the study which the phantom author entered via a secret staircase and wrote in voluminously before breakfast; they saw only Scott, the leisured laird and genial host, brimming with romantic anecdotes.

A fluent wordsmith with a fertile brain, Jeffrey was well equipped to write major works, to create an *œuvre* of his own, but he seems to have been more than satisfied to pour his talent and energy into anonymous journalism. It was a curious feature of his career that practically all his writing took the form of unsigned contributions to the *Edinburgh Review*. What, wondered Bulwer Lytton, might Jeffrey (and Sydney Smith) have achieved in the 'vigour of their age' if they had been less 'industrious' as reviewers? It remains a pertinent question. Still, reviewers, too, are authors, and the fact is that Jeffrey achieved a great deal. The *Edinburgh Review* – large portions of which he wrote himself – was Jeffrey's grand project, the 'scheme of literary eminence' of which he dreamed in his youth. The insouciant disclaimer prefacing his *Contributions*, in which Jeffrey described his reviews as mere 'miscellaneous papers, written hastily in the intervals of graver preoccupations', cannot be taken entirely seriously. Jeffrey's reviews *were* his books, the books of a fastidious Edinburgh lawyer and gentleman, who sought fame from writing – without actually seeming to write.

Social and intellectual snobbery intermingled where the *Edinburgh* reviewers were concerned. Jeffrey the gentleman reviewer saw the realm of letters as menaced by hacks, brazen and unprincipled Grub Street 'scribblers' against whom the cultivated amateur like himself was honour-bound to speak out. In its early years especially, the *Edinburgh Review* was something of a *Dunciad*, scourging literary fraud and folly. Regularly, the *Review* deplored the 'demon of scribbling', alleging that it would soon be as rare not to have written a book as not to have learned to write. There was, the reviewers believed, no more degenerate sign of the literary times than 'book-making', a modern vice which became the subject of endless *Edinburgh Review* strictures. Mixing humour with deadly seriousness, Jeffrey remarked that it was the reviewer's job to 'rid the kingdom of noxious literary creatures', to cull the swelling ranks of 'bookmakers'. Noxious literary creatures excoriated by the *Edinburgh Review* included Thomas Holcroft, William Godwin and John Thelwall, the latter charged by Jeffrey with an 'impatience of honest industry' – to say nothing of 'presumption and vanity'. Such writers were characterised by Jeffrey and his colleagues as mere tradesmen – literary interlopers, who also happened to be radicals and egalitarians, thereby invoking in the minds of Whig reviewers the dread spectre of Jacobinism. In his sneers at Thelwall and others, Jeffrey's sense of the Olympian height from which the *Edinburgh Review* gazed down on the literary ruck found all too copious expression.

Coleridge was to concede that the *Edinburgh Review* had done sterling work in diffusing knowledge and establishing the principle of reviewing only those books worthy of what he termed 'argumentative criticism'. But he protested that Jeffrey was forever betraying the *Edinburgh Review*'s selective prospectus and reviewing books with no claim to public notice – merely to indulge his vindictiveness, or to boost the *Review*'s sales by flattering the 'malignant passions of human nature'. Jeffrey would have been disingenuous to pretend that Coleridge's charges were baseless. Yet there were many instances where books of no special literary merit were noticed in the *Edinburgh Review* less out of spite than because their contents were reckoned worth bringing to public attention. This was especially true of travel books, a species of literature flourishing as mightily then as now, countless unremarkable examples of which were discussed in the *Review*. Such books were plundered for information by reviewers who were eager to test philosophical hypotheses about social development and the nature of man, as formulated by Enlightenment thinkers like Hume and Adam Smith.

'We have collected a super-abundance of materials', declared William Hazlitt, writing about the progress of the periodical press in the *Edinburgh Review* itself. 'Now the grand *desideratum* is to fashion and render them portable.' This was precisely what Jeffrey the editor, orchestrating the intellectual efforts of scholars, writers and critics, aimed to accomplish. Like Diderot's *Encyclopédie*, the *Edinburgh Review* was, in a sense, an attempt to make of many books one definitive book, an *omnium gatherum* that rendered all other works redundant. Jeffrey's ideal was the Enlightenment ideal of the inclusiveness of knowledge and the unity of discourse. The *Edinburgh Review* accordingly mingled discussions of politics with articles on philosophy and law, reviews of novels and poetry with essays on scientific subjects. For Jeffrey, all subjects belonged to the same continuum of knowledge, or 'letters', the terms 'letters', 'literature' and 'knowledge' being practically cognate during this period. Indeed, if a new volume of verse could be hailed by the *Edinburgh Review* as a 'literary event', so too could a work on entomology. Specialisation, the emergence of discrete disciplines and the growing rift between 'literature' and 'science' which in recent times dismayed C.P. Snow – none of this was anticipated by the *Edinburgh* reviewers.

However, even in Jeffrey's day, faith in the inclusive intellectual ideal upheld by the *Edinburgh Review* was becoming increasingly precarious, ever more hard-won. At times, Jeffrey himself felt burdened, not to say, overwhelmed, by the sheer proliferation of modern knowledge, as the volume of new publications grew apace. Think what a man now needed to know, he complained, in order to 'pass current' in 'informed circles of society'. Jeffrey's alarming sample of subjects claiming any self-respecting educated person's attention included: political economy, chemistry, mineralogy, geology, painting, sculpture, architecture, German and Spanish literature, Indian and Chinese learning and history, trade and agriculture – not to mention the philosophy of politics and a 'more extensive knowledge of existing parties and factions and eminent individuals, both literary and political, than was ever required at home or abroad, in an earlier period of society.' In modern circumstances, according to Jeffrey, a 'taste for miscellaneous information is formed almost before we are aware and our time and curiosity irrevocably reduced to a sort of Encyclopaedical trifling.' In his frustration about the difficulty of 'passing current', Jeffrey remains a remarkably topical figure – even if, by contemporary standards, his work as an editor and reviewer seems less like trifling than hard mental graft. We are all, perhaps, 'Encyclopaedical triflers' now.

Henry Cockburn maintained that the *Edinburgh Review* 'taught the public to think' – a claim that was to be echoed in the twentieth century by F.R. and Q.D. Leavis, who extolled periodicals such as the *Edinburgh Review* as mouthpieces of a public-spirited clerisy, expounding standards of taste and judgement which became authoritative throughout society. Such tendentious cultural nostalgia is, however, worth contrasting with the very different opinion voiced by the early nineteenth-century Dissenter, Josiah Conder. Conder argued that if Reviews like Jeffrey's enjoyed popularity, it was precisely because they pandered to people seeking 'ready-wisdom'. For this stony-faced naysayer, the expansive, opinionated, omniscient mode of reviewing pioneered by the *Edinburgh Review* afforded a 'new and royal road to knowledge, of which the indolent and superficial are glad to avail themselves'. For William Hazlitt, too, though gratified to be an *Edinburgh* reviewer himself, the issue of the educational benefits of discursive reviewing provided grounds for a certain amused scepticism. Hazlitt joked that the reviewing style of his own day, as distinct from the former laconic kind, appealed especially to those 'whose object is less to read the book than to dispute upon its merits and to go into company clad in the defensive and offensive armoury of criticism'. And, of course, there must have been not a few readers who turned to the *Edinburgh Review* and its like out of such motives, flibbertigibbets avid for predigested facts and opinions which they could parrot for effect on social occasions.

That the *Edinburgh Review* served as a potent source of intellectual stimulus is, however, beyond dispute. Consider its cultural standing in the eyes of serious-minded contemporaries. Among those who eagerly awaited the latest issue of Jeffrey's journal were Napoleon and Stendhal, while Madame de Staël's son, Auguste, declared that if there came a being from another planet, to whom he wished to communicate a noble idea of the human race's cultural achievements, it was to the pages of the *Edinburgh Review* that he would direct him. Among British readers, Macaulay was but one example of a future eminent Victorian on whom the *Edinburgh Review* left a more or less indelible mark. As literary apprentices, Carlyle and John Stuart Mill were likewise soaked in the *Review*'s – which is also to say Jeffrey's – influence. (The young Mill was obliged to read the first twenty years' issues of the *Review* in order to equip his father, James Mill – previously an *Edinburgh* reviewer himself – with background material for the monumental critique of Edinburgh Whiggery with which the *Westminster Review* was launched in 1824.) Comprising as it did a formative episode in the mental evolution of these and other leading Victorian figures, the *Edinburgh Review* played a major part in the shaping of nineteenth-century intellectual life.

In many respects, Jeffrey was editor of what amounted to a university-in-print. As such, his Review was to furnish something of a blueprint for London University. Set up in 1826, 'The London University' pioneered a modern, 'comprehensive' approach to higher education which corresponded to the *Edinburgh Review*'s 'enlightened', polymathic, secular ethos, for it was an important feature of the university that it was free from the high Anglican, aristocratic exclusiveness of Oxford and Cambridge. The original projector of the new academy was the poet, Thomas Campbell. Like Jeffrey, whose friend he was, Campbell attended Glasgow University, later contributing from time to time to the *Edinburgh Review*. Travelling in Germany, he saw a model for his scheme in the University of Bonn, but his thinking was scarcely less guided by Scottish attitudes to knowledge and education, as epitomised by Jeffrey's journal. The backwardness and inertia of the old English universities was, to be sure, a long-standing *Edinburgh Review* theme, and in the 1820s Jeffrey published impassioned polemics by Brougham and Macaulay endorsing Campbell's plan. The *Review*'s campaign to establish 'The London University' paralleled its commitment to parliamentary reform: both were aspects of the same Whig endeavour to advance the cause of the rising middle class.

Jeffrey and his contributors were not Campbell's sole supporters. The poet's project was also backed by an assortment of Dissenters, Utilitarians and Jews – though no single individual was to play so decisive a part in realizing Campbell's scheme as Henry Brougham. The autocratic Brougham took charge of vetting staff for the new college, and *Edinburgh* reviewers were conspicuous amongst them. J. R. McCulloch, author of endless *Edinburgh Review* articles, was appointed to London's first chair of Political Economy; Jeffrey's old friend the anatomist, Charles Bell, became Professor of Clinical Surgery; and the Italian exile, Antonio Panizzi – who later founded the British Library – was enrolled as Professor of Italian. Others – notably Thomas Carlyle – tried to exploit their *Edinburgh Review* connections without success. Jeffrey playfully proposed Carlyle as 'Professor of Mysticism' at the new college, but Brougham clearly considered the future 'Sage of Cheyne Walk' to be an unsuitable candidate for an academic post of any sort.

Karl Miller has written that 'The London University' could pardonably be described as the *Edinburgh Review*'s new university in London, the journal translated into stone. It does seem particularly fitting that a monument to the *Review*, one of the Scottish Enlightenment's greatest intellectual contributions, should have been erected in Britain's capital city, London having so compelled the attention of Jeffrey and his *Edinburgh Review* circle. Several *Edinburgh* reviewers – Brougham, Horner, John Allen and Sydney Smith – moved there at the earliest opportunity; if Jeffrey himself preferred to stay in Edinburgh, he nonetheless deferred to the literary and political canons of London's Whig salons, even as he worked as a parliamentary reformer for Scotland's greater incorporation within the British Constitution. It was as someone who somehow seemed to be rejecting, if not betraying, his own country that Jeffrey struck Scottish Tories like Walter Scott and the zealous critics of *Blackwood's Edinburgh Magazine*. 'Little by little,' Scott once warned his Whig friend, 'whatever your wishes may be, you will destroy and undermine until nothing of what made Scotland Scotland shall remain.'

This anguished outburst by Scott – he wept on the night he

gave way to it in 1806 – was provoked by looming Whig reforms of the Scottish legal system; yet its significance went far deeper. For Jeffrey – his love of living in Scotland notwithstanding – was hardly the stuff from which Scottish nationalism was to stem. There was indeed much about him and his fellow *Edinburgh* reviewers that clashed with the claims of Scotland and its indigenous traditions. With their rationalism and their cosmopolitanism, they were less concerned to celebrate the Scottish past than to identify themselves with the British future. Given all this, it was probably inevitable that in due course the *Edinburgh Review* would cease to be a specifically Scottish publication. Although the *Review* was to survive until 1929, as early as 1850 its offices were transferred to London; and thereafter, as Henry Cockburn ruefully remarked, it was 'Edinburgh' in name alone. Here was a development of a piece with the accelerating diaspora of Scotch intellectual talent during the early nineteenth century – a process at which Jeffrey and his colleagues can be said to have more or less consciously connived.

Following his death in 1850, Francis Jeffrey's reputation sank dramatically. Henry Cockburn's claim – that his friend was the 'greatest of British critics' – was to remain a decidedly minority opinion. Least of all has the memory of the 'prince of reviewers' been cherished in Scotland, where subsequent generations seem to have had trouble recognising this notable North Briton as a Scotsman at all. The fact is that Jeffrey and his Review have inspired little in the way of national pride, and that Scottish writing on the subject has been conspicuous by its absence. By 'English Studies', meanwhile, Jeffrey has been portrayed as a dogmatic Scotch critic, who aped metropolitan standards of taste already antiquated in his own day. Consequently, the true import of his career has seldom received proper recognition. Judged by the Scottish writer, G. Gregory Smith, to have suffered the 'obloquy of the pioneer', Jeffrey was a seminal figure in the history of journalism, the founder of a medium of communication that was to enable great numbers of British writers and intellectuals to comport themselves as high priests of civilised discourse.

II

The Age of the Monthly

'If you open the [monthly Reviews] you will be quite astonished by the number of questions which interest a cultivated Englishman. The Egyptian Question, the modern Spanish drama, the position of children in the factories, prison reform, the principles of ethics, etc., etc ... Every number of a Review is an encyclopaedia of the questions of the day ... The English are of the opinion that any question can be thoroughly dealt with in the space of not more than 16 pages.'

A view of English Reviews,
from the Russian Review, *Russkoie Bogatstvo*, 1899

John Morley

4. Blackburn's Diderot

Increasingly identified with ageing Whigs, Jeffrey's 'electrical' Review ended up seeming stiff and official, an ossified organ of the British governing classes. It bemused a younger generation to learn that the *Edinburgh Review* had been a sensation in its time. The idea that a Scotch dignitary, scandalised by its subversive tone, had once kicked the *Review* into the street, seemed barely credible. Writing in the mid-1850s, Walter Bagehot noted that the journal now seemed like the work of 'privy counsellors', a repository of ministerial pronouncements which exuded an air of constitutional gravity. Aside from anything else, a quarterly like the *Edinburgh* was simply out of step with the quickening tempo of modern communications: in the world of journalism, four months had begun to seem a very long time; moreover, in an era of mounting publicity, with literary celebrities as conspicuous as Dickens and Carlyle, the anonymity in which the old Reviews still cloaked themselves was rapidly falling from favour. If the times insisted on more frequent stimulus, they also demanded articles with names attached to them. By the 1870s, anonymous quarterlies were being upstaged by a new breed of 'monthlies', modern organs such as the *Contemporary Review*, the *National Review*, the *Nineteenth Century*, and the misleadingly named *Fortnightly Review*, none of which made any secret of its contributors' identities.

What Jeffrey had been in the early years of the nineteenth century, the *Fortnightly Review's* editor, John Morley, became in this fresh phase of the 'higher journalism': a directing intelligence, a central figure. Morley edited the *Fortnightly* from 1867 until 1882, and during the latter part of his tenure he was also editing the celebrated London evening paper, the *Pall Mall Gazette*, with the young W.T. Stead as his rampageous assistant. Thereafter, Morley devoted his talents to high politics. To become a great man had been his childhood ambition. Now, in mid-life, he would become 'Lord' Morley, the famous Liberal statesman, who served as Secretary of State for both Ireland and India. But he went on enjoying literary fame, too. His hagiographic life of Gladstone – whose commitment to Irish Home Rule he had been very nearly instrumental in sustaining – was an Edwardian best-seller. The historian, G.P. Gooch, remarked that Morley was a man of letters among men of affairs and a man of affairs among men of letters. A self-conscious apostle of light, steeped in European culture, he made raising the tone of public discussion the chief object of his existence. High-mindedness was the very stuff of his being. The worldly Lloyd George confessed that he never met John Morley without having to stifle an impulse to take off his hat.

Morley rose to prominence during an increasingly democratic era, a time when, thanks to the Second Reform Act of 1867 and the Education Act of 1870, there were more readers and more voters than ever before. It was an era that would see practitioners of the 'higher journalism' vying for public attention with an ever more rampant popular press, whose prime mover, Lord Northcliffe, was a very different kind of dignitary from Morley. The growth of the 'democratic spirit' was something which Morley, a 'new man' from Lancashire, welcomed, but if his principles were democratic, his temperament was severely aristocratic: he looked down, so it was said, 'with infinite contempt upon most of the trifles that interest the British tomfool'. As editor of the *Fortnightly Review*, Morley felt his responsibilities keenly – was he not engaged in the 'immeasurably momentous task of forming national opinion'? The new 'system of signature' found in him a leading, if always cautious, advocate. To publish signed articles, Morley made plain, was no light matter – but then, for this most circumspect of pundits, hardly anything was.

Morley's thoughts on anonymity are a subject in their own

right. Reviewing the work of the early *Edinburgh* reviewers in 1867, he argued that anonymous journalism had suited men like Jeffrey and Brougham, writers united in their Whig assumptions, in their commitment to a specific Whig programme. But his own era, one of flux and mounting scepticism, was different. Now, it seemed, the only motto that could be safely inscribed on the flag of a liberal Review was 'Progress', a piece of advice which each contributor interpreted according to his own special lights. The Review as as medium of oracular certainty was yielding place to the Review as open pulpit – a state of affairs for which 'signature' seemed the natural condition. Nevertheless, dispute about signature's pro's and con's was slow to subside – even if, in an era which made much of 'free speech', Morley was by no means alone in identifying anonymity with the obscurantist, undemocratic past. Founded in 1902, the *Times Literary Supplement* upheld the tradition of literary anonymity as a matter of principle until as recently as the 1970s, regular outbreaks of controversy over the issue notwithstanding. Signed reviews, successive editors of the *TLS* seem to have felt, were out of place in a paper that aspired to exercise authority.

The matter was one about which Morley himself seems never to have stopped equivocating, although he was eventually to conclude that the merits of signed journalism were less than he had once supposed. It was true that anonymity made possible the 'monstrous charlatanry' of the 'editorial We'. Equally, it enabled a vain editor (like Jeffrey) to re-write reviewers' copy with more or less total impunity. Yet, on the other hand, the reviewer who signed his name was apt to turn into a mere performer, a crowd-pleaser who wrote only what was expected of him. And what of the effects of signed journalism on the reading public? Were not such readers liable to frivolous curiosity, to indulging in idle gossip, to thinking more of the 'man who speaks' than of the 'precise value of what he says'? Still, when all was said, signature had one advantage that Morley prized above all others – it broke the old taboo on plain-speaking about religion. Thanks to the 'removal of the mask', the issue of religious belief could be publicly canvassed with a candour that would have been unthinkable just a few years earlier. To Morley this was a source of ineffable relief.

Born in Blackburn, Morley was the son of a Nonconformist doctor and brought up in an atmosphere stiff with piety. But at Oxford in the late 1850s he became a rationalist, a devotee of John Stuart Mill (to whose spare, ascetic physique his own bore a certain resemblance) and grew increasingly sceptical about the credibility of the Bible. When Morley professed himself an unbeliever, his God-fearing father was so mortified that he stopped his son's allowance. Morley left Oxford prematurely with a undistinguished degree – an anguished martyr to his new-found rationalist faith. In London, he dabbled in teaching, flirted with the law and finally poured his energies into freelance reviewing. Even during this hard-pressed early phase as a nameless 'bravo' contributing to the boisterous Tory pages of the *Saturday Review*, Morley was adopting the loftiest of postures, the most elevated of tones. Despite his penchant for spelling God with a provocative small 'g', he remained a prisoner of his evangelical upbringing. With his finely honed conscience and zeal for public duty, he struck many as an essentially religious figure, a minister *malgré lui*. 'Cut him open,' remarked George Meredith, 'and you will find a clergyman inside him.'

Morley's early work, *On Compromise* (1874), a richly rhetorical plea for uncompromising truthfulness, reveals him at his preachifying best – or worst. For there is much about this paragon of high principle that now seems remote, if not positively alien. From the pages of John Gross's study, the *Rise and Fall of the Man of Letters* (1969), Morley emerged as the chilliest of eminent Victorians. Nor, for all its mildly satirical, Stracheyesque trimmings, is Gross's sketch of him mere caricature. Morley's lofty literary manner barely hints at the private man – the convivial, if thin-skinned and sometimes prickly, human being, who drank champagne at breakfast, adored pet animals and enjoyed a wide circle of friends in the overlapping literary and political worlds of his day. In print, Morley felt bound to put on the robes of metropolitan authority – he was, after all, editing the *Fortnightly Review* at a time when much of the world was under British rule – and his mandarin prose might have been an advertisement for the moral sublimity of British civilisation. In an age of god-like British reviewers, none managed to be more god-like than Morley.

A talker of epigrammatic brilliance, Morley was quick to make his mark in London society. Not only was he a devotee of John Stuart Mill's, but during his days as a fledgling *Saturday* Reviewer, he had struck up a relationship with the philosopher, often visiting him at his home in Blackheath. Another of his early friendships was with that very different figure, the self-made Birmingham businessman, Joseph Chamberlain, an impetuous, power-hungry man of action, in whom Morley seems to have found something of an *alter ego*. Provincial 'new men' hostile to inherited privilege, Morley and Chamberlain felt themselves to be kindred spirits. Morley was far from sharing Chamberlain's empire-building instincts, though, his own belief in the British *imperium* having nothing to do with territorial expansionism. The falling out which occurred between the pair (over Irish Home Rule, the case for which Morley believed to be compelling) was perhaps inevitable. As they grew estranged, Morley found more and more to admire in Chamberlain's arch-rival, William Ewart Gladstone, whose ardour for Home Rule seemed to match his own; both found Chamberlain's brand of tub-thumping imperialism abhorrent. Playing philosopher to the king, Morley became Gladstone's chief confidant. His voluminous biography of the 'Grand Old Man' (or 'GOM') – published in 1903, in the wake of his hero's death – was a monumental act of homage.

It was through the Francophile Oxford don, Cotter Morison, that Morley became acquainted with the founders of the *Fort-*

nightly Review, a circle that comprised Anthony Trollope, the publisher George F. Chapman, and that versatile littérateur and consort of George Eliot, G.H. Lewes. The latter was the *Fortnightly's* first editor, and an able one, but hardly two years had elapsed since the *Review's* inception in 1865 when the strain of his multifarious activities began to tell on Lewes's fragile health. On Morison's recommendation, the job was offered to Morley. At the time, Morley was 27, a little known literary tyro, anxious to prove himself. For the next fifteen years – a stretch of time he later called *grande mortalis aevi spatium* – the *Fortnightly Review* was to be his life, the focus of his zeal and ambition. During that time, he was to turn what had been a promising, if precarious, venture into a Review of great contemporary significance.

Inspired by the Parisian *Revue des Deux Mondes*, the *Fortnightly's* founders aimed to 'further the cause of Progress by the illumination of many minds' – to which end articles in the Review were to be signed, with each contributor taking responsibility for his own views. They also planned to mix criticism with fiction and poetry – a new departure in the field of the 'higher journalism'. Morley stuck to this formula, while bringing to the *Fortnightly's* pages a new dynamism, an intellectual stringency peculiarly his own. With John Stuart Mill and Auguste Comte among his mentors, he launched a concerted attack on received ideas. Under his iconoclastic, freethinking aegis, the *Review* impugned theology, called for a national system of elementary education that was at once secular and free, championed Trades Unions, stood up for women, put the case for republicanism, and returned again and again to the issue of Ireland's historic grievances. In all this, Morley was able to exploit an extraordinary array of literary talent: Leslie Stephen, T.H. Huxley, Walter Pater, Frederic Harrison, Mark Pattison, Anthony Trollope, George Meredith, Walter Bagehot, Algernon Charles Swinburne, George Eliot, Matthew Arnold – such were the contributors who helped Morley to establish the *Fortnightly Review* as the Bible of Victorian rationalism.

What made Morley's success all the more remarkable was that it was achieved with exiguous resources and a comparatively modest circulation. During the early years of his editorship, the *Fortnightly Review's* readers numbered hardly more than 2,500 – a circulation much smaller than that of the *Edinburgh Review* under Jeffrey. However, if it was seen by few, the *Fortnightly* was read by many who mattered: politicians, clergymen, dons, lawyers. And so consistently stimulating and challenging did the journal contrive to be that it acquired devotees not only among those who were sympathetic to its progressive gospel but among those who were unsympathetic to it also. Morley's feat – a feat performed in the twentieth century with comparable success by Kingsley Martin as editor of the *New Statesman* – was to imbue radical journalism with a literary allure that intelligent readers – whatever their politics – found hard to resist. Required reading for the 'thinking part of the nation', its articles regularly quoted by the *Times* and other newspapers, Morley's *Fortnightly* enjoyed a special authority and centrality. Reviewing his editorial career in 1929, Leonard Woolf hazarded that Morley had probably had more practical political effect than was subsequently achieved by editors of mass circulation newspapers.

It was common enough for individual contributions to the *Fortnightly* to outshine the rest of the *Review*, commanding the kind of public interest once reserved for some famous – or notorious – pamphlet. Thus controversy raged when Morely published an article by Frederic Harrison defending the controversial new movement of trades unionism. But it was scientific articles – direct challenge to religious orthodoxy that they could seem to be – about which feeling ran highest. Morley achieved his greatest editorial coup with his publication of what amounted to an attack on the validity of the Bible by T.H. Huxley – 'Darwin's bulldog', as Huxley liked to style himself. The substance of Huxley's article, the 'Physical Basis of Life', may seem innocuous enough now, but in 1869, its substitution of evolution for Genesis scandalised conventional opinion, precipitating what Morley termed a 'profound sensation'. Much to its editor's delight, this issue of the *Fortnightly* had to be re-printed no fewer than seven times. Such unabashed scepticism caused some to see the *Fortnightly Review* as a revolutionary publication, sapping the foundations of the established order. In certain quarters, Morley was even taken to be some sort of Jacobin, a latter-day Saint-Just baying for blood. The Edwardian editor, W.A. Spender, recalling his boyhood, remembered an atrabilious old relative who nearly had a fit when he found him with a copy of Morley's Review. Writhing with disgust, the old man wrested it from the young Spender's grasp and pitched it onto the fire.

Vis-à-vis religion, Morley *was* of subversive intent. When it came to politics, however, he was very far from being an extremist. In common with Francis Jeffrey, Morley was a creature of eighteenth-century rationalism, an heir of the *philosophes,* who was also a disciple of the their arch-critic, Edmund Burke. Coming after the revolutionary deluge, these influential editors were alike in believing that abstract schemes of progress needed to be tempered by Burke's conservative wisdom, by his intuitive distrust of all proposals for tampering with the existing institutions of society. If, in short, they were on the side of 'progress' and 'enlightenment', they were equally in favour of tradition and the avoidance of precipitate change. Perhaps the only *philosophe* who commanded their complete sympathy was the purposefully moderate Turgot.

Morley wrote with polish and panache about Burke and about the 'philosophical cabal' – the French thinkers for whom Burke felt such loathing. Published in book form, his study of Voltaire was to be reprinted three times. But of all the contributors to what he termed the 'literary preparation for the French Revolution', it was Diderot who seems to have appealed to Morley most. His two volumes on Diderot and the *Encyclopédie* were an erudite and empathetic exploration of the roots of his own generation's liberal beliefs. The *Encyclopédie* – whose editorial address Voltaire called an 'office for the instruction of the human race' – was after all the prototype of the *Fortnightly Review*, of his own intellectual endeavours. Like Diderot, Morley the editor was setting out to establish a 'centre for the best observation of fresh-flowing currents of thought, interest and debate.' Like Diderot, he busied himself with recruiting 'active-minded men of all kinds', exhorting them to pool their mental resources. But could he succeed where Diderot had failed, and forge a fresh intellectual synthesis appropriate to an age of transition, a time when men seemed bereft of their bearings? This was Morley's dream in his capacity as Victorian encyclopaedist – though it was not often that Morley was accused of dreaming.

As he replaced the many volumes of Diderot's *magnum opus* on his shelf, Morley mused that their pages would seldom be disturbed by himself or others ever again, for they had long since served their historic purpose and were now little more than a noble ruin. The possibility that the same fate awaited his own endeavours seems not to have bothered Morley too much. From his study of Diderot, he drew the conclusion that the business of the encyclopaedist had little to do with making great literature. His mission was to educate his age, to be effective in his own time. Diderot's example inspired him to think that men of letters like himself – specialists in what he called 'dispersiveness' – were society's new directors, inheritors of the role that had traditionally been occupied by the clergy.

While he was editing the *Fortnightly Review*, it was possible for Morley to feel that the status of the 'higher journalism' was rising by the day, and that the *Fortnightly* itself was an almost integral part of the machinery of state. An 'eminent Review editor' once boasted to Morley that he felt himself to be equal in importance to twenty-five members of parliament. Morley affected to find this claim a trifle excessive, but appears to have had no doubt that the *Fortnightly Review* and its like were powerful instruments. Reviews, he remarked, betokened a 'very considerable revolution' in intellectual habits. Promoting freethinking, helping to rid the world of ignorance and superstition, they had brought 'abstract discussion' from the library down to the 'first man in the street'. Thanks to them, the general public was increasingly exercised by questions which, twenty years earlier, would have been discussed only in 'obscure debating societies' and 'little secularist clubs'. Speculation had become wholly democratised. Now everybody who read anything at all serious was reading a dozen essays a year about the existence of god and the survival of the soul, and the eternal riddles lay on the table alongside the popular magazines.

▼▲▼

In the early 1880s, Morley was at the height of his journalistic renown. By now he was editing both the *Fortnightly Review* and the *Pall Mall Gazette*, the evening newspaper beloved of Gladstone, which had been founded by Frederick Greenwood with the express purpose of bringing the 'higher journalism' to the attention of a wider public. Somehow, Morley also found time to compile a hefty biography of the late Liberal statesman, Thomas Cobden. Championing free trade, international peace, mass elementary education and Home Rule for Ireland, Morley was beginning to assume Cobden's mantle as the conscience of British Liberalism. Indeed, with socialism an embryonic movement still, he was widely regarded as the standard-bearer of 'progressive' politics.

Morley briefly edited the popular literary magazine, *Macmillan's*, but by the mid-1880s he had given up being a full-time editor. Aspiring to be an actor, not just a spectator, to make history, not just to write it, he entered Parliament as MP for Newcastle in 1883, after which he rapidly rose to ministerial office.

The major literary works on which he might have embarked would never be begun. In later years, Thomas Hardy said that he could have become the author of a great historical epic, the Gibbon of his day, but Morley had long suspected that, compared with being a great statesman, the fame of a Gibbon was a paltry thing. Yet whether it meant more to influence human destiny by means of literature or by means of legislation was a dilemma that continued to haunt him as he held the fates, first of Ireland, then of India, in his imperial hands. In the event, Morley was to devote his later years to a career in politics that his friend, J.H. Morgan, would euphemistically describe as a 'triumph of character over achievement'. Like Richard Crossman in more recent times, Morley became that peculiarly awkward, fallible figure, the intellectual in politics, fated to be judged according to his own stringent standards.

During his years at the India Office (1906–1911), the former editor of the *Fortnightly Review* ran the risk of losing his reputation for enlightenment. Fearful of public disorder and swift to crack down on native unrest, Morley the liberal turned into something of an autocrat where the people of India were concerned. Indeed, many of his admirers were appalled by the speed with which he ordered the arrest and imprisonment of Indian dissidents, by his readiness to invoke *raison d'état*. Perhaps, for all his 'civilisation', Morley could not entirely conquer a tendency to regard non-Europeans as lesser breeds. At all events, without ever visiting India, he ruled some 300 million Indian people by telegraph and dispatch from an office in Whitehall; and when Indians visited him, he was tempted (so he privately confessed) to dispense with 'Parisian', 'cosmopolitan', or even 'London' 'varnish'. Still, if Morley had difficulty in regarding Indians as fellow human beings, he began reforms that ultimately issued in Indian independence. His record at the India Office was at once liberal and illiberal.

To T.H. Huxley Morley confided that he had set out to improve politics – only to find that politics was 'dis-improving' him. Embroiled in public affairs, he must sometimes have rued the moral absolutism of his early writings, the high-minded rejection of compromise that had earned him the soubriquet, 'Honest John'. This said, his political career was by no means a story of erstwhile principles betrayed. In his opposition to imperial expansionism and war-mongering, Morley was unswerving. The Boer War – of which his old friend, Joseph Chamberlain ('Jingo Joe' as he became known) was perhaps the chief instigator – found in him one of its harshest critics. And when Britain went to war against Germany in 1914, Morley resigned his Cabinet post, desolated by a turn of events hardly anticipated during the glad, confident rationalist morning when he was editing the *Fortnightly Review*. Subject – like so many doubting Victorians – to fits of gloom about the ultimate meaning of the universe, Morley had nevertheless entertained a firm belief in human progress. Now he confessed himself 'half-sorry' to have lived long enough to see 'such ship wreck'.

Quitting the public stage, Morley immured himself in the library of his Wimbledon home. Surrounded by 11,000 volumes – his own collection of books had been augmented by the library of the late Liberal historian, Lord Acton – he 'brooded among the ghosts of centuries'. In front of guests, he seldom mentioned the war, preferring to talk about the great masters of European literature and indulge his taste for edifying aphorisms (on his mantelpiece was carved Bacon's saying, 'The nobler a soul, the more objects of compassion it hath'). To some, he had become 'Lord Morley of Borley', the personification of elderly sententiousness. George Bernard Shaw referred to him as that 'solemn piece of literary obsolescence'. And by insisting on the destruction of his private papers, Morley did what he could to ensure that posterity's knowledge of him would be confined to his lapidary public utterances. To this day, much about this Victorian Pharaoh – who seems to have had a Puritanical aversion to being painted or photographed – remains inscrutable. Despite his objection to literary anonymity, Morley could not have kept his own *incognito* more completely. The two volumes of memoirs that he published in 1917, under the title *Recollections*, are works of unyielding reticence. About his marriage to Lady Morley – with whom he was seldom ever seen – the world knows next to nothing.

Before he died in 1923, Morley had the satisfaction of seeing Ireland gain Home Rule. Nevertheless, the society that emerged in the wake of the First World War was one he found largely alien. For socialism – rapidly displacing Liberalism as the dominant political creed among 'progressive' intellectuals – he had scant sympathy. To him, it signified collectivism, the death of individual liberties. It is strange, at first glance, that he should have got on so well with the socialist firebrand and communist-sympathiser-in-the-making, Harold Laski. What united the two men was that they were both alumni of the Enlightenment, for whom rationalism was tantamount to a religion. 'The life of reason burned the more brightly for his presence,' wrote Laski after Morley's death. Perhaps it did. 'Perhaps', incidentally, was a word for which Morley, with his scrupulous scepticism, had profound respect.

▼▲▼

Morley vacated his editorial chair when the enfranchisement of the working classes and the introduction of mass education were new and imponderable developments. Subsequent years were to witness far-reaching changes in the world of journalism – changes in which nobody would play a more pervasively influential part than Alfred Harmsworth, the future Lord Northcliffe. The launching of Harmsworth's *Daily Mail* in May 1896 was nothing less than a turning-point in British social history. Comprising terse, easily digested news items, brimming with 'human interest' stories and all manner of piquant trivia, the *Daily*

Mail marked the sudden arrival of the mass circulation newspaper, which purported to reflect all aspects of human life. Never again would a handful of dignified daily titles – like the *Times* and the *Daily Telegraph* – together with a phalanx of magisterial quarterly and monthly Reviews, overshadow the rest of the press. The 'higher journalism' was not facing extinction, but its heyday – the period when it was possible for John Morley to envisage the earth being inherited by *Fortnightly* reviewers with elegant prose styles and well-furnished minds – proved short-lived.

'We must educate our masters' was the maxim of earnest editors like Morley, haunted by the spectre of 'King Demos' and anxious to teach the new mass reading and voting public how – and even what – to think. For Alfred Harmsworth, by contrast, such high-mindedness was really snobbery-in-disguise. Fancying himself the champion of the common man (the parallels between him and that latter-day uncommon common man, Rupert Murdoch, are in many ways striking), Harmsworth set about supplying readers with an undemanding diet of entertainment and gimmickry. His overriding aim was to build up the maximum possible circulation – and in the process to establish lucrative links with the burgeoning advertising industry. Making people think barely entered his calculations; and in the unsentimental figure of Kennedy Jones – who insisted that journalists made sure that their work appealed to readers of the meanest intelligence – he found the ideal henchman. 'You left journalism a profession,' Jones would one day tell John Morley. 'We have turned it into a branch of commerce.' Alas, there seems to be no record of Morley's reply. That it was Olympian seems certain.

The vast success of the *Daily Mail* – palpable proof of King Demos's progress – unnerved many among the ruling classes. The great boast of papers of quality, such as the *Pall Mall Gazette*, was that they were written by gentlemen for gentlemen. Here was an organ that appeared to be written and read by mere office boys – or so sneered the Tory Prime Minister, Lord Salisbury, himself one of the higher journalism's loftiest Victorian exponents. Yet if the *Daily Mail* inspired patrician distaste and unease, it was soon prompting more worldly-wise reactions as well. Fears that the *Mail*, with its sensationalism and vast, semi-educated readership, amounted to a recipe for revolution gave way to the realisation that the *status quo* had actually found a fresh bulwark. Indeed, the paper's loyalty to the established order became proverbial. According to the great Edwardian newspaper editor and columnist, A.G. Gardiner, shrewd aristocrats discovered that the safest way to deal with office boys was to ply them with copies of the *Daily Mail.*

What few were inclined to dispute was that, following the revolution wrought by Harmsworth, the gap between serious and popular journalism had grown wider than ever, and was now an inexorable cultural fact which it was useless to challenge. For what common ground was there between a newspaper like the *Daily Mail* and an intellectual Review like the *Fortnightly* – or between their respective readerships? Yet, during this time, there emerged a quixotic figure who dreamed of human fellowship and unity and who made the bridging of gulfs, whether in journalism or in any other sphere, his life's work. Brought to metropolitan prominence by John Morley, this self-styled barbarian from the north of England was bent on achieving the impossible. With one foot in Morley's world and the other planted in the brazen new journalistic world of Alfred Harmsworth, he aspired to be both high-minded *and* popular, to capture the attention of gentlemen *and* office boys. His quixotic quest was to make for one of the most extraordinary public lives of modern times.

W.T. Stead

5. 'The Chief'

A bronze plaque on the Thames Embankment memorialises the exploits of the ubiquitous Victorian pressman, William Thomas ('W.T.') Stead. An insatiable communicator who would have been hugely at home in the age of the internet, Stead frankly propounded the case for 'government by journalism' and dedicated all his energies to practising what he preached. The Victorian political fixer, Reginald Brett (later Viscount Esher), doubted if any major public event of the late nineteenth century was innocent of Stead's influence. However, this ambitious editor-cum-journalist was not content simply to stamp his personality on the present. Much given to forecasting the future, he also aspired to play the part of history's midwife. Long before the First World War, Stead was championing the cause of European unity (he talked of the desirability of a common currency) and advocating a merger between what he feared was a tottering British Empire and the United States, of whose growing power he was ever mindful. How extraordinary that during a time when books on all aspects of Victorian culture have poured from the presses, Stead has been so neglected by posterity. Only now, thanks in some degree to the work of the American scholars, Joseph Baylen and Grace Eckley, (editor of the informative journal, *NewsStead*), is his many-sided career being re-discovered. In many ways, it is as though Gladstone had slid from view.

A self-trumpeting showman, Stead was also an earnest crusader, an aspirant 'philosopher-king' with a zeal for education and social progress. Prodigious in his self-belief, he button-holed heads of state, fought injustice, proclaimed the joy of knowledge, celebrated outdoor exercise – he was an ardent cyclist at a time when the bicycle was new – and paraded his faith in what we now call the 'paranormal'. With his unkempt beard and brilliant blue eyes, his scruffy clothes and lust for living, Stead was the kind of psychological extremist we associate with the novels of Dostoevsky. His sudden death in April 1912 – sailing to New York, he went down with the *Titanic* – was the somehow inevitable climax to a life charged with headline-grabbing drama.

Stead's fame was a feature of that increasingly remote time when a large part of the world was under British rule. For many years, Stead himself was convinced that the English-speaking peoples were fortune's favourites. In this, he was at one with his empire-fixated friend, Cecil Rhodes, whose conquistador image in the eyes of the late Victorian public he helped to fix. Underlying his main publishing enterprise, the *Review of Reviews*, launched in 1890, was the goal of imbuing English-speaking people everywhere with a sense of their historic destiny. A triumphant success during the first decade of its existence, the *Review of Reviews* was the pulpit of Stead's maturity, the platform from which he lectured mankind. From it sprang an American and an Australian *Review of Reviews*, publications with independent editors but which also played some part in promulgating Stead's grand, if nebulous, vision.

Stead was a Nonconformist, a cradle Puritan whose faith in the Bible never weakened. Born in 1849, in the village of Embleton, near the Scottish border, he was the son of a Congregational Minister and attended the celebrated Silcoates School in Wakefield. Even as a boy, he was railing against wrong-doing, dashing off letters of furious protest to the local press. In 1871, aged just twenty-one, he became editor of the *Northern Echo*, the Darlington-based Liberal paper which Harold Evans, conscious of his forebear's formidable example, was to edit in the 1960s. Five years later, Stead rose to national fame when, in print and at public meetings, he anathematised Turkish atrocities against Bulgarian Christians, dwelling with characteristic horror on the violation of women. 'Arouse the nation or be damned', he heard

God telling him. His righteous stand inspired Gladstone – who read the *Northern Echo* avidly – to write his inflammatory pamphlet, *The Bulgarian Horrors and the Question of the East*. Stead was particularly anxious to deter the pro-Turkish Tory Prime Minister, Disraeli, from starting a war in which Britain would end up allied with Turkey not only against the beleaguered Bulgarians but also against Russia. A romantic Slavophile who grew intimate with the intriguing pan-Slav propagandist, Madame Novikoff, the editor of the *Northern Echo* would in due course be honoured by the Bulgarian National Assembly for his contribution to Bulgarian independence.

In 1880, Stead decamped to London, to work under John Morley on the prestigious evening paper, the *Pall Mall Gazette*. Morley and his colleague were to be described as a 'union of classical severity and rude Gothic vigour', and it was true that, for all his bombast, Stead had none of Morley's patrician *hauteur*. In many respects, as a self-appointed people's tribune, he was the heir of those earlier plain-dealing Puritans, Daniel Defoe and William Cobbett. Like them, he was a strange Protestant compound, a self-engrossed do-gooder, a champion of co-operation whose career was to be a one-man show.

When Stead voiced his premonition that Morley was going to become an MP and that he himself was about to occupy the latter's editorial chair, Morley reacted with 'chill disdain'. In 1883, though, Morley did indeed quit the 'higher journalism' for politics, and Stead duly became the *Pall Mall Gazette*'s principal director. It was now that his self-advertising genius for journalism made itself abundantly apparent. By the end of the 1880s, Stead had played a central role in transforming journalistic practice, effecting changes that did much to shape the press's whole subsequent evolution. Banishing the grim sobriety of the Victorian newspaper with its endless columns of anonymous print, Stead introduced illustrations, went in for sensational headlines and crossheads, and adopted that typically American practice, the interview, as the most efficient means yet devised of 'extracting the ideas of the few for the instruction of the many'. What Stead was ambitious to bring into being was a newspaper that 'palpitated with actuality' – while also palpitating with the personality of W.T. Stead. Soon Matthew Arnold was superciliously identifying him as the father of that seductive, if only too democratic and essentially 'featherbrained' fashion, the 'New Journalism'. Styling himself an 'imperialist plus the ten commandments and common sense', the New Journalism's exponent-in-chief set out to run the British Empire from his editorial desk in Northumberland Street. The latter part of 1884 found him employing his innovative approach to concentrate national attention on the situation in the Sudan, where British troops and civilians were threatened with annihilation at the hands of a messianic Muslim warrior known as the 'Mahdi'. Perhaps influenced by contacts in high places, Stead concluded that only one man could be expected to deal with this troublesome tribesman: the single-minded, God-fearing British general who had quelled the Taiping Rebellion on behalf of the Emperor of China, and who was known to the British public as 'Chinese Gordon'.

At the beginning of 1884, Gordon chanced to be in Southampton, on his way to the Congo to work on behalf of King Leopold of Belgium. Wasting no time, Stead went and sought the peripatetic military mystic's views. On January 9th, the *Pall Mall Gazette* carried a voluminous interview in which the general – himself a sometime governor of the Sudan – spoke with an air of great authority about the Mahdi and what might be done to tackle the crisis. The paper also carried a lively leading article by Stead crying up Gordon's unique qualifications for the task in hand. In the wake of Stead's well-timed scoop, the entire British press became consumed with Gordon fever, and before long crowds on the streets of London were chanting: 'Gordon must go ...' Hitherto loath to do anything, Gladstone, now Prime Minister, and his Cabinet, found themselves obliged to defer to what appeared to be the popular will. By January 18th, 'Chinese Gordon' was being dispatched to the Sudan.

Perhaps Stead saw in the Bible-besotted, empire-smitten Gordon a sort of military *alter ego*. Certainly, he bore much of the responsibility for creating the overblown public impression of him as a superman figure, as an infallible national saviour. Not that the editor of the *Pall Mall Gazette* seems to have felt all that much remorse over the bloody catastrophe that overtook his headlong hero at Khartoum. Early and late, Stead was adamant that Gordon had been undone by stupid statesmen who denied him a free hand and failed to furnish him with adequate support. Above all, he blamed Lord Cromer, Britain's Agent in Egypt, making him out to be an unimaginative bureaucrat who would long be remembered for having fatally obstructed a soldier of genius. The whole sorry saga only stiffened Stead's conviction that it was the editor, not the politician, who knew best.

As the débâcle in the Sudan unfolded, Stead was becoming exercised by evidence that Britain's much-vaunted navy was turning into an out-of-date liability. In September 1884, acting on information supplied by Captain (later Admiral) John Fisher, he drew up an exhaustive inventory of the navy's shortcomings. As well-documented as it was acutely embarrassing, Stead's *Pall Mall Gazette* report, the 'The Truth about the Navy', charged the British government with systematic negligence, and called for the immediate construction of modern 'Iron-Clads'. As in the case of his interview with Gordon, Stead contrived to launch a crusade which the rest of the press was swift to join; and, as before, Gladstone and his colleagues were confronted by a mounting popular agitation which they could not ignore. Acceding to many, if not all, of Stead's demands, the government stumped up £3 million for a programme of naval renewal. Little wonder if the editor of the *Pall Mall Gazette* began to think of himself as the Prime Minister of British journalism.

It was in the following year that Stead embarked on the most emotive and effective of all his *Pall Mall Gazette* campaigns. Understandably impressed by his record of getting things done, the philanthropists, Benjamin Scott and Josephine Butler, entreated him to support them in awakening British consciences about the scourge of child prostitution and about the so-called 'White Slave Trade', the thriving international commerce in under-age girls. This pair of genteel Victorian reformers, both of whom were lobbying to get the age of consent raised from thirteen to sixteen, could hardly have recruited a keener coadjutor. At the age of eleven, Stead had picked a fight with the school bully for leering at a girl as she stooped to adjust her garter, receiving a beating for his pains. Throughout his life he was to nurse a positively theatrical penchant for knight-errantry.

Stead's Holy War against Victorian vice was melodramatic stuff. In pursuit of suitably shocking copy, he took to leading a nocturnal existence, going into London brothels and quizzing brothel-keepers and prostitutes. Over a period of weeks in the first part of 1885, he managed to amass a vast and incriminating body of information about the secret lives of wealthy men, pillars of society who were private debauchees. Abetted by a former madame, he even staged the procurement of a twelve year old girl, with a view to writing a plausible eye-witness account of just how simple it was to perform such a transaction. A certain Eliza Armstrong lay doped in a candle-lit room, while Stead, got up as a gentleman roué equipped with a cigar and a glass of champagne, paid her a fleeting visit. Later, she was spirited away to France by the Salvation Army (with whose chief-of-staff, William Bramwell Booth, he enjoyed a close rapport). The aim, apparently, was both to ensure her safety and to enable Stead to emphasise the ease with which such a child might fall prey to the White Slave Trade.

Entitled 'The Maiden Tribute of Modern Babylon', and mingling in-depth reportage with fulminating moral outrage and lurid sensationalism, Stead's revelations were serialised in the *Pall Mall Gazette* during the first two weeks of July 1885. The result proved to be perhaps the greatest newspaper furore of the nineteenth century. Scandalising polite London, Stead's exposé of British upper-class decadence aroused the curiosity of people everywhere – this being a time when news travelled faster and reached more readers than ever before. Demand for the *Pall Mall Gazette* was such – particularly in the United States – that copies of the paper began selling on the black market at astronomical prices. A contemporary print shows the *Gazette*'s offices besieged by a vociferous mob. According to the writer, Hugh Kingsmill, it was not until the First World War that Britain was to see anything like this display of mass emotion again.

On August 13th 1885, barely a month after 'The Maiden Tribute' was published, Parliament passed the Criminal Law Amendment Act, which raised the age of consent to sixteen (and which also, incidentally, proscribed all homosexual relationships). Yet because he had abducted Eliza Armstrong without the consent of her putative father, the triumphant crusader suddenly found himself under arrest; and, at the Old Bailey, on November 13th, he was actually sentenced to three months in Holloway Gaol. Rather than resenting this seemingly galling turns of events, however, Stead seems to have relished the chance to comport himself as a martyr in the cause of righteousness, and while behind bars he wrote on, more carried away than ever by feelings of his own moral and political significance. In a self-intoxicated contribution to the *Contemporary Review*, entitled 'Government by Journalism', he argued that in the new democratic era, with its speeded-up communications, newspapers were reducing politics to subordinate status. For had not the press – a parliament that was always in session – become the 'eye and ear and tongue of the people'? Was it not the 'visible speech if not the voice of democracy'? Were not those who ran it, being closer to the public, the 'wielders of real power'? As if drafting a charter for the reputedly 'over-mighty' barons of today's media, Stead exalted the editor as the 'uncrowned king of a modern democracy'.

It must be said that Stead prompted some to think of him not as an uncrowned king but as a sex-obsessed zealot. Following 'The Maiden Tribute' episode, he set about hounding the Liberal Party's rising star, the allegedly adulterous Sir Charles Dilke, with a fury that made even his well-wishers wince. And when it emerged that Charles Stewart Parnell had for years been conducting an affair with the wife of a fellow MP, Kitty O'Shea, he hounded the Irish leader with the same immoderate, not to say fanatical, tenacity. Both figures were to be badly damaged by a Fleet Street persecutor who in reality was an ardent, if mostly platonic, womaniser himself. Indeed, it seems safe to say that Stead's rabid censoriousness when it came to sexual morals was rooted in his own guilty conscience. Yet despite – or perhaps because of – his own promiscuous urges, this monogamous Puritan would always insist that marital fidelity was the bedrock of the social order, the very foundation of Britain's imperial success.

The forty-one year old Stead was a powerful figure when he launched the *Review of Reviews* as a novel kind of monthly in 1890. Like his school friend and initial sponsor in the venture, George Newnes, he was keen to make the most of the publishing opportunities conferred by the diffusion of literacy. But unlike Newnes, who had founded the magazine *Tit-Bits* in 1881 – thereby placing Northcliffe and all subsequent popular press magnates in his debt – Stead was far from seeing himself as a purveyor of mere entertainment. The age of mass circulation journalism was still to dawn in 1890, and Stead, the pioneer sensation-monger, was about to enrol himself among those British intellectual editors who have aspired to create a thinking democracy, convinced that high-minded reviewing has a vital contribution to make to the improvement of mankind.

Stead's proselytising enthusiasm for education was bound up with his sense of the Anglo-Saxon race's special destiny. The *Review of Review*'s mind-boggling manifesto conveyed Stead's ambition to circulate a periodical that would be to the English-speaking world what the Catholic Church had once been to the 'intelligence of Christendom'. No ordinary monthly, the *Review of Reviews* was to be read as men used to read their Bibles – not to waste an idle hour but to discover the will of God. Meant both to educate and inspire, the *Review of Reviews* was going, Stead believed, to attract devotees throughout the world, men and women who would thrill to the vision that he shared with Cecil Rhodes: that of an English-speaking empire capable of sustaining peace and justice *ad infinitum*. Here was a scheme of things in which perhaps only God – whom Stead routinely called the 'Senior Partner' – had a more central role to play than the editor of the *Review of Reviews*.

It says much about Stead's ebullient optimism in the 1890s that the *Review of Reviews* opened with a section entitled 'The Progress of the World', a trenchant summary of events throwing into relief the great drama of history-in-the-making. Illustrated with photographs and cartoons culled from both the British and foreign press, the rest of the Review comprised a profile of some newsworthy personality and a copious critique of a 'book of the month', plus an extensive critical digest of the latest periodical literature. The vibrant vehicle of the opinions, schemes and crusades of W.T. Stead, the *Review of Reviews* also embodied a prodigious quantity of distilled research; and since this was a time when the periodical press was in a state of relentless expansion – its size trebled during the first ten years of the *Review*'s existence – Stead and his small staff had ever more ground to cover. That they carried out their work with such unfailing efficiency is something for which posterity can be grateful. A wide-ranging, well-organised repository of contemporary news and views, Stead's monthly illuminates the fateful years leading up to the cataclysm of 1914 like no other.

Pricing his Review at sixpence – a Review such as the *Fortnightly* cost five times as much – Stead made the contents of the higher journalism available to the new mass reading public. Among those who appreciated his efforts to 'democratise thought' was that faintly ludicrous figure in the early history of British trade unionism and local government, John Burns. Burns, an autodidact with a booming voice, hailed the *Review of Reviews* as a blessing to those – like himself – who hungered for intellectual stimulus but were too poor to afford all the Reviews that they would like to buy. His Battersea home bulging with books, Burns was typical of many working-class men and women of his day to whom education seemed at once glamorous and liberating. To such people, Stead's Review was calculated to make a special appeal. But his Review's popularity was not confined to the less privileged. The monthly known as the 'Busy Man's Magazine' was also appealing to all who felt helpless in the face of the floodtide of new books and new information. Present-day feelings of being overwhelmed, of simply never being able to keep up, have a long pedigree. Such feelings were widespread in the 1890s, before the end of which Stead was claiming an international circulation of some 200,000 (and taking special pleasure in the discovery that his readers included a Chilean sheep farmer).

During the 1890s, Stead operated from Mowbray House, a grand Victorian edifice in Norfolk Street, a thoroughfare off the Strand demolished in the 1970s. Known as the 'Sanctum', his office looked out onto the Thames, then thronged with maritime traffic of every description. It was there, at the top of a long flight of stairs and flanked by photographs of public figures and animals, with the newly invented telephone forever ringing, that Stead held court. 'The Chief', as he was known to his staff, was often to be found deliberating with politicians and with dignitaries from across the Atlantic or the Indian subcontinent, but by all accounts, his door was equally open to the humble and obscure, to anybody seeking help. Those who approached him ranged from exploited workers to abused women, from childless parents to would-be suicides. For Stead, as for that earlier 'Great Cham',

Dr Johnson, playing the sage and dispensing charity were aspects of the same moral mission. If Mowbray House stood as a beacon of light, a source of British intelligence and instruction, it was also something of a welfare centre, the headquarters of a Christian editor who pleaded for the 'union of all who love in the service of all who suffer'.

Stead delighted to play the part of genial host, diffusing the spirit of fellowship and fraternity. At one stage, he and his wife were throwing regular *Review of Reviews* parties, to which anyone could apply for an invitation. Held in the Sanctum on Friday afternoons, between four o'clock and six, the Steads' 'At Homes' appear to have been popular events. Elizabeth Banks, a journalist on the staff of the *Washington Post,* made them the subject of an effusive dispatch. As Mr Stead poured tea and passed round cake, she reported, guests found themselves mingling with a cosmopolitan assortment of guests – including people from Japan, India, Austria-Hungary, France, Spain and Germany. Mowbray House, she added, was the place to meet one's favourite actors and actresses, who kept dropping in from local theatres; or to shake the hand of one's favourite author; or, if one happened to be a journalist, to make the acquaintance of one's favourite editor. One met many a clergyman, too, as well as men and women whose only reason for being present was that they were subscribers to the *Review of Reviews* – but who invariably proved to be the most cultivated and interesting people. The temptation to quote liberally from this flattering write-up in the very next issue of the *Review of Reviews* was one which Stead made no effort to resist. At a later date, he published a photograph of one of his 'At Homes', showing the Sanctum crammed with guests, many of them well-dressed ladies wearing hats and veils. In the corner of the picture stands a gentleman with a beard and a turban, evidently a Sikh.

Seldom, though, was Stead at his leisure for long. Puritanism had implanted in him an abhorrence of idleness, a dread of wasting a single moment. Not only was Mowbray House the address of the *Review of Reviews* – from the same premises, Stead published cheap abridged editions of the literary classics; ran a circulation library (from which stout boxes of books were sent to provincial subscribers); launched a scheme for adopting babies; set up a correspondence society on behalf of the lonely and isolated; and encouraged the learning of languages by letter-writing. Stead himself took a particular interest in Esperanto, Ludwig Zahmenhof's newly-devised *lingua franca*, whose use as an antidote to international misunderstanding he did much to promote.

Briefly, Mowbray House also served as the headquarters of another magazine edited by Stead, *Borderland*, the first publication to be devoted exclusively to the exploration of the occult. Making common cause with Madame Blavatsky, Annie Besant, Conan Doyle and others, Stead identified himself as an exponent of 'Spiritualism', then a novel development. Like Arthur Koestler in more recent times, he aspired to establish the study of unexplained phenomena as a respectable field of inquiry. Prone to bursts of 'automatic writing', Stead insisted that he himself was psychic and that a certain Julia Ames, an American journalist of his acquaintance, who had died young, had chosen him as her medium. If he had any doubts about the reality of the spirit world, they were dispelled entirely following the untimely death of his son, William, in 1907 at the age of twenty-four. Stead was delighted to inform his readers that his son was maintaining regular contact with him from beyond the grave. It was in the aftermath of William's death that he set up the psychic information exchange known as *Julia's Bureau* for the sake of those who were anxious to communicate with the departed.

Nevertheless, temporal power was to remain Stead's chief preoccupation. Great potentates – his Puritan forebear, Oliver Cromwell, prominent among them – beguiled his imagination (though he also liked to identify himself with the Pope, and established 'Vatican' as the the *Review of Review*'s telegram address). It was Stead's fascination with power that underlay his rapt interest in the apparently inexorable progress of the United States. Here, he felt, was a phenomenon of the utmost significance, not just for the British but for the whole world. During his later years, Stead grew ever more convinced that, by virtue of its vastly greater population and superior spirit of enterprise, the USA was destined to supplant Britain as the dominant world power of the twentieth century. Admittedly, he was by no means alone in his incipient doubts about Britain's imperial prospects. Kipling nursed similar forebodings, as did Cecil Rhodes. What kept up the spirits of these despondent (and in some ways, perhaps, rather sinister) 'race patriots' was the dream that the English-speaking peoples as a whole might yet join forces to form the greatest empire of all time.

Stead's gathering sense of the precariousness of the British Empire was reinforced by the Boer War, that 'strange and sordid tragedy', as he called it, in which a quarter of a million British soldiers struggled to subdue a mere 15,000 Boer farmers. As it turned out, the war – which lasted from 1899 till 1902 – was to mark a turning-point in Stead's career, if not in his whole view of things. For despite his earlier fervour for Cecil Rhodes's empire-building exploits in South Africa, Stead believed that the Boers were a wronged people and that British aggression against them was a crime. It was a stand for which he would pay a high price. With war fever raging among the British populace, the editor who had so often advertised his credentials as a British patriot was smeared by the 'yellow press' as a traitor. Meanwhile, sales of the *Review of Reviews* plummeted, and Stead found himself painfully at odds with his old friend Rhodes. Though the two men stayed on polite terms, the South African War – which saw British soldiers herding Boer women and children into what became known as concentration camps – shook Stead's faith in the vision that had bound him and Rhodes together.

The deterioration of his relations with Rhodes probably upset

Stead more than the enmity directed at him by British jingoists: some of his favourite preoccupations had sprung from têtes-à-têtes with the chiliastic diamond magnate – not least his vision of a select body of men dedicated to promoting the unity of the English-speaking people with the kind of zeal that Loyola and the Society of Jesus brought to the rescue of Catholicism in the seventeenth century. Such was the rapport between the pair, moreover, that Rhodes nominated Stead as one of the executors of his Will, thinking that his friend would make an ideal administrator of his scheme to bestow Oxford scholarships on selected students from America, Australia and South Africa. But Stead's opposition to the Boer War and all those party to it caused the sickly millionaire to rescind his decision. The editor of the *Review of Reviews* was, he decided, 'too eccentric' for his grave purposes.

During the last fifteen years of his life, aghast at the 'arms race' in which the European powers seemed increasingly caught up, Stead committed himself to the cause of international peace. Following Tsar Nicholas II's 'Peace Rescript' in 1899, he busied himself with promoting the First Hague Peace Conference (which led to the creation of the International Court of Justice in the Dutch capital). The Tsar was among the heads of state to whom the great champion of 'government by journalism' paid a visit as he travelled to country after country on a 'Peace Crusade', endeavouring to awaken public concern about the mounting menace of militarism. That the Tsar was regarded by many of his subjects as a gruesome tyrant Stead somehow contrived not to notice. What mattered to him was that the Russian Emperor was capable of making an enlightened gesture, and that he had the good sense to subscribe to the *Review of Reviews.*

Prior to the First World War, nobody worked harder than Stead to foster friendship between Britain and an ever more emulous Germany, with its Kaiser who jibbed at British imperial pre-eminence and dreamed of his own 'place in the sun'. In 1906, he played a leading role in arranging a visit of German editors to Britain as a means of generating goodwill among leaders of national opinion. The following year, he took part in a reciprocal visit by English editors to Germany. This is not to suggest, however, that he was prepared to see Britain and Germany enjoying parity in defence terms. In the time that remained to him, Stead launched a fresh and highly effective press campaign to strengthen the British navy. 'Build "two keels to one"', was his advice to the British government faced with the Kaiser's palpable ambition to achieve naval supremacy.

The Titanic went down on April 15th 1912. Stead had been on his way to a Peace Rally in New York, and was one of the ship's most famous passengers. It was the end of a publicist who once characterised his time as an 'age of miracles', an epoch when, with knowledge growing at an ever more dizzying pace and each year bringing fresh discoveries and inventions, anything seemed possible – from the making of an 'unsinkable' ocean liner to the penetration of human existence's ultimate mysteries. A figure of boundless energy, ambition and curiosity, Stead had aped Icarus, striving to fly ever higher, as though blind to human limitations. Now this imperial Englishman was fated to sink to the bottom of the sea.

Latterly, Stead was seen by many as an ageing crank; and it is true that with some of his activities – for instance, the posthumous psychic interview that he conducted with Disraeli in 1909 on the budget crisis of that year – he seemed to be deliberately courting public ridicule. Nevertheless, his death was mourned throughout the world. Forgetting his excesses, fellow journalists remembered him for his humanity and for the blows that he had struck on behalf of decency and truth. A.G. Gardiner portrayed him as a man apart, unique and incomparable. 'He did not belong to our narrow ways and timid routines,' wrote Gardiner. 'The wide waters of the Atlantic are a fitting grave for his bones.'

James Knowles

6. Distinguished Functionary

Stead's perihelion coincided with that of his suave contemporary, James Knowles, founder and mainstay of the Review known as the *Nineteenth Century.* While infinitely more discreet than the publicity-fixated proprietor of the *Review of Reviews*, Knowles, too, was a British journalist avid for renown and influence. Not surprisingly, perhaps, Stead and Knowles, masterful personalities both, were jealous rivals, keenly conscious of one another's activities. It was in Knowles's pages that Matthew Arnold condescended to note the emergence of the 'New Journalism', loftily ascribing this dubious development to a 'certain young man'. For his own part, Knowles regarded Stead as a 'filthy ex-convict' and branded the *Review of Reviews* (in which articles published by him were regularly subjected to critical scrutiny) an exercise in literary piracy. Launched in 1877, the *Nineteenth Century* was an undertaking of consummate superiority, an organ of the higher thought addressed to the higher classes; pre-eminent among its readers were the Victorian statesmen and aristocrats, the ecclesiastical dignitaries and London literati immortalised in the novels of Anthony Trollope.

Conducting his Review as though it had nothing to do with mere commerce, Knowles projected himself as the least earth-bound of editors: everything about him was Olympian. Yet despite his celestial pretensions, he was a shrewd entrepreneur, whose taste for fine writing was matched by his flair for business. When – after being employed for six years as editor of the *Contemporary Review* – he resolved to start a Review of his own, his father agreed to underwrite the venture with a loan of £2,000. So swiftly, though, did the *Nineteenth Century* establish itself as a lucrative concern that Knowles found no occasion to take advantage of his father's generosity. By the time of Knowles's death in 1908, his

Review was a national institution, as well-known as it was profitable. To his heirs, Knowles bequeathed a legacy of £31,000 – a small fortune by the standards of Edwardian England. The 'higher journalism' never had a more prosperous exponent.

Born in 1831, James Knowles grew up in Clapham at a time when the neighbourhood was still identified with the 'Clapham Sect', the Evangelical movement with which morally and intellectually earnest families such as the Macaulays were associated. Knowles's father was a high-minded, upwardly mobile architect from Reigate. A small, dapper bundle of nervous energy, Knowles was to become a high-minded, upwardly mobile architect too. As a young man, he helped his father to design the Grosvenor Hotel, that monument to Victorian Gothicism which still stands next to London's Victoria Station. His own architectural claims to fame were to include the laying out of the garden of Leicester Square and the designing of Aldworth, Tennyson's pseudo-medieval manor house on the Sussex Downs. However, from the earliest age, Knowles took an intense interest in the topics of the hour, developing a penchant for eclectic discussion. The case for and against religion in general and Christianity in particular engrossed him; so did much science; so did Arthurian legend, the subject of his only book (and an enthusiasm that he shared with Tennyson). Years before the periodical press began to consume his whole attention, Knowles was dabbling in amateur journalism, editing miscellaneous literary and scientific articles for a local Review named the *Clapham Magazine*. Not that it is all that difficult to reconcile Knowles the architect with Knowles the editor: the buildings and Reviews of this conscientious craftsman were alike in their ample yet symmetrical proportions, in their Victorian grandeur.

Knowles's ardour for the 'higher journalism' was complemented by his ardour for high society. If he was a born Review editor, beguiled by well-chosen words and interesting opinions, he was likewise a born socialite – and a good deal of a snob. His eagerness to recommend himself to Tennyson and

Gladstone, to be able to claim Poet Laureate and Prime Minister as his friends, made him the target of caustic comment. But his was a case where intellectual fervour and the activity disparagingly referred to as 'tuft-hunting' appear to have been more or less inseparable. It was through talking to Tennyson, not long after the completion of Aldworth in 1868, that Knowles conceived the idea of the dining and debating club for eminent Victorians that became known as the 'Metaphysical Society'. Acting as impresario, Knowles persuaded leading public figures – churchmen, politicians, scholars, scientists and editors – to meet regularly in London and engage in frank debate about Christian evidences, about fundamental theological questions. Open to both believers and unbelievers (its model was the Apostles, Cambridge's secret conversation society), the Metaphysical Society was a well-timed novelty, a ministry of philosophical talents that was to last for just over ten years, generating during that time a vast volume of rarefied discussion. Out of the papers read to it, Knowles saw the possibility of shaping a *magnum opus*, a work of encyclopaedic reach. His dream was to compile the definitive guide to modern mental and moral speculation – to make an historic contribution to what Victorians termed the 'March of Mind'.

Gladstone, Ruskin, T.H. Huxley, John Morley, Dean Stanley, Arthur Balfour, Herbert Spencer, Fitzjames Stephen, Leslie Stephen, F.D. Maurice and R.H. Hutton, the respected editor of the *Spectator* – all these, and more, took part, in greater or lesser degree, in the deliberations of a Society that was to form the cornerstone of Knowles's editorial career. By 1870, when he was appointed editor of the *Contemporary Review*, a publication founded as a vehicle of Anglicanism, Knowles was on cordial terms with most of the British intellectual and literary luminaries of his day, and was accordingly well-placed to secure their services as reviewers. When, seven years later, irked by the uncompromising orthodoxy of the *Contemporary Review*'s proprietor, he decided to set up a Review of his own, he found it easy enough to muster influential backing. Grandees galore were quick to make public their support for his scheme. Before long, Knowles's star-studded monthly was enjoying a circulation of 20,000, and reckoned to be perused by five times that number.

By way of epigraph, the *Nineteenth Century*'s inaugural issue boasted a sonnet by Tennyson, specially composed for the occasion and portraying Knowles and his coadjutors as intrepid mariners setting sail on uncharted seas. Among the rest of the issue's distinguished contributors were Cardinal Manning, Matthew Arnold and Gladstone, the latter writing on the influence of authority in matters of opinion, the first of some sixty-seven compositions that the 'GOM' was to publish in the *Nineteenth Century* before his death in 1898. That every item in it bore what we now call a 'by-line' was a feature of the Review of which its editor was to make much. Professing a principled aversion to anonymity, Knowles spoke up for avowed authorship as a means of elevating the whole tone of public discussion. Of course, his habit of emblazoning the cover of the Review with the names of notabilities was hardly free from commercial calculation. Yet if Knowles's tendency to court celebrities (he had a decided weakness for titled contributors) was commercially astute, it was not the only reason why the *Nineteenth Century* met with such extraordinary success; for, like all great editors, Knowles was a shrewd reader of the *Zeitgeist*, prompt to divine the public mood and prompt to commission timely comment. Consider his concern with the late nineteenth century crisis of Christian faith, with the implications of living in a godless universe – a preoccupation which was all but universal during the years of his editorship. Little that Knowles published precipitated reactions quite so fevered as the article, 'Is Life Worth Living?' (1877), by W.H. Mallock, the Victorian Tory sage who was much given to pondering the fate of morality and the meaning of human existence in a world bereft of Christian belief. Others were to write for the *Nineteenth Century* on themes such as 'Worry' and 'Weariness', and in general Knowles's pages are rich in testimony to the underlying neurosis of Victorian society. 'An age of anxiety was his platform', remarked his solicitous modern biographer, Priscilla Metcalf.

What made the *Nineteenth Century* unusual among Victorian Reviews – and what surely enhanced its appeal in an increasingly democratic, freethinking era – was the width of its viewpoint. From the days of the Metaphysical Society, Knowles had taken his stand on 'full, free, friendly and frank discussion' as the road to wisdom, as the soundest means of establishing the truth about anything. This was at the root of his Socratic liking for 'symposia', for bringing together debaters of more or less diametrically opposed outlooks. Often in the *Nineteenth Century*, Tory reviewers were pitted against Liberals while both were apt to clash with champions of the embryonic Labour movement. For his own part the reverse of radical, Knowles nevertheless published expositions of socialism by Keir Hardie and company, licensed Prince Kropotkin (in whose eyes he was one of the 'best-informed men in Europe') to write in defence of anarchism and made ample space available for reports by genteel philanthropists like Beatrice Potter (the future Mrs Webb) on what was becoming an ever more vexed question during this period: the condition of the poor. Pricking the consciences of the privileged was work to which Knowles devoted much time and energy. Indeed, the emergence of the moral climate that was to culminate, four decades after his death, in the creation of the British Welfare State, could be said to have owed something to his educative efforts.

Where, though, Knowles indulged his taste for untrammelled debate most was over the rival claims of science and religion. The war of words that he sparked off in the mid-1880s between the devout Gladstone and the agnostic T.H. Huxley turned into one of the most abrasive intellectual show-downs in the history of periodicals. Launched in 1885 – and resumed in 1890 – Huxley's scientific attack on Gladstone's adamant affirmation of the essential truth of the Book of Genesis excited keen public interest at a time when public challenges to scriptural authority were still relatively rare. Here was absorbing intellectual sport: Britain's elder statesman, pillar of Church and State, locked in excoriating verbal combat with a largely self-educated man of science – and, as many appear to have felt, being made to look foolish. Of all Victorian polemicists, Huxley was the most formidable – a reviewer whose 'episcopophagous' copy could make the pulses of a Review editor such as Knowles race. For some fifteen years, he was to be one of the *Nineteenth Century*'s leading contributors, receiving much deferential treatment – even if it was often found necessary to subject his all too rampant rhetoric to editorial restraint. Like the Metaphysical Society, Knowles's Review was animated by the principle dear to Tennyson – that science had taught human kind to separate heat and light. It was a principle which, with all his scientific training, the headlong Huxley tended to honour more in the breach than the observance.

For Huxley, the *Nineteenth Century* served as an influential mouthpiece, affording him regular and well-paid opportunities to promote the cause of science and popular education – in which respect, he could be said to have been furthering the missionary work begun by Francis Jeffrey and the *Edinburgh* reviewers at the start of the nineteenth century: like them, he objected to the predominance of Britain's old universities, with their social exclusiveness and academic narrowness; like them, he was an exponent of the 'democratic intellect'. It so fell out that Huxley was hard at work on Knowles's behalf assailing the case against agnosticism propounded by Britain's future Tory Prime Minister, the cerebral Arthur Balfour, when he breathed his last, on 29 June 1895. Only the first instalment of Huxley's refutation – what he termed the 'cavillary charge as distinct from the 'heavy artillery and bayonets' that were scheduled to follow – could be printed. His loss was keenly felt – especially by the editor of the *Nineteenth Century*.

James Knowles presided over his Review as though it was a journalistic version of the House of Commons, a parliament of reviewers enshrining his country's vaunted belief in intellectual liberty. Yet there were two topics in particular about which the ostensibly open-minded Knowles was altogether loath to countenance divergent points of view. One was female suffrage, a cause for which – in common with large numbers of thinking Victorians, men and women – Knowles had little patience. The other was the Channel Tunnel. Belatedly brought to fruition in the 1990s, the proposal to build a tunnel linking Britain and France was being mooted in the 1870s, and might have been realised before the turn of the nineteenth century but for the implacable opposition of the editor of the *Nineteenth Century*. The whole notion of a tunnel connecting Britain with France and the rest of Europe filled Knowles with unease. Was not such a development going to render Britain vulnerable to subterranean invasion? Would it not make nonsense of Britain's hard-won naval supremacy? Here was an issue which transformed this otherwise poised and polished English man into a panic-stricken zealot.

In the 1880s, while Parliament was debating the pro's and con's of the Channel Tunnel, Knowles was doing his utmost to discredit and frustrate the scheme. The issue of the *Nineteenth Century* for April 1882 opened with two pages of weighty names protesting against the Tunnel, including Tennyson, Browning, Herbert Spencer, Huxley, John Murray, R.H. Hutton and the Labour leaders, George Howell and Thomas Burt. Knowles himself – who as a rule wrote little – composed a six-page editorial in which he pointed out that British admirals and generals vehemently opposed to the Tunnel but were under professional constraint to keep their opinions to themselves. In the May issue of Knowles's Review, more figures of note added their names to the list of those who were opposed, and the same issue carried several anti-Tunnel articles. Knowles did not entirely abandon his commitment to fair and free discussion, however. He published, for instance, a fiery article by the French journalist, Joseph Reinach, accusing the English people of 'walking backwards from civilisation'. Still, readers could be in no doubt where the *Nineteenth Century* stood on this matter. The Review's unmistakable message was that the Channel Tunnel was a national catastrophe in the making. At a time when controversy is raging over illegal immigrants, it must be said that Knowles's animus against the Tunnel is not without topicality.

The collapse of the Channel Tunnel proposal stemmed in large measure from Knowles's fervent campaigning, as indeed did the official disfavour which went on dogging the whole question. For if the concept of the Channel Tunnel refused to die, so did Knowles's hostility to it. Gladstone, who did not support Knowles's stand, was not being flippant when he charged him with having murdered the scheme: 'The aborted tunnel cries out against you from the bottom of the sea', he admonished the jubilant editor. Totally impenitent, Knowles remained proud of the part that he had played in killing off the Tunnel. In 1907, a year before his death, he was still missing no opportunity to voice his belief in the necessity of preserving Britain's age-old isolation from Continental Europe. The prospect of the 'un-islanding' of Britain seems to have been the stuff of James Knowles's nightmares. Whereas the lustily patriotic W.T. Stead thought of Britain as 'vagina gentium', Knowles clearly preferred to regard his native land as 'virgo intacta'. However liberal-minded, he was a quintessentially imperial figure, an Anglocentric man of letters with a chauvinistic conviction that 'Britain' and 'civilisation' were more or less synonymous terms. How fitting that when he died – in Brighton in 1908 – he was buried in a coffin wrapped in the Union Jack.

Until 1883, Knowles did much of his editing in the study of his Clapham home. Afterwards – elated by the triumph of his anti-Tunnel crusade – he bought the lease of a handsome eighteenth century house in central London known as Queen Anne's Lodge. Overlooking St James's Park, Knowles's new residence stood but a stone's throw from the Houses of Parliament proper – and but a stone's throw, too, from Pall Mall, with its numerous gentlemen's clubs, fecund recruiting-grounds for well-bred practitioners of the 'higher journalism'. Here, surrounded by paintings and *objets d'art*, Knowles set himself up as arbiter-in-chief of British public taste, while thrilling to what he termed the 'great pulses of national life'. Almost certainly, it was of Knowles that John Morley was thinking when he referred to that 'eminent editor' who congratulated himself on being equal in influence to no fewer than twenty-five Members of Parliament. Knowles himself was in the habit of remarking that his editorship gave him the income of a Cabinet Minister, but with the palpable advantage that, by contrast with a real Minister, he was never out of office. It is obvious that Knowles was not given to false modesty, but it is equally clear that his high opinion of himself had some foundation. Knowles's position as editor of the *Nineteenth Century* gave him great prestige – quite as much as was enjoyed by the editor of the *Times*. With Queen Anne's Lodge as his court, the twice married editor (his first wife died prematurely) took to leading the life of a metropolitan lion, becoming much sought-after, much-consulted and much-flattered – not least, perhaps, by aristocratic literary ladies, for the publication of whose work Knowles seems to have nursed a special predilection. There was a time, it was said, when not to know James Knowles, was not to be known.

By the same token, there was a time when virtually everyone of contemporary consequence seemed to belong to Knowles's reviewing circle – though he was too scrupulous an editor to enrol people as contributors simply because they were famous. Frederic Harrison may have been joking when he declared that the only notable figures never to have been published by Knowles were Bismarck and the Pope. Nevertheless, it is true that there were few enough British celebrities of the period whose names did not at one stage or another adorn the *Nineteenth Century*'s cover. But then this was a time in which social prominence and the capacity to write with passable distinction tended to go hand in hand. British political life – British public life in general – teemed with individuals who were both able and willing to satisfy the request of a Review editor such as Knowles for a well-turned article on some topical issue. For a century or more, hardly a leading statesman was not also a competent man of letters. The odd example of this vanishing breed – think of Roy Jenkins, or of Roy Hattersley, perhaps – is discernible still, but in the media age, literary skill among politicians is increasingly rare. Editing the *London Review of Books* in the 1980s, Karl Miller complained about the dearth of politicians who were prepared to attempt the kind of expansive, argumentative articles that his paper went in for. Such frustration was seldom, if ever, the lot of Miller's illustrious Victorian forerunner.

A well-known architect who turned into a celebrated editor, Knowles was a man of parts whose Review was said to have become the voice of the representatives of 'all that was most interesting in England'. Aside from anything else, he was perhaps the last Review editor to attempt to take the whole of knowledge as his province, to make a strenuous effort to embrace all facets of mental endeavour. Regularly publishing articles on 'recent science', he was reluctant to concede that the pursuit of intellectual comprehensiveness was turning into a lost cause – that what Morley called the 'day of the circumnavigator' was over. He himself was an amateur student of geology and evolution, who at the same time brimmed with curiosity about the springs of mental activity. In common with not a few of his contemporaries – W.T. Stead amongst them – he was fascinated by unexplained phenomena, by the central mysteries of existence. In 1899, he rejoiced to learn about Marconi's invention of wireless telegraphy, having for years been speculating about 'brain waves' and the possibility that an exceptionally energetic mind might trigger off some kind of 'electrical manifestation'. Now the question occurred to him why, if electricity could be transmitted by a battery, it might not just as well emanate from the human brain, especially a brain such as Gladstone's. That science has latterly found a means of measuring electrical activity in the brain would, his biographer suspected, have been a source of gratification to him.

Following Knowles's death, old *Nineteenth Century* hands celebrated a 'myriad-minded' editor with a talent for nurturing the gifts of others. He was indeed a classic instance of the editor whose value is best appreciated by colleagues, by those exposed to the direct impact of his personality. A great devotee of the stage, he was like some charismatic theatre director, who excelled at stimulating bravura performances, at getting the best out of his troupe. Maybe his closest counterpart in the higher reaches of contemporary journalism is the long-standing editor of the *New York Review of Books*, Robert Silvers, a literary figure who – without being well-known to the world at large – has won the admiration of scores of his contributors. Like Knowles, Silvers has written little – even less perhaps than his cisatlantic predecessor – yet been the cause of much writing by others. Curiously enough, this New York literary impresario and Anglophile has also been susceptible to the lure of English high society. For many years, the contributors' list of his paper was often notable for the names of titled British reviewers – figures such as (Lord) Hugh Trevor-Roper and (Lord) Noel Annan. It might even be suggested that something of the spirit of the *Nineteenth Century* has survived in the *New York Review*. The spacious spirit in question has much to do, no doubt, with imperial self-confidence, with the great power status which, in Knowles's time belonged to Britain still, but which has long since been inherited by the United States. The patriotic Knowles would probably be grieved by the extent to which British global hegemony has passed into American hands – though it can hardly be said that he had not been adequately forewarned. Signs of British decadence – the amateurishness of the country's administrators and the widespread physical unfitness brought to light by the Boer War – received plenty of attention in the panoptic pages of his own Review. So did evidence of the USA's latent supremacy.

Walter Bagehot remarked that, with the *Edinburgh Review*, Francis Jeffrey transformed the editor, once a mere bookseller's drudge, into a 'distinguished functionary'. In James Knowles, intellectual servant of the British establishment (on whom Edward VII bestowed a knighthood in 1903), this grand literary type may be said to have reached its highest point of development. Perhaps it is worth adding that Knowles also took after his Edinburgh exemplar in being that seeming paradox, a distinguished Review editor with a remarkably undistinguished collection of books. Indeed, Knowles would appear to have set little store by books in their own right. On principle, he believed that the 'ideal library' ought to comprise the 'fewest books possible'. Confronted by what would later be termed the 'knowledge explosion', Knowles was inclined to think that books were becoming obsolete, and that the key role of interpretation now resided in periodicals (and therefore in editors like himself). He once disconcerted an elderly Vice Chancellor with the suggestion that universities should invest in chairs of Periodical Studies. A creature of the golden age of magazine culture for whom articles were a uniquely effective medium of communication, Knowles strove to make the 'higher journalism' culturally pre-eminent. Contributions to his pages, though often enough occasioned by new books, were routinely presented as free-standing essays. The trend towards literary self-aggrandisement on the part of the periodical press was pushed by the editor of the *Nineteenth Century* to its ultimate extreme. Not only in terms of political power was James Knowles an imperialist.

At the end of 1900, Knowles renamed the *Nineteenth Century* the *Nineteenth Century and After*. A sly opportunist, it turned out, meaning to hold the respected editor to ransom, had already patented the title the *Twentieth Century*. Its cover henceforth emblazoned with the symbol of a Janus-head, gazing both forwards and backwards, the Review was to outlive its *onlie begetter* by more than half a century. But of its later editors, perhaps only Knowles immediate successor, his conscientious son-in-law, William Wray Skilbeck, made anything like the mark that Knowles himself had made. A barrister and powerfully built sportsman (in his youth he was a famous rugby footballer), Skilbeck consolidated his father-in-law's legacy with widely admired aplomb. When, with the First World War barely over, he died suddenly, aged only fifty-six, he, too, was much mourned. Grief-stricken friends paid homage to his sense of public duty, to his selfless devotion to king and country. Keeping up publication of a monthly organ of the higher journalism throughout a period of grave national crisis – while also serving as a special constable – was said to have been too much even for Skilbeck's tremendous constitution.

An obituarist of Skilbeck's, T.F. Wyatt, pointed out that contributors to his pages learned to expect reactions to their work from the most far-flung places; to write for the *Nineteenth Century and After* was to command the attention of the world. Wyatt went on to ask whether it was not a fact of real significance that, only a few days earlier, as a train bearing demobilised soldiers was about to pull out of London bound for the North of England, some thirty copies of the *Nineteenth Century and After* were purchased at a station news-stand. That this was a significant – not to say startling – fact, few today would be likely to dispute. Indeed, less than a hundred years later, the very idea of such a publication being so popular strains credulity – even granting that wartime, with its disruptions and *longueurs*, has been known to make readers of people like almost nothing else.

Yet this most Victorian of Reviews never really recaptured the kudos it had enjoyed under its original title when the career of James Knowles was at its zenith. Well before the First World War, modish literary opinion among the younger generation was inclined to ridicule the *Nineteenth Century and After* as a grandiloquent anachronism, and it cannot be denied that Knowles and his successor were less than attentive to fresh literary developments. Busy reading Dostoevsky, Arnold Bennett thought that they would have done better to re-christen their Review the 'Middle Ages'. As the years rolled by, the *Nineteenth Century* and *After* became best-known simply for being old and established – like some vintage brand of marmalade. The twilight years of its existence, the 1950s and 60s, witnessed a procession of well-meaning editors struggling to revitalise a monthly that had long since been eclipsed in public favour by comparatively inexpensive intellectual weeklies, such as the *New Statesman* and the *Listener*. By that stage – and with comical belatedness – it had at least been renamed the *Twentieth Century*.

Fleetingly, at the beginning of the 1950s, Knowles's old Review was enlisted by the CIA-backed Congress for Cultural Freedom as a means of combating communism – a task that was to be more systematically executed by the Congress's magazine, *Encounter*, launched in 1953. During the same period, its then editor, Michael Goodwin, got it into his head to assemble an anthology of writing done for Knowles and to invite contemporary contributors to discuss the result. For all its worthiness, the exercise hardly betokened a Review that was keeping pace with the times. Perhaps it was a tribute to the cultural tenacity of the nineteenth century that the era's journalistic namesake endured as long as it did. Not until 1972 did the curtain drop for good on this monument to the higher journalism of Victorian Britain.

III

The 'Higher Journalism' in the Twentieth Century

'A friend has described to me how, as a youth, he saw Frederic Harrison, the famous positivist (whatever that may be), seated in a railway carriage, and reading the *New Statesman*. As he read, the veins of his forehead swelled, his hands holding the journal shook with rage, and occasionally a strangled cry broke from his lips.'

Malcolm Muggeridge,
The New Statesman, April 19th, 1963

'Not enough can be said, surely, about the excellence of British weekly journalism ... Like the green lawns of Britain, it is simply an art that has been cultivated for a long, long time.'

Karl Meyer, *The Washington Post*, January 16th, 1966

The Editor at work

Kingsley Martin

7. King of Conscience

Kingsley Martin and the *New Statesman* seem to have been made for each other. It was because of Martin, its editor from 1931 until 1960, that the *New Statesman* became a periodical which mattered to an unusual degree, changing minds and changing lives. The intellectual weekly which still goes by that name bears but a glancing resemblance to the one that Martin created. Publicising the virtue of rational argument and pressing the case for a just social order, Martin and his paper were among the makers of the Britain that emerged after the Second World War – the Britain so objectionable to Margaret Thatcher, with its Welfare State and 'liberal consensus'. Cyril Connolly wondered what England would have been without the *New Statesman* – and equally what the *New Statesman* would have been without Kingsley Martin. Nobody has been moved to pose such questions in relation to any of Martin's numerous successors, or to the more recent versions of the *New Statesman* which they have edited. Peculiar to the middle decades of the twentieth century, Martin's achievement proved inimitable.

Kingsley Martin inspired extreme reactions. But few thinking people were wholly indifferent to this emotional intellectual, who turned the *New Statesman* into a legendary title, a British journal of left-wing protest that commanded attention all over the world. Thriving on publicity, Martin was better-known in Britain than any newspaper editor, while his commitment to the cause of anti-imperialism brought him celebrity-status in India and many other colonial societies struggling to gain independence. If he has no contemporary counterparts, it is partly because there is no longer a British Empire. Fervently anti-imperialist, Martin was nonetheless a child of empire, with the assumption of moral authority and zest for foreign travel that long characterised a certain kind of Englishman.

What made Martin so compelling a communicator was his genius for bringing himself alive on paper. An aficionado of the theatre, he was something of an actor manqué who – like his self-dramatising forerunner, W.T. Stead – developed an extraordinary intimacy with his readers. The *New Statesman* was the stage on which Martin agonised about the world's woes, parading his dilemmas and projecting himself as a conscience-stricken humanitarian. Often photographed for newspapers and magazines, a battered figure with a shock of stiff grey hair and a long, care-worn face, Martin came to personify the intellectual Left. 'He is our own fever and pain', wrote Malcolm Muggeridge, adapting the words of an old music hall song and mocking Martin as the archetypal liberal in distress, a journalist who wore his bleeding heart on his sleeve.

In Muggeridge's eyes, Martin was an intellectual mountebank, a pedlar of leftist illusions. Yet not even this sardonic fault-finder disputed Martin's editing achievements – achievements behind which lay much assiduous artistry. 'Influence is style,' Martin liked to remark, availing himself of a maxim thought up by his sole predecessor as editor of the *New Statesman*, Clifford Sharp, an able journalist who was ruined by drink. And perhaps it was his strict observance of this precept which, more than anything else, made the *New Statesman* such a journalistic success. At any rate, Martin practised his craft in the belief that a well-timed article, 'written with distinction', might not merely capture public attention but even stimulate a 'whole movement of thought' and ultimately deliver practical results. Working in great turmoil, surrounded by manuscripts and galley proofs – how, colleagues wondered, did he ever get the paper out at all? – Martin endlessly redrafted the *New Statesman*'s pages. It is doubtful whether an editor ever stalked *le mot juste* with such neurotic ardour. Week after week, the paper's printer was confronted by copy rendered all but illegible by editorial corrections, an inky riot of second, third, fourth and fifth thoughts. The printer called Martin the 'Spider' – and one or two other, rather less charitable, names, no doubt.

If anything rivalled Martin's passion for weekly journalism, it was his passion for the opposite sex. His early marriage to Olga Walters, a young woman of literary leanings for whom angst became a way of life, went wretchedly wrong. Subsequently, however, he formed what seems to have been a rewarding relationship with a buxom, self-assertive lady of the Left named Dorothy Woodman – while reserving the right to pursue other women. This he not infrequently did – generally with consequences that brought frustration to all concerned. Yet whether any of his female friends mattered to him nearly so much as the *New Statesman* seems doubtful. 'I ate, drank and slept with the paper', wrote Martin. Nor is there any reason to think that he was not in earnest when he propounded the advice that an 'editor's paper should be his mistress'. Henry Cockburn once remarked that Francis Jeffrey *was* the *Edinburgh Review*; it would be no great exaggeration to say that Martin *was* the *New Statesman*. His reluctant retirement from the the paper after an uninterrupted stint of thirty-one years was probably the most painful experience of his life.

Taking things lightly was not in Martin's nature. Behind him stretched a long line of God-fearing Puritans. Like his contemporary and fulminating antagonist, the Cambridge critic, F.R. Leavis, he sprang from Huguenot stock. Among his forebears were the Flemish Protestants who settled in London at the end of the eighteenth century after being thrown out of Catholic France. But Scottish Calvinists formed part of his pedigree, too. With such a background, Martin might well have followed in the footsteps of his father and grandfather, both of whom set themselves up as Nonconformist preachers, bent on saving souls. From his father, the infuriatingly moralistic Basil Martin, he got his zeal for reform, his horror of war, his nagging sense of guilt. He also inherited his father's highly-strung constitution. Now blazing with enthusiasm, now prostrate with nervous exhaustion, father and son led febrile lives – lives of a kind which seem to have been not at all uncommon among the Puritanical.

Born in 1894, Kingsley Martin grew up in Hereford and in the north London suburb of Finchley. As a child, he attended his father's Congregationalist chapel every Sunday and witnessed him acquiring a reputation for militancy and bloody-mindedness. Often, when Basil Martin mounted his pulpit, it was to preach against inequality and injustice – a stance much liked by Hereford's Nonconformist poor but apt to make the town's well-to-do seethe. His father was to incur far more widespread unpopularity during the Boer War, of which he became an outspoken opponent. Martin never forgot how the family's windows were smashed in by rampaging 'Jingos', for whom his father's pacifist posture was indistinguishable from treason. Yet none of this seems to have bothered him too much. Had he not been brought up to believe that the righteous were blessed, that the last would one day be first – however dim their present prospects? What did come to worry him, it seems, was his inability to see any but heroic qualities in his father. Burdened by filial piety, he was to become absorbed in a more or less conscious search for alternative father figures – men with whom he did not find it a wrench to disagree.

The author of a memoir entitled *An Impossible Parson* (1935), Martin's father was an early example of the sort of clergyman who seems to care more about radical causes than the existence of God, but there was one respect in which this progressive clergyman could not have been more traditional, and that was in his reverence for the word. Reading aloud – from the Bible and from the works of English novelists like Dickens and Scott – was a daily occurrence in the Martin household; and when not reading aloud to their children (there were two sons, one of whom died young, and two daughters), Basil Martin and his wife were engaging them in edifying conversation about issues of politics and morality. Keen to foster the intellectual development of sons *and* daughters – a rare thing at this time of course – these high-minded Edwardian parents equated education with individual and social betterment, extolling the value of public service. The lives led by their children were to match their expectations exactly. Concerning herself with the problem of urban slums, Martin's older sister, Irene, became Britain's first female surveyor, while his younger sister, Peggy, dedicated herself to what would now be termed child psychotherapy. As for Martin himself, he aspired to contribute to the commonweal through journalism, taking charge of a public-spirited weekly – in which capacity he could be said to have been sustaining his father's ministry by secular means.

When the First World War broke out in 1914, Martin was a somewhat sickly youth of seventeen, attending Mill Hill School, a Nonconformist foundation not far from his Finchley home. Called up for military service, he refused to fight, following his father's pacifist example. Instead he served as an ambulanceman in France. In 1919, he went to Magdalene College, Cambridge, to read history. As an undergraduate, he emerged as a socialist who was also a frantic socialite, declared himself an agnostic, excelled at chess-playing – he was, perhaps, always calculating his next move – and studied hard, crowning his efforts with a First. Following Cambridge, he went to America, spending a postgraduate year at Princeton. During that time, he completed the thesis that became his first book, the *Triumph of Lord Palmerston* (1924), a Stracheyesque study of press-inspired jingoism during the Crimean War. But for America itself, he evidently felt no special affection, tending to view it as a country of political conformists, philistines and gangsters – a view which he seems to have found little reason to modify in later years. Returning to Cambridge in 1923, he was awarded a history

Fellowship and made himself busy. While tutoring Cambridge students and teaching for the Workers Educational Association, he began work on a study of the French *philosophes*, eventually published in 1929 under the title, *French Liberal Thought in the Eighteenth Century*. If this erudite examination of the work of Bayle, Voltaire, Diderot and others was a useful work of reference, it was also Martin's manifesto, the testament of an aspirant British *philosophe*.

John Freeman said that Martin's *New Statesman* was a weekly lesson in the application of reason, honesty and compassion to public affairs. Nevertheless, many found this donnish editor frivolous, jibbing at his grasshopper mind, his tendency to adopt – and as quickly discard – the opinions of the person to whom he had just been speaking. Beatrice Webb accused him of being a 'flibbertigibbet'. Martin, whose vanity was notorious, seems not to have been especially stung by this taunt. Indeed, if anything, he appears to have taken it as a compliment, proof that he had chosen the right line of work. For it was plain to him that to be an effective editor was to be a human barometer, swift to register the least change in the mental atmosphere. Despite all this, he earnestly identified himself with the same historic movement of public enlightenment so steadfastly championed by Mrs Webb. If he was a flibbertigibbet, he was a flibbertigibbet with a mission. Little about Kingsley Martin was clear-cut.

The privileged Mrs Webb and her submissive husband, Sidney, were presiding spirits of Martin's paper. Founded in 1913, it was after all their creation, the counterpart-in-print to the London School of Economics, which they had set up in 1895 as a means of creating an educated ruling class committed to 'scientific socialism'. Taking the name 'Fabians', the Webbs envisaged a society purged of poverty, waste and inefficiency, a rational polity run by well-briefed experts – by, in a phrase, 'new statesmen'. The Webbs' work was an integral part of Martin's intellectual heritage, as was their defining Fabian faith in what they termed the 'inevitability of gradualness'. In the years before he took over the *New Statesman*, Martin used to make regular pilgrimages to Passfield Corner, the Webbs' Surrey home, returning to London suffering from 'mental indigestion' after hours of political argument. Towards both of them he never ceased to feel a certain piety – though he did not entirely share the bureaucratic, collectivist conception of socialism which turned the couple into such fervent supporters of Stalin's Soviet Union. For all his own Soviet sympathies – and they were certainly warm enough – Martin stopped short of hailing Stalin as a Messiah.

The *New Statesman* that Martin edited was also much influenced by the Webbs' sometime Fabian colleagues, H.G. Wells and George Bernard Shaw. With the latter Martin was familiar from youth, the great Irish dramatist having turned out on winter evenings to address sparse gatherings of Dissenters at his father's Finchley chapel; Wells he got to know a little later. In the 1930s – by which time both believed that capitalism was doomed – Martin shrewdly turned the long-standing rivalry between the two men to journalistic advantage. When Wells came back from Russia in 1934, he published a critical interview that the writer had conducted with Stalin, and then goaded Shaw – whose own susceptibility to Soviet propaganda had done much to confirm the Webbs in theirs – into passing judgement on Wells's performance. The feline exchange that ensued between this pair of bumptious old literary lions – it precipitated a voluminous *New Statesman* correspondence on the meaning of socialism – was a favourite episode in Martin's editing career. Dazzling where the Webbs – who lived for facts and figures – were dull, Shaw and Wells could be seen by Kingsley Martin as modern versions of Diderot and Voltaire. With their faith in reason, taste for polemics and encyclopaedic range of interests, they supplied him with glamorous contemporary images of the 'artist-philosopher' bestriding his age and directing human destiny. In his memoirs, Martin declared that he had learned from them almost everything that he knew.

From no book had Kingsley Martin learned more than the *Outline of History* (1923), H.G. Wells's grand attempt to do for the twentieth century what Diderot, with the *Encyclopédie*, had done for the eighteenth – i.e. compile a 'directive synthesis of knowledge', a Book of Books designed to dispel public ignorance and serve as an instrument of progress. When it came to Wells the prophet of science, however, Martin was to prove an indifferent disciple at best. It was, admittedly, in the *New Statesman* that C.P. Snow first aired his anxiety about the 'two cultures', about the growing gulf between the literary and scientific worlds. But early and late, Martin's paper was read for the quality of its writing on politics and literature, not for its scientific coverage, which remained exiguous. The biologist, Laurence Hogben, flayed Martin for failing to rise to the challenge of scientific advance, for neglecting to explore what science and technology had to contribute to socialism. To this pugnacious Marxist, Kingsley Martin and the *New Statesman* exemplified 'genteel Whiggery', a 'liberal culture' in terminal decay. It was a charge for which Martin seems to have been stuck for an answer.

If Martin was slow to espouse the cause of science, it was hardly from want of encouragement. The Cambridge known to him in the 1920s was, after all, the Cambridge of Rutherford and the Cavendish Laboratory, a place of great scientific dynamism. During his years there, moreover, he became besotted with a female science student named 'Verity', who endeavoured to stimulate his scientific curiosity. Yet it was not for any scientist that Martin would cherish memories of Cambridge, but rather for that now seldom mentioned man of letters, Goldsworthy Lowes Dickinson. Much enamoured of ancient Greece and equally enamoured of ancient China – he liked to sport the cap of a Chinese mandarin – Dickinson was a liberal humanist whose faith in mankind was severely tested by the First World War, and who spent his later years – he died in 1932 – championing the

League of Nations. Throughout his life he had dreamed of a democracy where everybody aspired to be an intellectual aristocrat – while also fearing that the many, preoccupied with making themselves comfortable, might throw away the 'pearl of great price', the art and the culture that had been handed down by the few. One of Martin's most treasured books was Dickinson's *A Modern Symposium* (1905), which – among other things – voiced an Edwardian Englishman's dismay at the prospect of an Americanised world pledged to speed and materialism. For lucidity of expression and cogency of argument he thought the book incomparable and used to urge aspiring contributors to study it.

Despite a gap between them of forty years, Martin and Lowes Dickinson became intimate. In the early 1920s both were suffering romantic agonies, Martin as a late-developing heterosexual, Dickinson as an ageing, perennially unfulfilled homosexual. Together, they found solace in ruing the state of the world. On holiday with Dickinson, absorbed in wide-ranging conversation, Martin discovered that it was possible to be gloomy and elated at the same time. It would often be noted that Kingsley Martin never seemed happier than when anticipating the worst. His friend, J.B. Priestley, remembered the occasion when Martin turned up at his house prophesying that total, final, ruinous war was imminent – as though bringing Priestley and his family a special treat. That he played the part of Jeremiah with peculiar relish may help to explain why, during the nerve-wracking years preceding the outbreak of the Second World War, his journalism was found to be so readable.

It was at Cambridge that Martin met the imperious John Maynard Keynes, who, as one of the principal directors of the *New Statesman*, was to figure large in his life. Martin was an undergraduate when Keynes acquired an international reputation on the strength of his pamphlet, *The Economic Consequences of the Peace* (1919), in which he denounced as morally and politically ill-judged the punitive reparations imposed on Germany following the First World War. Keynes's tract for the times was to serve as something of a rationale for those who favoured 'appeasement' in the 1930s. One of its immediate effects was to establish him as a hero in the eyes of young socialists like Kingsley Martin, though Keynes himself was far from left-wing. The rhetorical vehemence with which he railed against his elders – his charge was that the Victorian ruling class bore responsibility for embroiling Britain in a disastrous conflict - made him seem rather more of a rebel than he really was. Like Beatrice Webb, Keynes was an upper-middle-class paternalist, with more than a passing resemblance to the sages and philanthropists of Victorian times, but unlike Mrs Webb and her fellow Fabians, Keynes was planning to save capitalism from itself, not to get rid of it altogether.

Both Keynes and Lowes Dickinson were members of the secret Cambridge society known as the Apostles. Something of a model for the Bloomsbury Group, the Apostles stood for the importance of personal relations, aesthetic contemplation, the pursuit of truth. Their plain-speaking, conscience-searching ethos owed more than a little to the Quaker background that Keynes shared with the influential Cambridge philosopher, G.E. Moore, but it was rooted, too, in reverence for ancient Athens – as typified by Lowes Dickinson's *A Modern Symposium*, with its homage to the dialogues of Plato. Never an Apostle himself, Martin always felt aggrieved that he had been denied a chance to join the magic circle, whose members included not only Keynes and Dickinson but also Leonard Woolf, Bertrand Russell, Desmond MacCarthy, Lytton Strachey and Roger Fry. In later life, he came to feel that the Apostles were ivory-tower dwellers who made light of the significance of the class struggle. But the image of the Cambridge Apostle as questioner and truth-seeker, as a modern Socrates, meant much to him. It was as a latter-day Socrates, bearing weekly witness to the virtue of the examined life, that he liked to think of himself when editing the *New Statesman*.

THE

EDINBURGH REVIEW,

OR

CRITICAL JOURNAL:

FOR

JULY 1819..... OCTOBER 1819.

TO BE CONTINUED QUARTERLY.

JUDEX DAMNATUR CUM NOCENS ABSOLVITUR.
PUBLIUS SYRUS.

VOL. XXXII.

EDINBURGH:
Printed by David Willison,
FOR ARCHIBALD CONSTABLE AND COMPANY, EDINBURGH:
AND LONGMAN, HURST, REES, ORME AND BROWN,
LONDON.

1819.

THE

FORTNIGHTLY

REVIEW.

EDITED BY

JOHN MORLEY.

VOL. VI. NEW SERIES.

[illegible]

[illegible]

12.

LONDON:
CHAPMAN AND HALL, 193, PICCADILLY.
1869.

[*The Right of Translation is reserved.*]

THE

NINETEENTH CENTURY

A MONTHLY REVIEW

EDITED BY JAMES KNOWLES

No. 192, FEBRUARY 1893

LONDON: SAMPSON LOW, MARSTON, & COMPANY, LIMITED

PARIS: LIBRAIRIE GALIGNANI, 224 RUE DE RIVOLI

AGENTS FOR AMERICA: THE LEONARD SCOTT PUBLICATION COMPANY, NEW YORK

1893

Price Half-a-Crown

THE NEW

STATESMAN AND NATION

The Week-end Review

Vol. XXX. No. 754 SATURDAY, AUGUST 4, 1945 SIXPENCE

CONTENTS

LABOUR COMES OF AGE

Martin's debt to Keynes was deep. In many ways indeed, the great economist was his patron. Shown Martin's Cambridge thesis, Keynes sent him a letter extolling his work as 'learned, subtle and interesting'. It was on the strength of this letter that Martin introduced himself to Keynes's colleague, Leonard Woolf, who was literary editor of the liberal weekly, the *Nation*, which Keynes had bought from the Rowntree family in 1922. Woolf enrolled Martin as a reviewer, and the two men embarked on what was to prove a lifetime of close co-operation and squabbling, the grave, judicial Woolf often editing the *New Statesman* in Martin's absence. With the same letter, Martin managed to make a favourable impression on the stern director of the London School of Economics, William Beveridge. Swayed by Keynes's flattering testimony, Beveridge offered Martin a full-time academic position, and, in 1924, he joined the staff of the LSE, becoming assistant to the college's recently appointed Professor of Political Science, Harold Laski. Apt to romanticize himself as a soldier in the liberation war of humanity, this voluble socialist from Manchester was to be perhaps the most significant of the several mentors who shaped Kingsley Martin's view of things.

A dandified, bespectacled, Chaplinesque manikin seldom seen without a cigarette, Harold Laski was a brilliant intellectual showman. Everybody, from politicians down to the man in the street, knew who he was. Indeed, the 1930s have even been dubbed the 'Age of Laski'. Following the Labour Party's débâcle in the economic crisis of 1931 – when the Labour leader Ramsay MacDonald formed a Conservative-dominated coalition, filling the Left with disgust – Laski threw himself into the task of injecting fresh intellectual life into the Labour movement. As author, prolific journalist and tireless public speaker, he trumpeted the blessings of democratic socialism, while pressing the case for bringing the British Empire to a speedy end. Over the years, the educated classes of India and other British colonies came to abound in former LSE students of Laski's, who were also avid readers of the *New Statesman* – in which, thanks to Martin, many articles by Laski were published. Not exactly a great thinker, Laski was nevertheless a great teacher, with a flair for communicating with what A.J.P. Taylor called the new public of 'mass intellectuals' spawned by the spread of literacy. In concert with Martin and his paper and Victor Gollancz's Left Book Club, Laski greatly influenced the public opinion of his day, promulgating the message that to be a thinking person was to be a socialist. Eric Hobsbawm has remarked that it was to Laski, more than to any other single figure, that the Labour Party owed its historic victory in the 1945 General Election.

Yet there were many things about Laski – his egomania, his name-dropping, his penchant for intrigue – that antagonised even his own side. Furthermore, once Labour gained power after the Second World War, his outspoken left-wing sympathies became an acute embarrassment to a party that found itself presiding over a bankrupt economy and much beholden to American capitalism. 'A period of silence from you would be welcome,' was the much-quoted piece of advice he received from the Labour Prime Minister, Clement Attlee. Laski's premature death in 1950 – he was only 56 – may even have been brought on by the brusqueness with which the Labour élite rejected him; certainly his health was adversely affected by the unsuccessful libel action which he mounted against the *Daily Express* and other papers for portraying him as a partisan of violent revolution. Anxious to preserve his old friend's memory, Martin made haste to prepare a life of Laski, a work of hagiography much of which was actually to be written by Laski's former student, Norman MacKenzie – though Martin, for reasons hardly creditable, made no haste to acknowledge this. But, with the Cold War under way, the ideologue known to the popular press as the 'Red Professor' rapidly faded from public memory. It was a fate that would have seemed inconceivable a few years earlier, when Laski was an omnipresent celebrity, mingling with Churchill and Roosevelt and statesmen all over the world.

At the LSE, Laski and Kingsley Martin were part of a socialist coterie whose chief academic ornament was the historian, R.H. Tawney. Uncompromising in his moral revulsion against the 'acquisitive society', Tawney was revered, not to say sentimentalised, by many on the Left, Martin included, as something close to a saint. Another of the LSE's left-wing lecturers was the budding authority on public administration, W.A. Robson, with whom Martin founded the *Political Quarterly* in 1930, a journal which was to serve as an academic counterpart to the *New Statesman*. Despite its recent Fabian origins, however, the LSE was not dominated by the Left even at this early stage. Rent by ideological factions, the college was turning into a microcosm of the age's political divisions, a place in which socialists jostled with zealous exponents of *laisser-faire*. Beveridge himself, even though he became the architect of the Welfare State, was in many ways a conservative, with fewer qualms about right-wing members of his staff than about those on the Left. Much given to petitioning American foundations for sponsorship, he – like the leadership of the Labour Party – found Laski's habit of sounding off in public about the iniquities of capitalism more than a little irksome.

When Martin published a left-wing pamphlet concerned with the General Strike of 1926 – which criticised Beveridge's own role in the government's commission on the state of the coal industry – the director of the LSE was incensed. Henceforth, relations between Beveridge and his impetuous new recruit were less than cordial, and seemed likely to remain so. But, as things fell out, Martin soon got the chance to escape from Beveridge's jurisdiction – and seized it. In 1927, C.P. Scott, the respected editor of the newspaper then known as the *Manchester Guardian*, offered him a position as a well-paid leader writer. Exchanging academic life for journalism, Martin decamped from London to Manchester to work for a broadsheet that had long been identified with

Liberalism. With his new employer, a man of causes whose roots lay in northern Nonconformism, he seemed to have much in common. A gimlet-eyed Victorian patriarch with a bushy white beard, who was reputed to have made righteousness readable, Scott conducted the *Guardian* as though it was less a newspaper than a church. In 1927, the days were not so remote when *Guardian* leader writers had done their work in top hats, setting down their magisterial pronouncements on world affairs in an atmosphere of hushed solemnity.

It was on the *Manchester Guardian* that Martin encountered Malcolm Muggeridge, a young man with a sharp tongue and a poison pen, whose opinion of Scott stood in sharp contrast to his own. Scoffing at its editor's high moral tone, Muggeridge pointed out that the very existence of the esteemed but hardly profitable *Guardian* depended on the commercial success of Scott's other journalistic property, the *Manchester Evening News*, an altogether more 'popular' publication with which Scott did not go out of his way to identify himself. When Martin met him, the then leftist Muggeridge was on the verge of emigrating to the Soviet Union, appalled by MacDonald's 'betrayal' of socialism in the economic crisis of 1931. Before leaving, though, he dashed off a satirical *roman à clef*, in which Scott figured as a self-satisfied old humbug and Martin himself cropped up as a narcissistic left-wing careerist. Oozing libellous vitriol, Muggeridge's *Picture Palace* was perforce suppressed, not to be properly published until half a century later.

Both products, in their different ways, of Puritanism, Martin and Muggeridge were to become two of the most influential intellectual journalists of their time, and over the years they would see much of one another, despite deep differences in their political outlooks. Bitterly disillusioned by his exposure to Russian communism, Muggeridge abandoned all faith in efforts to improve the human condition, reserving a special scorn for left-wing progressives like Martin. Martin, on the other hand, steeped in Victorian moral optimism, committed himself to aping Scott as a high-minded British crusader dedicated to civilising mankind. Indeed, even though he failed in the event to get on with him much better than he did with Beveridge, Martin remembered his old editor with reverence. It thrilled him to think that Scott had transformed a small, provincial British newspaper into a publication of world renown, an 'organ of criticism and thought which no one of intelligence could afford to miss' and which was spoken of with respect 'on farms in the mid-West and in remote villages in the Balkans'. To enjoy such prestige was his own consuming ambition when he became editor of the *New Statesman* in 1931. He can hardly have foreseen how spectacularly he was destined to fulfil it.

▼▲▼

The editorship of the *New Statesman* was offered to Martin by Arnold Bennett – then a grand old man of English letters and one of the paper's directors – over breakfast at the Savoy Hotel. Behind the appointment lay the influence of Keynes, who in 1931 was bringing about a merger between the *New Statesman* and the *Nation*, the old liberal weekly which – like the Liberal Party – had known better days. It was to Keynes as the most active director of the paper that would be known as the *New Statesman and Nation* that Kingsley Martin found himself accountable for his editorial decisions. Keen to establish at the outset that Martin shared his commitment to attacking the old liberal dogma of free trade, Keynes plainly saw the *New Statesman* as a platform for promoting his own economic doctrines. Not that Martin was Keynes's intellectual puppet, or that Keynes, whose commitment to free expression was of Voltairean intensity, expected him to be – though why he was prepared to assent to the recruitment of an editor with whose politics he disagreed is not altogether clear. It may be that there was an element of flirtation in the great economist's relationship with the *New Statesman*, and that the paper enabled this complex man of privilege to dabble in politics that appealed more to his heart than his head.

What is certain is that, during a period when Britain was experiencing the consequences of the Wall Street Crash of 1929, with the Labour movement divided and demoralized, Keynes and Martin seldom saw eye to eye. Rebuking him for his incurable 'minority-mindedness', Keynes accused his colleague of being 'defeatist', of harbouring grievances and of concocting the kind of articles that got the *New Statesman* known as the 'bilious weekly'. The quality which Keynes was anxious that the *New Statesman* should exemplify was the one upheld by the Bloomsbury Group as the hallmark of civilised discourse: *urbanity*. Perhaps the endless disputatiousness of these pre-eminent new statesmen contributed to the creation of a weekly that was at once bilious *and* urbane. However, there was one issue about which editor and director, with their plain-living pedigrees, were at all times in furious accord – namely, the wisdom of maintaining the tightest of budgets. Despite – or possibly because of – the considerable wealth which he himself had shrewdly amassed, when it came to setting the *New Statesman*'s rates of pay, Keynes was parsimony personified. Grouses about the paper's notoriously niggardly fees he reacted to by affecting incomprehension that anybody should expect to be handsomely rewarded for undertaking work so obviously enjoyable as writing for the *New Statesman*. Such work, he said, was surely its own reward. Besides, he liked to add, he himself could, if necessary, write the whole paper in three hours. No one doubted it.

Martin, meanwhile, paying contributors by the inch and employing a ruler to measure off precisely how much (or little) they were owed, made a fetish of frugality. To write for his paper was to write for honour, not for money. Even as he preached socialism, in other words, Martin practised capitalist thrift – and did so to palpable effect. In the course of the 1930s, when money for many was scarce, the *New Statesman* grew steadily more prosperous.

By the end of the 1950s, helped by able business managers, Martin was overseeing a flourishing publishing concern, a weekly renowned as the sole socialist paper ever to have been run at a profit. To have scotched the myth that the only people who ever got involved with such a paper were either bankrupts or cranks gave him considerable satisfaction.

Yet the *New Statesman*'s true wealth was intangible, bound up with cultural traditions. Innumerable ingredients formed the character of this historic Review – not least, of course, the magpie mind of Kingsley Martin himself. The *New Statesman*'s character almost certainly owed something to the example of A.R. Orage's *New Age*, the progressive, concise, sharply written Edwardian weekly, on which Martin's predecessor, Clifford Sharp, learned the art of editing. Without doubt, it owed much to the sociological approach of the Fabians, as well as to the tradition of liberal dissent kept up by the *Nation*, whose pertinacious editor, H.W. Massingham, brought to his work the moral fire of an Old Testament prophet. To all this was added a little of the levity cultivated by Gerald Barry's *Weekend Review*, a title absorbed by the *New Statesman* in 1934. Barry's weekly gave Martin's paper its brain-teasing competitions, plus the droll weekly catalogue of British dottiness, 'This England'.

The desirability of eschewing excessive zeal was a lesson learned by Martin from C.P. Scott. As celebrated for its arts coverage as for its commitment to causes and crusades, Scott's *Guardian* achieved exemplary balance. Himself (like Scott) preoccupied with politics and public affairs, Martin nonetheless set out to publish a paper with broad human appeal. The *New Statesman* would probably never have commanded so much attention had Martin not taken care to capitalise on the work of the paper's early literary editors, J.C. Squire, and the Bloomsbury essayist, Desmond MacCarthy. In MacCarthy's fastidious protégé, Raymond Mortimer, Martin found an ideal colleague, a literary editor with attributes that he lacked but which he knew to be journalistically indispensable. If Martin was a Puritan with small interest in the arts, the homosexual Mortimer was a Francophile aesthete for whom the visual arts were a passion. On paper the two men seemed incompatible, yet it was on paper that they formed a famous partnership. Cyril Connolly said that they complemented each other like the hands of a pianist.

In terms of politics, Mortimer stood closer to Keynes than he ever did to Martin. Despite his 'progressive' views – he wrote damningly about the public school system – he was far from left-wing. A gentleman reviewer with a private income, and a fascination with Victorian bishops, he was if anything a high Tory. Whether his reviewers were socialists was hardly a consideration uppermost in Mortimer's mind – though whether they were gentlemen may well have been. Hence arose what was to be satirically known as the *New Statesman* 'pantomime horse', the curious (perhaps exaggerated) phenomenon whereby reviewers of conservative tendency in the literary back half of the paper could appear to be at odds with the left-wing contributors predominant in its political front half. Not that Kingsley Martin fretted too much about any of this. Readers who tried to vex him by saying that they only ever bought his paper for the back half, preferring the small ads, competitions and reviews to the rest, failed. Martin likened them to people who are forever running into the pub 'just to buy cigarettes'. What he could feel certain of was that the breadth of opinion found in the *New Statesman* made it interesting to different kinds of readers, a fair proportion of whom were not socialists. When, years later in the 1980s, the *New Statesman*'s literary and political pages were brought into rigid ideological accord, Martin must have turned in his grave. It was the end of an era – and not just for the *New Statesman*.

When Martin and Mortimer worked together in the 1930s and 40s, the *New Statesman*'s address was an alleyway off High Holborn called Great Turnstile, a name once as resonant as that of the paper itself. At the top of an old office block close to the heart of legal London, and not far from the London School of Economics, Martin and his drawling literary colleague ran a talking shop much frequented by journalists and critics, politicians and diplomats. Often figuring among their guests were refugees from oppressive regimes and colonial leaders, notable among them Krishna Menon and Jawaharlal Nehru, in whose eyes Kingsley Martin counted as a powerful metropolitan ally. Here was a vibrant liberal coterie – one to which British society no longer offers any parallel – where men of letters routinely mingled with men of affairs. Sometimes wearing odd socks, and even odd shoes, always the image of the grubby intellectual, Martin presided over Great Turnstile as though it was a court-in-exile, an alternative Establishment. Like his lordly Victorian forerunner, Sir James Knowles, he might have claimed that the influence of a score or more parliamentarians found embodiment in his own person – though he was surely the last exponent of the 'higher journalism' who could have made such a claim without seeming to be nursing delusions of grandeur.

Keynes and Laski were much in evidence at the *New Statesman*. But no one did more to enliven Kingsley Martin's *salon des refusés* than Richard Crossman. The overbearing son of a Chancery judge, 'Dick' Crossman was an Oxford classicist who became both a Labour MP and a left-wing journalist of belligerent brilliance. Originally, Crossman made his name with the book, *Plato Today* (1937), which attacked Plato as the ancient precursor of modern fascism, the archetypal authoritarian. It is a book which says much about Crossman himself, the logic-chopping upper-middle-class intellectual, who, in common with Keynes, little doubted that he knew what was best for people. In the *New Statesman*, Crossman discovered his favourite mouthpiece, employing the paper to instruct society in general and the Labour Party in particular. Each Monday morning for many years, a blistering row broke out between him and Kingsley Martin and other members of the *New Statesman* set, which provided the inspiration for the week's leading article. 'Ideas were our ammunition,' wrote Crossman, certain that British socialism would soon wither unless fortified by regular doses of *New Statesman* polemic.

Crossman argued that the socialist journalist must cultivate the art of the impossible – until a climate of opinion emerges that makes the impossible possible. Yet, schooled in Platonic paradox as he was, he questioned whether real progress would ever be achieved until philosophers became kings or kings became philosophers. In 1964, Britain's new Labour Prime Minister, the self-confessed pragmatist, Harold Wilson, enabled Crossman to try his own hand at playing the philosopher in politics, making him a minister in the ill-starred administration that he formed in that year. Whether Crossman was half as effective a minister as he was a political journalist remains a moot point. Today, his six years of high office are remembered less for statesmanship than for what might be termed 'New Statesmanship' – for the expansive political diaries that he kept during that time, aiming to demonstrate that, democratic pretensions notwithstanding, Britain is really an old-fashioned oligarchy, a state where the many are subject to arbitrary rule by the secretive few.

Kingsley Martin did not mind in the least when this bespectacled bully outraged *bien pensant* leftists' pieties – as he so often did. For Crossman the colleague, however, he found it increasingly difficult to muster much enthusiasm. The truth was that Crossman yearned to take over the editorship of the *New Statesman*, and made no attempt to disguise his designs. When, in 1955, he was offered a lucrative contract by the *Daily Mirror*, Crossman delivered Martin an ultimatum, threatening that unless guaranteed the editorial succession he would leave the *New Statesman* for the *Mirror*. Much to Crossman's surprise and indignation, Martin urged him to accept the *Mirror*'s offer. Deeming him incapable of either pledging or inspiring loyalty, Martin was convinced that if Crossman ever became editor of the *New Statesman* he would be the paper's ruin.

In the aftermath of Martin's death in 1969, and with his own ministerial career by that stage over, Crossman would belatedly get the chance to prove Martin wrong. But his brief tenure of the post that for years he had so much coveted – he edited the *New Statesman* from 1970 until 1972 – turned into a melancholy fiasco. Protesting against British political integration with the rest of Europe, and suffering from what was scathingly dubbed 'ex-minister-itis', Crossman made the *New Statesman* the vehicle of the anti-European Left. Many found the paper tiresomely doctrinaire and predictable – a complaint seldom, if ever, made about the *New Statesman* in Martin's day. The irony was that unpredictability was precisely the quality that Martin had prized in Crossman's journalism. 'Kingsley is having the last laugh now', Crossman ruefully confessed as sales of the *New Statesman* slumped.

In their days as contentious colleagues, Crossman and Martin were sometimes reconciled by a world-weary Scotch cynic with a pointed beard named Aylmer Vallance. One of the rummer members of the Great Turnstile circle, Vallance was a former editor of the *News Chronicle*, a journalist of fabled versatility, best-known perhaps for a series of influential *New Statesman* articles on the state of the British fishing industry. During the First World War, he had worked for the Secret Service – at one point, it seems, fighting a duel with revolvers in the Himalayas, like some character out of John Buchan. Following the outbreak of the Second World War, he startled staff at the *New Statesman* when he suddenly metamorphosed into a Lieutenant Colonel employed by the Intelligence Department of the War Office. Every morning at eleven o'clock, he used to turn up at the *New Statesman*'s offices, where he would deliberately torment the doom-laden Martin with his own prophecies of doom – prophecies which, stemming as they apparently did from official sources, Martin felt bound to take especially seriously.

Crossman, who also served as a wartime Intelligence Officer, had reason to believe that Vallance was under instructions to keep an eye on Martin and to prevent him from being 'silly', from paying too much attention to communist friends who kept telling him that the war was the work of 'wicked capitalists'. Yet Vallance was suspected of being a covert communist himself. Martin, who eventually lost patience with him, said that Vallance's politics could be guessed from the fact that he named his son 'Tito'. Almost certainly, this intriguing, chronically impecunious figure was some species of double agent.

If Crossman and Vallance were *New Statesman* habitués, so were G.D.H. Cole and Noel Brailsford, the latter an ardent champion of Indian independence and a writer as romantic and rhetorical as Cole, a stickler for statistics, was pedestrian. Martin's heterogeneous entourage also included: the whimsical Irish essayist, Robert Lynd; the GP-cum-journalist, Harry Roberts, who – anticipating the heroic career of the late David Widgery – wrote about health in relation to social conditions; the ex-student of Harold Laski and sometime communist, Norman MacKenzie, who became Martin's put-upon assistant, writing on politics and education; the enigmatic movie reviewer, G.W. Stonier, who was to vanish into the wilds of Africa; the drama critic, T.C. Worsley; and the bearded, lubricious philosopher, C.E.M. Joad, who brimmed with books, articles and reviews on subjects of every description. Acclaimed by Martin as the 'prince of the popularisers', Cyril (otherwise known as 'Professor') Joad knew considerable renown as a radio personality during the 1930s and 40s, often taking part in the BBC's programme, the 'Brains Trust'. Like J.B. Priestley – who also enjoyed a long association with the *New Statesman* – Joad was an early instance of what would now be called a 'media pundit'. Puffing at their pipes – a common enough habit among *New Statesman* literati – Joad and Priestley became sages of the airwaves, seasoned opinion-mongers with deferential followings. It dismayed the elderly Beatrice Webb to learn from Martin what a hold broadcasting was giving these 'new intellectuals' over the younger generation. As an advocate of 'scientific' thinking about society's future, she found them glib.

More than a little patriarchal by the standards of today, Kingsley Martin's circle was nevertheless far from being an all-male enclave. Indeed, so far as opening his paper to the opposite sex was concerned, Martin had an excellent record – rather more respectable than many editors of his day. One of the women who contributed most to the *New Statesman* was Janet Adam Smith. A genteel Scottish bluestocking with a passion for mountaineering, she served as the paper's literary editor during the 1950s. A number of other bookish women were, in greater or lesser degree, associated with the *New Statesman*, among them Virginia Woolf, Naomi Lewis, Elizabeth Bowen, Rebecca West and Olga Katzin. Employing the pseudonym, 'Sagittarius', the latter for many years diverted *New Statesman* readers with satirical verses of ephemeral brilliance.

It is also worth remembering that there was more to *New Statesman* than polished prose and that Kingsley Martin published much by the left-wing cartoonists, David Low and Victor ('Vicky') Weiss. The antipodean Low – with whom Martin collaborated on a benign travelogue about the Soviet Union – contributed to the paper prior to the Second World War. A memorable cartoon by him evokes Kingsley Martin himself. Perched on a desk with shirt sleeves rolled up, Martin is scratching his head and peering at a galley proof with a disgruntled expression on his face, as though about to subject what he had written to the sort of drastic revision that so often reduced the *New Statesman*'s printer to despair. Vicky, too, found Martin an irresistible subject. Perhaps the vividest of the several caricatures that he executed of him appeared as an illustration for Olga Katzin's versified squib, *Let Cowards Flinch*, published in 1947 and inspired by the Tory image of Britain's new socialist rulers as Jacobin fanatics. Decking him out in ruff, pantaloons and buckled shoes, Vicky turned the editor of the *New Statesman* into '*Le Nouvel Homme d'État*', the supercilious Diderot of the British Revolution. An insomnia-prone refugee from Nazi Germany (by birth he was a Hungarian Jew), Vicky began to contribute to the *New Statesman* on a regular basis in the mid-1950s, his genial cartoons of statesman and celebrities mingling with darker work, with visions of a world at the mercy of cynics and madmen. When this depressive humorist committed suicide in 1966, Martin paid written tribute to his craftsmanship and humanitarianism. Emotional international socialists, with no love of the United States, editor and cartoonist were kindred agonised spirits.

Martin's own contributions to the *New Statesman* comprised leading articles, many book reviews and the famous feature known as 'Critic's London Diary', to which others contributed but which was essentially his mouthpiece. Inspired by the eclectic 'Wayfarer' Diary which H.W. Massingham had written for the *Nation*, this was a facet of his work over which he took infinite pains. An artful 'flibbertigibbet' with a 'promiscuous, unconcentrated' mind, 'Critic' retailed gossip and topical anecdotes, decried injustice and persecution (in the 1930s, he had much to say about the growth of anti-Semitism) and reported on sojourns in foreign parts with a regularity that made him seem a true citizen of the world. There were also times when he projected himself as a nature-lover, growing effusive about birds and cats and bees. Not infrequently, indeed, *London Diary* was effectively a countryman's diary, the nature notes of a metropolitan editor, who came to own a weekend cottage in Essex and who liked to quote (in faintly patronising terms) the crusty bucolic wisdom of a jobbing gardener named Mr Park. Dramatising Leftism as a way of life, always insistent that, despite it all, there is much to enjoy in human existence, *London Diary* was Martin's episodic autobiography, his discursive confessions. For thirty years, this sentimental diarist laid himself bare, turning the minutiae of his days – private embarrassments included – into arresting journalistic titbits. Once, during the Blitz of 1940, when German bombs were raining down on London, Martin described how he had been blown off the lavatory in the act of reading Jane Austen. The episode was widely savoured.

A weekly column of sustained panache (more than one person remarked that Martin wrote with the vigour and unornamented lucidity of a latter-day Tom Paine), *London Diary* had legions of devotees. But then, so did much else in the *New Statesman* – including the vivid, stylish, tantalisingly suggestive book reviewing of V.S. Pritchett. Like Martin, Pritchett was a roving Puritan who worshipped the word and strove to justify himself through journalism. For years the back half of the *New Statesman* soaked up Pritchett's inordinate literary zeal, his endless compulsion to perform and to preach. Indeed, the services rendered to the paper by this hugely individualistic, largely self-educated literary critic and writer of short stories were as monumental as they were poorly paid. Having first contributed to it in the late 1920s, Pritchett was still writing for the *New Statesman* in the late 1970s, the quality of his work by common consent unimpaired. Arguably, his finest phase at Great Turnstile, though, was the 1940s, a time of paper rationing and much-reduced book-production, when he immersed himself in classic European novels and perfected the art of seeming to say much in a short space.

Proud of Pritchett, Kingsley Martin even vouchsafed him a pay rise – though only after a long period of somehow failing to notice the hard-pressed reviewer's problems in raising a family on his slender *New Statesman* income. He took pride, too, in another self-taught London journalist, whose career was to be all but inseparable from Great Turnstile. A bookish ex-policeman of liberal temper, Bill Hewitt – better known to *New Statesman* readers as C.H. Rolph – devoted his energies to legal and social reforms. During the 1950s, when he campaigned tirelessly against capital punishment, Rolph became the *New Statesman*'s resident writer on crime and civil rights. His weekly journalism helped to shape the penal policy of the Tory Home Secretary, R.A. Butler. At the same time, he enjoyed a reputation as something of a Samaritan; troubled people were always turning up at the *New Statesman* and appealing to him for help. The affectionate biography of his old editor that Rolph published in the wake of Martin's death in 1969 was an act of homage by a protégé forever grateful for having been given the opportunity to do what he considered to be virtuous work.

Whether alumni of ancient English universities or well-read autodidacts, Kingsley Martin and his fellow new statesmen were lecturers-in-society, much-heeded publicists. Read by great numbers of the educated – by politicians, dons, lawyers, scientists and school teachers – their work was also read by not a few among the less educated, by fledgling V.S. Pritchetts and C.H. Rolphs, ordinary people anxious to 'improve' themselves. A readership survey of the mid-1950s threw what now seems quaint light on working-class subscribers who liked to base their 'Saturday night arguments' on some political or literary article that had appeared in the *New Statesman*'s current issue. At a stage when higher educational provision was still sparse, there were many for whom the paper seems to have served as a sort of extension class or home university. During an era, moreover, when British public life, including much journalism, still bore the impress of Victorian formality, all manner of readers were partial to the *New Statesman* simply because it was one of the few papers to challenge the prevailing stuffiness: here was a weekly that seemed refreshingly free from taboos – in which, apparently, *anything* could be discussed. Turning over its pages in a south London grammar school library in the 1940s, a bright teenager named David Jones – in the 1960s 'D.A.N.' Jones would work on the literary side of the paper – found the *New Statesman* to be 'pleasingly bold about God, class and sex'.

The *New Statesman* became the *vade mecum* of 'progressive' opinion. With his paper's absorption of the *Nation* and the *Week-*

end Review, Martin found himself with the opportunity to set himself up as the leading British, if not world, champion of journalistic dissent, and had made the most of it. Indeed, during what he was to recall as the 'great age of the weeklies', Martin came to dominate the entire field of weekly journalism. Apart from Wilson Harris, the prim editor of the Tory *Spectator*, his sole competitor of consequence was the formidable feminist, Lady Rhondda, who ran the weekly known as *Time and Tide*. The daughter of a Welsh coal magnate, and otherwise known as Margaret Haig, this high-minded heiress was Martin's female counterpart; her Review – which she claimed to think about for fourteen hours out of twenty-four – was her life, and she sank all her money into it. But despite attracting talented contributors, she could only watch as Martin's title steadily outstripped its rivals. A growing body of people proclaimed themselves *New Statesman* 'addicts'. By one such addict, Martin was said to have conjured up an intangible 'non-located' club. Perhaps the clue to the *New Statesman*'s mystique was that it had the air of an everyman's Bloomsbury Group. Devotees were able to fancy that they belonged to the intelligentsia, and in truth, the appeal of this famous socialist weekly was by no means free from snobbery. However, socialism and snobbery made the *New Statesman* what it was, a paper written by gentlemen for gentlemen, a select circle which anyone could join by paying sixpence on a Friday.

In fact, the typical *New Statesman* reader was less commonly reckoned a snob than a prig – the kind of self-righteous pacifist and vegetarian so dyspeptically caricatured by George Orwell in *The Road to Wigan Pier.* Sometimes mythologized as a gangling youth with damp hair and a copy of the paper under his arm, the '*New Statesman* reader' became the butt of many a satirical jibe. It may be that no one came closer to embodying this chimerical figure than Martin himself – though Martin was hardly a youth with damp hair, and if he was a prig, he was a peculiarly self-mortifying one. Seldom finding it easy to make up his mind about anything – not for nothing was the *New Statesman* nicknamed 'Staggers and Naggers' – he comported himself as the tortured conscience of liberal Britain. In one of his most memorable sallies, Muggeridge described Martin as an editor who every Friday underwent crucifixion for the sins and deficiencies of mankind, always rising again on Monday to bring out his paper anew. And this professional martyr was after all plying his trade during a phase of history when opportunities for agonising were legion. The Great Depression, the rise of fascism, the breakdown of the League of Nations, the Russian purges, the Second World War, the Jewish Holocaust, the dropping of the atomic bomb on Hiroshima and Nagasaki – how many eras have witnessed such a concentrated sequence of macabre events? Martin's cup was always running over.

A socialist of pacifist upbringing, bent on resisting the rise of fascism, Martin became a persistent performer of editorial somersaults. One moment he was advocating 'collective security', with the implication that Britain and other countries might have to take up arms in order to preserve democracy; at another moment he seemed to be ruling out military action altogether. His acidulous friend, A.J.P. Taylor called him a 'compendium of his time', an editor whose unending equivocations epitomised the mental conflicts of great numbers of bewildered Britons. Perhaps the one political issue about which Martin managed to be at all consistent during the 1930s was the Spanish Civil War. Such was his undeviating support for the beleaguered Spanish Republic in its struggle against Franco's fascists that he notoriously turned down dispatches George Orwell sent from Spain revealing the Republican cause to be riddled with murderous Stalinists, who were as contemptuous of democratic freedoms as the fascists. To have published Orwell's articles, he was later to insist, would have been to aid and abet fascism's progress – an explanation unlikely to have weighed much with Orwell himself, in whose eyes Martin had branded himself a pro-Soviet hack with the 'mentality of a whore'.

Martin's editorial line during the years leading up to the Second World War was anything but consistent. The Munich Crisis of August 1938 found him, after much hand-wringing, endorsing Neville Chamberlain's policy of appeasement towards Adolf Hitler. Except in concert with the Soviet Union, Martin seemed persuaded, Britain would never be able to guarantee the borders of Czechoslovakia in the teeth of Nazi aggression. Within weeks, however, he was to execute a remarkable *volte-face*: with the fate of the Czechs now sealed, Chamberlain, it suddenly transpired, was guilty of a shameful act of betrayal. It was Martin's bad luck that his earlier verdict was the one that was commonly remembered. Ever afterwards – like Geoffrey Dawson, the editor of the *Times* – he bore the stigma of having been among the leaders of opinion in Britain who publicly condoned the selling out of the Czech people. The words that he wrote at the time of Munich – and indeed the very circumstances in which he set them down – haunted him. In later years, dogged by the need to justify himself, he wrote that the *New Statesman* of the 1930s was a 'vivid reflection of all our perplexities'. This may have been true. Certainly, in August 1938, Martin was only blurting out what many of his compatriots, Keynes included, were saying in private. But he had made an irretrievable mistake, and he knew it.

Martin was not exactly the stuff of which war heroes are made; though, once war was declared, he could hardly be indifferent to the knowledge that his name was on a blacklist of public figures whom the Nazis were planning to deal with if they succeeded in taking Britain over. For some years he carried morphia tablets about him in case he found it necessary to kill himself. He even considered plastic surgery, thinking that, with his larger than average nose, he might be mistaken by invading Nazis for a Jew. Yet it was not just for his own skin that he feared. As he noted in a wartime memorandum, the First World War had gravely damaged the mental and physical health of thousands of British soldiers, and might not another war, with the threat now of constant aerial bombardment of civilians, have disabling effects on the whole nation? Moreover, what chance did Britain stand of escaping crushing defeat save through heavy reliance on American help, with the likely consequence that it would end up a mere American satellite? Employing an expression often heard in Britain in more recent times, Martin speculated that even if the British won the war, they might yet 'lose the peace', emerging not just as a 'second class power' but as something far worse: a 'second-class people'.

Martin feared that British civilisation was facing perdition – and with it the weekly paper, that irreplaceable medium of British high-mindedness, to which he had pledged his whole existence. Uncertain about so much else, he was unswerving in his belief in the *New Statesman* as a repository of the finer values. Underlying his entire editorship was his faith that the paper was an instrument of enlightenment, a means of engendering a critical public with a 'weekly journalism frame of mind'. At a time when newspapers and magazines were increasingly controlled by acquisitive, conservative-minded press barons like Rothermere and Beaverbrook, Martin made himself known as the proponent of a different kind of press altogether. He believed that, for all its minority status, the *New Statesman* might set a powerful example, demonstrating that there was more to journalism than triviality and sensation-mongering. Much concerned with the relationship between what people read and what people think – he took a great interest in the theory and practice of propaganda – Martin maintained that it was the job of guiding spirits like himself to teach the uninstructed how to read newspapers with a critical eye. And the 'uninstructed' included the otherwise well-educated – scientists, for instance, blinkered by their specialisms. The great contemporary desideratum, he wrote in 1930, shortly before becoming editor of the *New Statesman*, was for a 'map' explaining to men their whereabouts in the civilisation they were heir to, and enabling them to distinguish between the 'obvious lie and the more complicated truth'. Thus averred Martin, bringer of light, weaned as he had been on the rationalist optimism of Shaw and Wells – not to mention the *philosophes* of eighteenth-century France.

In his crusade against the press barons, Martin was not alone. During the 1930s and 40s, F.R. Leavis and his wife, Q.D. Leavis, were publishing their maledictory Cambridge journal, *Scrutiny*, actuated by remarkably similar anxieties. How curious it can now seem that Leavis saw Martin not as an ally in his own battle against the advertising industry and the rising tide of commercialism, but as a figure remorselessly to be reviled. In Leavisite demonology, the *New Statesman* ranked with the BBC's Third Programme as the plaything of frivolous London intellectuals, who – did they but know it – were sapping the foundations of the native culture. Fifty years on, Leavis and Martin look like *semblables,* British men of letters caught up in much the same cultural struggle. Were they not united in their horror of Americanised mass entertainment and their scepticism about the benefits of science? Besides, were they not both hereditary Huguenots, English Puritans for whom existence was a war between the forces of light and the forces of darkness? What Leavis seems to have found hardest to forgive about the *New Statesman* was its very success. During a period of what he took to be inexorable cultural decline, with habits of discrimination in decay, he seems to have been convinced that no *bona fide* Review could be other than an 'outlaw' enterprise. Hence, the more famous the *New Statesman* grew, the more it forfeited its claim to serious attention. *Scrutiny*'s circulation, on the other hand, Leavis was able to regard as honourably exiguous, priding himself on the quality as opposed to the quantity of the journal's readership – on the cachet that it boasted, for example, among 'key élites' of the Indian subcontinent.

The Leavises had ample cause to envy the phenomenal progress made by the *New Statesman* during the era of the Second World

War, for, in spite of all his fears, the war found Martin's paper prospering as never before. Nor was there to be any falling away thereafter. Indeed, in what was to prove the twilight of British power, Kingsley Martin reached the summit of his prestige, presiding over a publication whose circulation rose rapidly from 30,000 to over 90,000 copies per week. Here was what appeared to be an unstoppable cultural force.

To be sure, Martin's weekly was by no means the only publication to enjoy a good war. Bored, off-duty servicemen were hungry for printed matter of every description, and during the hostilities demand for books, newspapers and magazines boomed. Likewise a beneficiary of this reading fever was the literary magazine, *Horizon*, edited by that seasoned *New Statesman* contributor, Cyril Connolly. What perhaps gave the *New Statesman* special credibility was the fact that, during a period of pervasive propaganda, its editor bore witness to events with unmistakable honesty, never disguising the dilemmas that assailed him. In his memoirs, he was to recall the many letters he received during the War praising him for putting out a paper which, even if it was not right about everything, at least seemed to be trying to tell the truth. And after all, his own favourite causes – the establishment of a Welfare State in Britain (the *New Statesman* did much to publicise the work of William Beveridge) and the liberation of colonial peoples abroad – were the causes of the moment. Many a servicemen felt like Martin, that the fight against fascism would hardly be worth winning unless victory struck a decisive blow on behalf of democracy and social justice.

When the Labour Party swept the Tory Prime Minister, Winston Churchill, from office in 1945, Martin was jubilant. With good grounds for thinking that he had made a major contribution to Labour's success, Martin felt himself to be in the van of progress, a left-wing intellectual missionary whose time had come. When the *Daily Mail* celebrated its fiftieth birthday in May 1946, Martin remarked that mass circulation newspapers which supported the *status quo* had a new public to contend with. Were not the numbers of thinking people growing apace – thanks to broadcasting and to periodicals with small circulations like the *New Statesman*, thanks to books, pamphlets and discussion groups, and thanks not least to the painful lessons of the recent past? 'A race is run', he editorialised, 'between the commercial exploitation of public ignorance and the deliberate self-education of people who have discovered, through two world wars and a great economic slump, that democracy has no meaning unless it is based on knowledge and not disconnected snippets of information collected for their news value.' In the years following the Second World War, Martin's vision of an educated democracy seemed eminently realisable, and the future for serious weekly journalism looked bright.

▼▲▼

Sorting through the *New Statesman*'s mail one morning in December, 1957, Norman MacKenzie, got a surprise, for one of the envelopes he opened contained a lengthy letter on the subject of the arms race from the leader of the Soviet Union, Nikita Kruschchev. Or so it seemed. When Martin saw the letter – which had been translated from Russian and sent to Great Turnstile via the Russian Embassy – he was incredulous. Indeed, for a while, he was convinced that the *New Statesman* was the victim of a practical joke – one which, given the gravity of the arms race, he judged to be in singularly poor taste.

Proving to be perfectly genuine, Kruschchev's missive was inspired by the open letter that Bertrand Russell had published in the *New Statesman* in the previous month – itself provoked by the celebrated *New Statesman* article with which J.B. Priestley had launched the Campaign for Nuclear Disarmament in February of the same year. Russell was appealing to the Russian and American administrations to abandon attempts to propagate their respective creeds by force of arms, thereby sparing the human race from nuclear devastation. Kruschchev's letter was in large measure an endorsement of the elderly philosopher's sentiments, but with the proviso that the Soviet leader could not see why either the USSR or the USA need give up its ideology as well as its arms. It was now perhaps only a matter of time before the leadership of the latter felt compelled to join the debate. Sure enough, early in 1958, the *New Statesman* received a robust riposte to Kruschev's statement from the American Secretary of State, John Foster Dulles. Impugning the Russian leader's good faith, Dulles pointed out that the Soviet communist Party had never yet disavowed the use of force to promulgate its creed. Moreover, had not the Red Army but recently put down an uprising in Hungary rooted in resistance to Russian communist rule?

Seldom inclined to think well of America, Martin probably felt better disposed towards Kruschchev than towards Dulles, though by the 1950s – despite his horror of McCarthyism and unease about the Korean War – he was, it seems, yielding to the view that Russian communism and American capitalism were systems of equal nastiness. All this aside, however, what the aforementioned episode vividly illustrated was the extraordinary moral and intellectual stature the *New Statesman* had acquired. With the Cold War at its height, the very future of *homo sapiens* was being debated in the pages of Martin's paper by the Russian government, the American government and a British philosopher of world eminence. Enjoying a journalistic coup of historic magnitude, Martin was entitled to feel on top of the world. In due course, Kruschchev's letter was to be framed and put on prominent display in the *New Statesman*'s boardroom, a memento of the days when the fate of nations seemed to be bound up with the deliberations of Great Turnstile.

Together with the 'Third Force', the notion of Britain as an exemplary social democracy beholden neither to the Soviet Union nor the USA, the Campaign for Nuclear Disarmament bulked large among Martin's later preoccupations. Meanwhile, he travelled extensively, becoming a ubiquitous ambassador for British socialism – and, as such, an object of mounting suspicion to the CIA, which throughout the 1950s waged covert intellectual war on British Leftism through the medium of the Anglo-American Review, *Encounter*. Often stopping to deliver lectures, Martin traversed the whole of the middle East; spent time in China and Japan, India and Burma (the latter a country beloved of his companion Dorothy Woodman); and made himself familiar with many of the countries of Africa. Nor was Australia – where he was dubbed the 'most peripatetic editor in the world' – omitted from his packed and hectic itinerary. It was one of the boasts of Martin's declining years that he had visited no fewer than sixty countries – an impressive tally by any reckoning.

When it came to crusading for the dismantlement of the British Empire, Martin had few rivals; and when it came to nursing optimism about the upshot of the 'colonial revolution', he probably had none. It must be said, though, that this optimism seems to have been intimately connected with his faith that former British subjects would carry on deferring to the teaching of British mentors like himself. Martin's vision was of a post-colonial world shaped according to the 'enlightened' dictates of the *New Statesman* and the London School of Economics. It seems scarcely to have occurred to him that there would ever be a time when the *New Statesman* ceased to be revered by Indians, Africans and others as a source of metropolitan light. But then, this perhaps hardly occurred to the paper's colonial devotees, either. Many were the Indian intellectuals who regarded Martin as a messianic figure. Every Sunday afternoon, Jawaharlal Nehru sat down to read what Martin had found to say in the latest issue of the *New Statesman* to have reached the subcontinent. Indeed, it may be that, in the years following the country's independence in 1947, Indian foreign policy was in some measure being influenced by Great Turnstile editorials.

The end of British rule in India and elsewhere filled Martin with delight. Yet with the triumph of the anti-colonial cause, much of his mission in life was accomplished, and, increasingly, he found himself bereft of purpose, struggling to find a fresh *raison d'être.* So much of his editorial energy had gone into denouncing his own country's deliquencies in amassing an empire in the first place. Over what was he to wax morally indignant now? 'The Suez Crisis', the abortive Anglo-French invasion of Egypt in 1956, furnished Martin with a last grand opportunity to lash the British ruling-class for its overweening arrogance. Post-Suez, however, as British power dwindled apace, so did Martin's scope for raging against it – though old habits died hard. Maintaining that Martin ended up morally redundant, Muggeridge cruelly likened him to a shrewish wife who keeps scolding her impotent husband for imaginary infidelities.

It was not just as an enemy of empire that Martin suddenly began to be robbed of relevance. Steeped in the culture of print, he never really came to terms with radio – let alone with television, the revolutionary social impact of which was becoming daily more palpable during the final phase of his career. Indeed, if his tendency to mumble made him an indifferent radio performer, on television he proved to be altogether inept. In front of the cameras, the journalist who would be characterised by Bernard Crick as a 'television personality before television' was embarrassingly ill-at-ease. Desperate to keep his status as a leading commentator, Martin greatly envied the ease with which his intellectual contemporaries, Malcolm Muggeridge and A.J.P. Taylor, together with his *New Statesman* colleague, John Freeman, were taking advantage of the new medium, in the process becoming better known than he was – better known than they could ever have been by writing for the *New Statesman* (or any other publication for that matter).

The success of Freeman, who had been his protégé, Martin found especially galling. *Face to Face*, the celebrated series of the late 1950s in which Freeman, following the example of the American broadcaster, Ed Murrow, subjected public figures to what by the standards of the day were excoriating interviews, made its presenter a household name. He became rather more of a household name than face, in fact, since Freeman kept his back to the viewer at all times. With more sourness than was typical, Martin observed that Freeman was the only broadcaster who ever achieved fame by confronting the public with his behind.

It was Freeman who succeeded Martin as editor of the *New Statesman* in 1961. The son (like Richard Crossman) of a Chancery judge, Freeman was an upper-middle-class socialist who had been an enthusiastic reader of the *New Statesman* since his Oxford days in the early 1930s. After decorated service as a Guards officer during the Second World War, he entered Parliament in 1945 as MP for Watford, quickly rising to senior ministerial rank in the Labour government of Clement Attlee. When he resigned from government in 1951 – belonging to Aneurin Bevan's 'Keep Left' group, he opposed the future Labour leader Hugh Gaitskell's decision to cut health expenditure in the interests of defence – Martin invited Freeman to join the *New Statesman*. No doubt eager to exploit his inside knowledge, he employed him as assistant editor. Three years later, he made him his deputy.

Urbane, respected, soaked in Great Turnstile lore, Freeman was Martin's preferred choice as successor – in so far as anybody was. It was a sign of his confidence in him that he had delegated much of the running of the *New Statesman* to Freeman whenever he went abroad. However, once Freeman became editor proper, it was not long before relations between mentor and pupil grew strained, Freeman's views about the direction the *New Statesman* needed to take turning out to have little in common with Martin's. With the Cold War permeating the whole intellectual atmosphere, Freeman set about creating a new *New Statesman* – a paper which, among other things, was unequivocally anti-communist and which could no longer be accused of anti-Americanism. Breaking with tradition, he appointed the American journalist, Karl Meyer, as the weekly's American correspondent. At the same time, he found a new literary editor in Karl Miller, an anti-communist Scot with a keen interest in American literature. That the *New Statesman* – or, for that matter, society at large – had anything to gain from broader, more sympathetic, coverage of the American scene had almost certainly never entered Martin's mind. Latterly, the *New Statesman* contributor probably most favoured by him on the subject of the United States was J.B. Priestley, a gruff literary John Bull with a tendency to portray the United States as a mindless, materialistic dystopia.

And yet – for all his efforts to impart to the *New Statesman* a more timely ethos – Freeman himself now seems no more a figure of the 1960s than Martin. What struck many who met him was his antediluvian courtesy, his positively Victorian concern with punctilio. Freeman's extreme formality was sufficiently evident in the laconic character of his own journalism. Much the least agreeable aspect of the job that he had inherited seems to have been the weekly business of writing 'London Diary', the personalised *New Statesman* feature that long survived his predecessor's retirement. Baring his soul to the paper's readers or milking some private mishap for laughs, as when Martin reported his *contretemps* on the lavatory – such unbuttoned journalising was simply not Freeman's style. It was said that where Martin went before the public in a state of undress, the costive Freeman was loath even to take off his tie.

In the event, Freeman's editorship of the *New Statesman* was but a brief interlude. Reputed to have remarked that if the Labour Party won power in the 1964 General Election, the 'gates of paradise would open', Freeman was to be offered the ambassadorship of India by the incoming Labour Prime Minister, Harold Wilson – a post that he was quick to accept. The sense of betrayal felt by Kingsley Martin – who had evidently assumed that he and Freeman were at least united in regarding the editorship of the

New Statesman as a sacred trust – was acute. Nor did he draw much comfort from the arrival of Freeman's red-headed, militant successor, Paul Johnson, for, notwithstanding his prodigious talents as a polemicist, Johnson was a Catholic, a votary of a religion which the nominally Protestant Martin identified with dogma and obscurantism. Eventually, Martin would grudgingly admit that Johnson, under whose aegis the circulation of the *New Statesman* fleetingly rose, was not doing such a bad job. Whether, however, he would have succeeded in coming to terms with Johnson's subsequent transformation into a right-wing zealot, a Thatcherite free-marketeer, who rabidly repudiated nearly all the values for which the *New Statesman* was famous, is another matter.

In 1962, Martin published a short book called *The Crown and the Establishment*, arguing not for the abolition of the British monarchy – he was probably too much of an old-fashioned Englishman for that – but for its reduction to Scandinavian unobtrusiveness. But the following year – during which the *New Statesman* was celebrating its fiftieth anniversary, with congratulations pouring in from heads of state all over the world, including the new President of the United States, John F. Kennedy – he suffered a severe stroke. With difficulty, he nevertheless wrote on, setting to work on his memoirs and continuing to contribute occasional pieces to the *New Statesman*. His new-found causes for consternation included the growth of racism in Britain and the Labour Government's unqualified support for American intervention in Vietnam. All too plainly, however, the calibre of his journalism was not what it had once been. Besides, his high-minded agonisings hardly chimed with with an era whose tone was being set by pop stars and satirists. In the age of the Beatles and *That Was the Week That Was*, Martin's was the voice of a vanishing Britain.

Stung by the behaviour of Freeman, he was also stung by his treatment at the hands of the Labour Party. When Harold Wilson offered him a knighthood, he was the reverse of flattered. So far as this veteran Labour supporter was concerned, only a life peerage would have been acceptable. For all his socialism, for all his commitment to bringing about greater equality, Martin yearned for the highest honours that the British Establishment had to bestow – and yearned in vain. Still, if he felt that he was being snubbed and ill-used at home, outside Britain the former editor of the *New Statesman* was made much of. Indeed, all over the post-colonial world, he was hailed as a hero, receiving preferential treatment almost wherever he went. It so happened that he was in transit when he died in 1969, staying in Cairo with the Indian ambassador to Egypt, Apa Pant. There could hardly have been a better setting for this cosmopolitan editor's final days than the Egyptian capital, that symbolic meeting-point of East and West. Was it not to the creation of a united world that Martin – like his exemplar, H.G. Wells – had devoted so much of his energy?

It was Freeman's opinion that Martin had not only played a key role in equipping the Labour Party of the Attlee era with its moral categories, but that he had also moulded patterns of dissent all over the world. The sheer scale of his influence few were disposed to doubt – though many believed that he had done far more harm than good. By critics like Muggeridge and Arthur Koestler he stood charged with having indiscriminately promoted the 'progressive' line, with being criminally foolish and gullible. His detractors had special cause to despise him when, in 1952, referring to the alleged liquidation of one and a half million 'enemies of the people' in the wake of China's recent Maoist revolution, 'Critic' posed the breathtaking question: 'Were these executions really necessary?' Nor can it be denied that Martin was ingloriously slow in facing up to the mounting evidence of the Soviet Union's institutionalised inhumanity: for years, he preferred to think of Russia as a backward society with a heritage of oppression, attempting a noble experiment in the teeth of implacable capitalist hostility. It has also to be admitted that his socialist expectations about the outcome of decolonisation were hugely inflated. People with dark skins who had suffered colonial subjugation made Martin dewy-eyed; here, this paternalistic Englishman seems to have felt, were the meek who would inherit the earth. East of Suez, somebody jibed, he thought that God was left-wing – West of Suez, a right-wing reactionary.

Something of a Holy Fool, Martin was an unabashed humanist in an age that was making a mockery of the humanist case, and while always prepared to concede the strength of mankind's irrational and destructive impulses, he nevertheless refused to accept that human progress was a lost cause. Conor Cruise O'Brien called him a moral and political Micawber. In theological terms, he could be described as a follower of Pelagius, who demurred at the doctrine of original sin associated with St Augustine, believing rather that man's salvation lay in his intelligence, in wisely directed effort. However, by this stage in the evolution of the human species, it is surely the Augustinian pessimism of Martin's arch-adversary, Muggeridge, that has the less need to make excuses for itself. It was, incidentally, in the pages of the *New Statesman*, following Martin's retirement from the paper, that Muggeridge launched his most comprehensive attack on what he termed the 'Great Liberal Death Wish'. With what relish did this impish mentor of the 1960s' satire movement pour scorn on all that the *New Statesman*'s sometime editor had held dear.

At the time when Muggeridge was propounding his anti-liberal gospel, the *New Statesman* remained what Martin had made it: the most quoted journal of opinion in the world. Only now, perhaps, more than thirty years after his death, is it becoming possible to assess Martin's contribution, to gauge the height from which the *New Statesman* fell during the 1970s and 80s as – like Britain in general and the Labour Party in particular – the paper staggered from crisis to crisis. With all his obvious flaws, Martin was among the maestros of modern journalism, the creator of an intellectual paper of incomparable charisma. Remembering him in 1969, Paul Johnson – still a professed socialist at that time – wrote that Martin had communicated to all who worked with him a 'dramatic and inspiring sense of the validity of his paper and what it was trying to do'. That Martin's zest and zeal also rubbed off on many of his readers seems certain. There were those who in all earnestness believed that, if only more people read the *New Statesman*, the world would be a better place. Of what comparable publication would anyone be tempted to say that today?

Michael Josselson and Melvin Lasky

8. Ideologues of Destiny

Long identified with the Cold War, the monthly magazine *Encounter* died what could be reckoned a punctual death at the beginning of 1991. Considering how prominent a part it had played in intellectual affairs during the 1950s and 60s, the obsequies of this remarkable Anglo-American monthly were strangely muted. It was *Encounter*'s fate that the only thing many people remembered about it was that it had once been covertly sponsored by the CIA. Coming to light in 1967 (at a time of mounting unease over the Vietnam War), this information sullied the name of a highbrow Review that had purported to be an advertisement for the West's dedication to openness. Amid much public acrimony, the magazine was to be disowned by a swathe of literary celebrities, foremost among them Stephen Spender and his successor as the magazine's co-editor, Frank Kermode. Adamant that he had always been assured by American colleagues that *Encounter*'s funding (conspicuously generous from the outset) derived from irreproachable private sources, Spender protested that he had been deceived and ill-used over many years. Feelings of anger and outrage on the part of the defectors – most of them English – were extreme. Indeed, in Spender's case they seem never to have subsided. The reaction of the octogenarian poet to the news that *Encounter* had finally folded was blunt: 'I am glad,' he said.

Encounter was launched in London in 1953 under the auspices of the anti-communist Congress for Cultural Freedom, and boasted a prestigious Haymarket address, close to the centre of British power in Westminster. It began life as a transatlantic marriage of minds, with an ex-communist English editor in Spender and an ex-Trotskyist American editor in Irving Kristol, who came to London from New York to supervise the magazine's politics. What Spender, the winsomely diffident patrician, brought to the enterprise was English cultural prestige, together with the editorial experience and literary contacts that he acquired while working on Cyril Connolly's *Horizon*. Kristol, by contrast, brought to it the hard-bitten ideological polemicising associated with the magazine *Commentary*, which had been established in New York in 1945 as the intellectual mouthpiece of the American Jewish Committee, and on which Kristol served his editorial apprenticeship. If never exactly a London counterpart of *Commentary, Encounter* was in many respects the creation of Jewish intellectuals, with Arthur Koestler an important influence on its development. Author of the classic anti-Stalinist novel, *Darkness at Noon* (1940), and leading contributor to the seminal collection of essays by communist apostates, *The God that Failed* (1950), Koestler – a polymathic *littérateur* from Budapest – played a key role in organising the original public gathering of the Congress for Cultural Freedom in Berlin in 1950. In later years, his peculiar contribution to *Encounter*'s polished pages was to be a sense of dramatic – not to say melodramatic – urgency. No issue of the magazine proved more controversial than the one guest-edited by him in 1963, which addressed itself to the decline of Britain, and bore the portentously interrogative title: 'Suicide of a Nation?'

In the 1950s, *Encounter* exuded Anglo-American amity. This was a time when, prompted by the USA's freshly acquired status as the dominant Western power, anti-Americanism was a common enough European sentiment. But young British writers and intellectuals were becoming captivated by American culture, by its energy and novelty, affecting American English and sometimes even pseudo-American accents. *Encounter* was much of a piece with this trend. British well-wishers of the USA who were pleased to become contributors included the literary academic, Marcus Cunliffe, the political journalists, Henry Fairlie and Peregrine

Worsthorne, those 'angry young men' of the period, Kingsley Amis and John Wain, and the prolific Cambridge historian, D.W. Brogan, for whom *Encounter* was breathing new life into the tradition of intellectual journalism pioneered by the *Edinburgh Review*. Kristol, meanwhile, crossing the Atlantic and taking a benign, if quizzical, interest in the English scene, did what he could to reciprocate this goodwill; and when he moved back to New York in 1958, his diplomatic efforts were to be ebulliently perpetuated by Melvin Lasky, who became the longest-serving of *Encounter's* several editors. Likewise of New York Jewish background, Lasky said goodbye to Berlin, where he had been running the anti-communist cultural Review, *Der Monat*, made London his home and threw himself with gusto into the business of befriending leading members of Britain's literary and political establishment.

It is true that on the European Left almost everything about *Encounter* was eyed with suspicion. Detecting the hand of US imperialism at work, leftist opinion considered that *Encounter*'s contributors were enrolling themselves as American stooges. The British Marxist historian and Communist Party member, Eric Hobsbawm, declined to have any dealings with the magazine, despite being pressed to contribute to it by editors who were forever eager to proclaim *Encounter*'s independence and breadth of viewpoint. All the same, *Encounter* quickly came to enjoy the attention of readers all over the world, its fame far transcending its optimum circulation of 30,000 or so. And what justification could there be for imputing any very insidious intent to a periodical that had made a name for itself with a tart essay on the English aristocracy by Nancy Mitford, and which, if it published conservative views and pro-American outbursts by the chauvinistic mid-Western critic, Leslie Fiedler, also forged close links with the British Labour Party? No one, to be sure, ever supposed that *Encounter* was going to champion the politics of somebody such as Hobsbawm, but many were prepared to accept the magazine's *bona fides* as an open enough intellectual forum.

Yet *Encounter* was not entirely what it seemed. What the scandal of 1967 belatedly brought to public notice was that for years – via the ostensibly unaffiliated Congress for Cultural Freedom – the CIA had been underwriting an elaborate international network of intellectual periodicals, pledged to fighting the ideological battle against communism and to combating anti-American feeling. It also sponsored a number of European 'Encounters': in France, *Preuves*; in Italy, *Tempo Presente*; and in Spain, *Cuadernos* (this last aimed not just at Spain but at the whole of Latin America). Backing was also given to the journals *Quest* in India and *Quadrant* in Australia – not to mention *China Quarterly, Minerva* and *Censorship*, all published in England, and the journal *Transition*, which was set up in Uganda. Apart from anything else, this extraordinary operation now seems testimony to the great store that was still set by the 'higher journalism' in those days.

The secret history of the Congress for Cultural Freedom and its many magazines has been laid bare with a wealth of detail, albeit from sharply different perspectives, by Peter Coleman and Frances Stonor Saunders. The work of an Australian barrister and pro-Congress partisan, Coleman's book, *The Liberal Conspiracy* (1989), depicts the Congress's chief protagonists as heroic figures who became engaged in a momentous struggle for the 'mind of Europe' at a time when, in the aftermath of World War Two, European submission to Soviet totalitarianism was widely feared to be an ever-present threat. In her book, *Who Paid the Piper?* (1999), Frances Stonor Saunders hardly doubts the momentous nature of the struggle in question, but portrays Coleman's heroes in altogether less eulogistic terms. For all their commitment to truth and freedom, to the boasted values of western civilisation, they emerge from her sprightly narrative as compromised accomplices of US cultural imperialism.

Naturally enough, both writers have much to say about Melvin

Lasky, whose status as one of the most active of all cold warriors – intellectual or otherwise – is beyond dispute. Of Russian Jewish blood, this burly ideologue, with his spade beard, pipe and faint resemblance to Lenin, was reared in the loquacious, casuistic atmosphere of New York's City College in the 1930s – the same hotly politicised milieu that spawned Kristol and kindred intellectuals who later recanted their youthful radicalism. Long before he arrived in London to edit *Encounter*, Lasky was devoting all his time to prosecuting the Cold War. As a former combat historian in the American army and a seasoned linguist, Lasky had ended up in Berlin in 1945, where he tirelessly attended writers' conferences, issued denunciations of Soviet tyranny and lobbied the American military authorities to launch a paper aimed at countering communism and inspiring writers in the East who were suffering under communist repression. Something of a prototype for *Encounter* – but explicit about its official backing – *Der Monat* was established in Berlin in 1948, with Lasky as editor. Two years later, in concert with Arthur Koestler, Lasky was mobilising the mass Berlin gathering of anti-totalitarian western intellectuals known as the Congress for Cultural Freedom, which later crystallised into a formal body, backed by the CIA and charged with masterminding the intellectual offensive against the Soviet Union.

It was during this grim, post-war period in bombed and partitioned Berlin that Lasky first met Michael Josselson, fellow Jewish intellectual and fellow linguist, with whose career his own was to be indissolubly enmeshed. A peripatetic figure, Josselson had served in American Intelligence during the Second World War, afterwards being recruited by the embryonic CIA. Born in Estonia in 1917, Josselson came from a family driven into exile by the Bolshevik Revolution. Having attended university in Berlin, he migrated to Paris, where he worked his way up to become director of an American-owned department store. With the shadow of Nazism looming across Europe, Josselson migrated once more, this time to the USA. By 1942, he had acquired American citizenship. It was not in America, however, but back in Europe that he would carry out much of his most important work. Only in recent years, thanks to the efforts of Coleman and Stonor Saunders, has it become apparent how central to the Congress for Cultural Freedom's story was the part played by this unknown soldier of the Cold War. Both man of letters and CIA agent, Josselson was to discover his true métier as the Congress's executive director – a capacity in which, with the base of his operations in Paris, he travelled widely. To Josselson belongs no small portion of the credit (or discredit) for securing the CIA's sponsorship of *Encounter* and other magazines, an arrangement that committed him to years of increasingly uncomfortable secrecy. With his bruised eyes and receding hair, Josselson was a professional agoniser, a complicated, profoundly driven personality, whose fate was to bear the burden of what the French philosopher, Raymond Aron, dubbed the 'original lie'.

Aron was among the countless anti-communist writers and thinkers whose literary energies Lasky and Josselson made it their business to direct. Indeed, to list all their cold war coadjutors, all their associates for whom communism was the 'God that failed', would be to compile an intellectual Who's Who of the period. The more prominent parties to the 'liberal conspiracy' included the Italian writers Ignazio Silone and Nicola Chiaromonte; the Swiss writers Denis de Rougemont and François Bondy; the white Russian impresario Nicolas Nabokov (cousin of the novelist), who became the Congress for Cultural Freedom's Secretary; such American intellectuals as Sidney Hook, Dwight Macdonald and James Burnham; and that sometime British Intelligence Officer and endlessly voluble foe of the Soviet Union, Malcolm Muggeridge, who was happy to involve himself in the money-laundering that brought *Encounter* into being. Yet for sheer undeviating pertinacity in fighting the Cold War, Lasky and Josselson had few rivals. Even Koestler, with all his anti-Soviet zealotry, was to turn aside from purely political polemics, memorably exclaiming: 'Cassandra has grown hoarse'. Cassandras who remained in full cry, here were a pair of ideologues for whom the war of ideas against Russian communism comprised both a career and a crusade. One day in Berlin in the late 1940s, according to legend, they together witnessed trainloads of deportees being carried off to the Russian Gulag. This was the moment, in the exalted words of their friend, Edward Shils, when 'these two Russian Jews decided to save western civilisation'.

Lasky and Josselson, it is plain, saw themselves as men of destiny charged with an epic mission. Convinced that the responsibility for preserving freedom and democracy now lay in the hands of the USA, they became ambassadors for that country in a Europe still in the throes of post-war reconstruction. In common with anti-communists on both sides of the Atlantic, they saw the United States as all that stood between Europe and precipitate annexation by the Soviet Union. Signs of 'fellow-travelling', 'neutralism' and 'anti-Americanism' filled them with foreboding. Their sense that Europe was going to have to be saved from itself found early expression in a hortatory little volume – to which Lasky contributed – entitled *America and the Mind of Europe* (1951). The tightening of the bonds between Europe and America, the 'creation of a common European-American spiritual community' – such, Lasky asserted, had become the 'primary life-preserving task of western culture'. Hymning America as deliverer, this long-forgotten book, a relic of the early days of the Cold War, today reads like a manifesto for *Encounter*, which was established two years later, with the creation of a transatlantic community of the mind high on its agenda. It was shocking to the future editor of *Encounter* that in England the *New Statesman*, exculpatory in its attitude towards the Soviet Union but less than reverential about the USA, was meeting with such feeble opposition. Lasky and his like were only too conscious of the fact that Martin's socialist weekly, then at the height of its prestige, was being keenly read by great numbers of western intellectuals. Indeed, part of the whole purpose of *Encounter* was to sap the ideological influence of a paper which, in Lasky's view, was incapable of distinguishing between a 'free' and a 'slave' society.

This is not to say that there was anything blatant about the way in which *Encounter* pitted itself against the *New Statesman*. The received (anti-McCarthyite) wisdom in sophisticated American circles being that the safest antidote to communism resided in the non-communist Left, the magazine adopted a cool, left-of-centre stance, enshrining the emerging post-war consensus in the West on the virtue of welfare capitalism – the style of politics that Daniel Bell, a leading liberal conspirator, christened the 'end of ideology'. So far as British domestic politics went, this meant striving to establish a close rapport with the dominant moderate wing of the Labour Party. During the mid-1950s – while Lasky was still in Berlin, editing *Der Monat* – this work was assiduously carried out by Kristol, who for several years busied himself with cultivating a cordial, not to say 'special', relationship between *Encounter* and social democrats in the Labour Party who were well-disposed towards the USA It was in *Encounter* that the prominent Labour ideologue, Anthony Crosland, developed the arguments of his seminal work, the *Future of Socialism* (1956), with its vision of a Britain modernised and Americanised, purged not of capitalism but of the crippling effects of class prejudice. The godfather of neo-conservatism, Kristol wrote much for *Encounter* himself at this time, often twitting the British establishment over its hidebound traditionalism. Yet despite his sterling efforts, this future rhapsodist of Ronald Reagan found that he was obliged to justify his editorial activities to Josselson, who, on behalf of *Encounter*'s parent body or *apparat*, was seldom convinced that Kristol was doing all that he could to counter the *New Statesman*, or to stem the growth of anti-American sentiment. Josselson, it appears, grew altogether less anxious on this score once Lasky was installed as *Encounter*'s American co-editor – a development long looked forward to, no doubt, by Josselson and Lasky alike.

Stephen Spender, meanwhile, became a familiar figure on the international conference circuit, seemingly content to believe that *Encounter* and the Congress for Cultural Freedom were being subsidised by a non-profit making body named the Farfield Foundation. During the course of the 1950s, he and his wife, Natasha, were to become great friends with the Foundation's genial president, Julius ('Junky') Fleischmann, often enjoying Mediterranean cruises on his luxurious yacht and by all accounts never suspecting that their host's largesse was other than his own. Not a few observers were to conclude that Spender's involvement with *Encounter* was scarcely more than a cosmetic exercise. From the depths of a conspiratorial armchair at his club, the Athenaeum, Spender's old friend, the late Sir Isaiah Berlin, confided to the present writer that the poet's role was to supply the magazine with what the British intelligentsia would regard as a 'certificate of decency'. It is true that Spender published much characteristically ruminative writing in *Encounter*, and that he handled with aplomb the side of the magazine which Lasky cynically characterised as 'Elizabeth Bowen and all that crap'. But over the central issue of the magazine's political management, his opinions, it appears, were all but irrelevant – as was amply demonstrated by what happened when Kristol returned to America

Spender's favourite candidate to succeed Kristol as *Encounter*'s co-editor was probably the WASP New Yorker, Dwight Macdonald, who had served for a year or two as associate editor of the magazine and whose effusive anglophilia Malcolm Muggeridge believed would be of inestimable value in assuaging anti-American sentiment in Britain. However, the trouble was that, from the point of view of *Encounter*'s paymasters, Macdonald's penchant for the old world was complemented by a highly critical view of the United States; in fact, he had been anxious to publish a diatribe in *Encounter* depicting America as a hell of materialism and neurosis – an article which ended up being rejected. As it turned out, Spender's wishes in the matter of the editorial succession were simply ignored. Josselson and his Congress colleagues gave him no choice but to accept Lasky as his co-editor. The pairing was to prove far from ideal.

In the eyes of the Congress's director, Spender perhaps seemed insufficiently earnest about *Encounter* and its tremendous mission. Mindful of the cultural ecumenism of T.S. Eliot, Josselson watched over a global family of magazines, dreaming of a world-wide community of like-minded intellectuals, as anti-communist as they were pro-America and the 'free world'. But to Josselson and the Congress, *Encounter* always counted as 'our greatest asset'. It was clear that, in a world where English was becoming the dominant language, *Encounter* had the potential to reach far more readers than, say, *Preuves* or *Tempo Presente*. At the same time, *Encounter*'s directorate saw the chance to exploit the prestige that Britain and British journalism still enjoyed in many parts of the world. Intent on projecting *Encounter* as essentially a London Review, they spared no effort to pre-empt suspicions that *Encounter* was pursuing a hidden agenda on America's behalf. They were especially anxious not to offend the sensitivities of Indian intellectuals, among whom Martin's *New Statesman*, with its anti-American bias, had long enjoyed the status of holy writ.

How best to capitalise on the Congress's 'greatest asset' was to become Josselson's *raison d'être*, as he flew from capital to capital, an obsessive editor manqué, forever fretting that *Encounter* was failing to fulfil its mission. Still, so far as at least one major objective was concerned – *Encounter*'s courtship of the British Labour Party – he ultimately had no reason to rue the gradualist stratagem put into effect by Kristol. At an early stage, Kristol advised Josselson to disabuse himself of the notion that *Encounter* could 'save the Labour Party from itself'. What the magazine could do, counselled Kristol – who wrote a judicious *Encounter* piece on Machiavelli

– was to nurture a 'certain kind of intellectual/cultural milieu that could have far-reaching, if indirect, effects.' In short, a process of subtle subversion was the objective; and arguably, this was precisely what was achieved. Certainly, by 1960, Lasky was rejoicing in the warm relations that obtained between *Encounter* and the Labour Party. It is true that not all of Labour's leadership endorsed *Encounter*'s advocacy of British entry into the European Common Market – a step, for reasons of US *realpolitik*, much favoured by Washington policy-makers at the time. However, the Labour Party that would take power in Britain in 1964 after thirteen years in opposition was steeped at the highest level in *Encounter*'s philo-American ethos. The fact is that several senior members of the Labour government formed by Harold Wilson in that year – Richard Crossman, Roy Jenkins, Anthony Crosland and Denis Healey – were *Encounter* contributors. Moreover, but for his untimely death in 1963, Britain might have had, in Hugh Gaitskell – Wilson's predecessor as Labour leader – a philo-American, sometime *Encounter* contributor, as Prime Minister.

Nonetheless, when *Encounter* was at the height of its fame and success, Josselson was growing increasingly uneasy about the Congress for Cultural Freedom's hidden history. Tormented by the legacy of the 'original lie', he began to fear that the Congress's CIA connection was a mistake, a potentially ruinous hostage to fortune. Nor were his misgivings ill-founded. The first ominous sign of the catastrophe to come was a *New York Times* report on a congressional inquiry into the taxation of private foundations, which appeared in 1964, and suggested that certain bodies were conduits for CIA money. From that point, Josselson's life turned into a race to reconstitute the Congress in the face of the looming threat of exposure and scandal. Despairingly, he realised that what might have seemed excusable in the 1950s was likely to be viewed in a very different light in the altered circumstances of the 1960s. Then anxiety about the Soviet Union's intentions had been endemic; now, with tension between East and West much eased, the Russian menace seemed to many altogether less serious – even as, through its bloody intervention in South East Asia, the USA was arousing moral revulsion all over the world. Growing ever more frantic, Josselson toyed with the idea of giving the Congress a brand new name, attempted to get it funded exclusively by the Ford Foundation, and urged the Congress's sundry magazines to seek separate funding (a proposal which, in *Encounter*'s case, bore fruit when ownership of the magazine was assumed – or appeared to be assumed – by the press baron, Cecil King).

Josselson also took steps to soften the Congress's commitment to the Cold War, anxious to dispel any suspicion that it was an instrument of American foreign policy. Meanwhile, as the Vietnam War escalated, he found himself acquiescing in the opposition to the war being voiced by such long-standing Congress sympathisers as J.K. Galbraith, Arthur Schlesinger and Richard Löwenthal. Löwenthal, an *Encounter* contributor of long-standing, even got the opportunity to publish articles in the magazine which questioned the wisdom of American involvement in south-east Asia – though under the stewardship of Lasky opposition to the Vietnam War was hardly something for which *Encounter* was renowned.

Among the agents of the crisis that Josselson was trying so feverishly to avert was Conor Cruise O'Brien, in those days a leftist maverick known for his posture as an anti-anti-communist. When, in 1963, an *Encounter* anthology edited by D.W. Brogan was published to mark the tenth anniversary of the magazine's existence, O'Brien contributed a lethal critique of *Encounter* and everything that it stood for to the *New Statesman*. Josselson and his Congress colleagues are unlikely to have read his verdict on their 'greatest asset' with equanimity. Considering that this was a Review which prided itself on having no 'line' to promote, was it not curious, mused O'Brien, how often *Encounter* carried material prejudicial to the Soviet Union, and how seldom it published material critical of the United States? Among other things, O'Brien was scathing about the Cold War sophistries of Leslie Fiedler. In an essay of 1956 entitled 'The Middle Against Both Ends', Fiedler had mounted an elaborate defence of American comic books, which, with their fantasies of sadistic violence, were widely felt to be marring America's image. Brushing aside objections to such books as 'middle brow and petit bourgeois', Fiedler intimated that there was something far healthier about a society like the USA, where ordinary people could freely avail themselves of such 'literature', than about a country like the Soviet Union, where the masses were force-fed with propaganda and large editions of the Russian classics. But, expostulated O'Brien, would Fiedler have put the same case had it been Soviet presses that were pouring forth violent comic books for popular consumption and America where subway attendants read the classics? He doubted it. The point was that, where the truth was uncomfortable for Russia, *Encounter* was quick to make it known, and where it was uncomfortable for the United States, it was equally swift to play it down.

Three years later – in the wake of further *New York Times* revelations about the work of the CIA – O'Brien returned to the attack. In a New York public lecture, delivered in May 1966, he aired his conviction that, from the outset, the whole purpose of *Encounter* had been to execute America's will. So far from enshrining the spirit of free enquiry, he maintained, the magazine was part of a skilfully mounted intelligence operation aimed at blunting intellectual opposition to American foreign policy, above all in Britain. In a key passage, he wrote:

> A number of young British writers of moderate talents and adequate ambition co-operated actively in this anti-communist but liberal programme. Some of them were progressive Tories, more were moderate socialists on the right wing of the Labour Party. If today that

> party, in the throes of its success, seems too largely anaesthetised on issues to which its traditions should make it more sensitive – such as Vietnam – this is due not entirely to humdrum economic considerations, relevant though they are, but also to an effective cultural and political penetration of which *Encounter* was the spearhead ... Over the years, the magazine, shrewdly edited, adequately financed and efficiently distributed, attracted many writers who hardly noticed, and did not think it important, that this forum was not quite an open forum, that its political acoustics were a little odd, that the sonorities at the Eastern end were of a different character from the Western ones.

For O'Brien, *Encounter*'s cunning achievement was to have induced distinguished writers of high principle to lend unwitting support to the 'more purposeful activities' of lesser writers, themselves engaged in 'sustained and consistent political activity in the interests – and as it now appears at the expense – of the power structure in Washington'. The image he conjured up was of a Trojan horse, which plausible American friends had wheeled into the camp of the British intelligentsia by stealth. On Josselson and the *Encounter* circle, the effect of O'Brien's remarks was incendiary. It might have been expected that if anyone at *Encounter* was going to defend the magazine against O'Brien's charges, it would have been Lasky; instead, that task was to be undertaken by Lasky's turbulent Welsh colleague, Goronwy Rees, a sometime friend of the British defector to the Soviet Union, Guy Burgess, who may once have spied for the Soviet Union himself but who had long since turned into the most rabid of cold warriors.

In his regular *Encounter* column, which was simply signed 'R', Rees declared that O'Brien's case scarcely deserved serious consideration. Nevertheless, he was to attempt a protracted rebuttal, replete with sarcasm and personal abuse. Indeed, the result was such that, on reading it, O'Brien decided that he had good grounds for suing for libel, and gave *Encounter* notice of his intentions. Not long afterwards, he has recalled, a friend of his found himself being accosted by a close colleague of Lasky's, the conservative journalist, Anthony Hartley, and urged to warn O'Brien that *Encounter* possessed a suitcase bulging with embarrassing material relating to the Irish writer's controversial career in Africa as diplomat and scholar – material that would be made public unless O'Brien aborted his libel action. Perhaps more amused than intimidated, O'Brien was about to enter a Dublin court (he believed that he had a better chance of getting a fair hearing in the Irish capital than in London) when events took a dramatic turn, making further action superfluous.

For in March 1967, a San Francisco scandal-sheet named *Ramparts* ran an in-depth exposé of covert activities by the CIA, which was quickly followed by publication in the *Saturday Evening Post* of the bombastic but highly revealing memoirs of a former CIA operator named Thomas Braden. Together, *Ramparts* and the *Saturday Evening Post* provided conclusive evidence that *Encounter* had indeed been sponsored by the CIA and that there had been considerably more to the Congress for Cultural Freedom than met the eye. With their case against him robbed of credibility, Lasky and his *Encounter* colleagues opted for an out of court settlement with O'Brien, and agreed to print an apology for defamation of character in the magazine. It was at this point that Spender and Kermode (who had recently taken over as *Encounter*'s English co-editor) broke ranks, voicing bitter indignation against their American colleagues and plunging *Encounter*'s whole editorial corps into highly publicised civil war. Had they not received repeated assurances from Josselson and Lasky that *Encounter* had never had anything to hide? Bristling with injured innocence, poet and critic professed themselves victims of systematic deception. Hurrying to the *Daily Mirror*, the offices of *Encounter*'s new owner, Cecil King, the incensed Kermode announced that he could only continue at *Encounter* provided that

Lasky was fired. King, however, never known for delicacy of conscience, was unmoved by Kermode's high moral stand. Indeed, he proved rather more anxious to retain Lasky's services than Kermode's, believing the former to be an editor of exceptional flair. In the upshot, and to the accompaniment of accusatory letters to the *Times*, and much mutual recrimination, *Encounter* was deserted by Kermode and Spender, along with a number of other prominent British intellectuals who took sides with them, including the philosophers Richard Wollheim, Stuart Hampshire and Isaiah Berlin. The unofficial conscience of Britain's liberal intelligentsia, Berlin pronounced that, through failing to tell the truth about *Encounter* and the CIA, Josselson and Lasky had 'compromised decent people'.

Josselson's anguish over all this was acute. What made his predicament all the more painful was that the débâcle at *Encounter* was but one aspect of a larger catastrophe, as the entire painstakingly constructed edifice of the Congress for Cultural Freedom, with its pan-continental ramifications, began to fall apart. With public feeling over the Vietnam War running high, criticism of the United States in general and of the CIA in particular had been growing ever more strident. In the *New Statesman*, the American journalist, Andrew Kopkind, published an acid article entitled: 'The CIA: The Great Corrupter'. Scornful of the 'spies who came in for the gold', Kopkind's indictment of American foreign policy typified much radical journalism of the period. For all the good that it might have done over the years, Josselson's beloved Congress was ending up with a blighted reputation.

Implacable in his hatred of communism, Josselson never doubted that he had been engaged in honourable work – work which, with the arrival of the Kruschchev era and its accompanying atmosphere of détente, he could feel was being vindicated. Now, however, tortured by remorse that he had not reconstituted the Congress at a much earlier stage, he watched helplessly as the efforts of a lifetime became enveloped in international obloquy. Nor could he tell himself that the Congress was being maligned by leftist hotheads, such as students too callow to know any better. Indeed, some of the Congress's hardest critics were right-wing intellectuals like James Burnham. For Burnham, the arch-exponent of American *realpolitik*, the Congress's discomfiture furnished conclusive evidence that the non-communist Left was simply not the shield against communism that Josselson and others had made it out to be.

Behind the scenes – unlike Melvin Lasky, he played scarcely any public part in the dramatic events of 1967 – Josselson concluded that the Congress for Cultural Freedom had no future, and resigned his directorship. Not very long afterwards, he suffered a stroke. Over the next few years, the former director's health deteriorated sharply. Rueful and dejected, he retired to Geneva, where, rather than composing his memoirs, he became absorbed in a curious biographical project. With the help of his wife, Diana, he set about writing a scholarly life of Barclay de Tolly, the Russian General who, assisted by 'General Winter', succeeded in repulsing Napoleon's advance into Russia but whose self-sacrifice and patriotism received scant credit at the time. The personal empathy underlying Josselson's interest in de Tolly's hapless career is sufficiently obvious. Like his hero, he felt himself to have been denied the 'heart's reward' of 'simple recognition'. Completing his book in doleful mood, he even began to wonder if the America whose cause he had once so ardently embraced had really been worthy of his allegiance after all. 'What a gruesome society it has become since you and I opted for it,' lamented Josselson in a letter to his old Congress colleague Nicolas Nabokov in 1975, a time when the United States was struggling to come to terms with the consequences of the Watergate Affair.

Three years later, he was dead. When, at his sparsely attended funeral, his widow was asked by a CIA officer what she wanted done with the medal which the Agency had conferred on her husband, she pointedly walked away. Heartfelt tributes from old friends like Raymond Aron poured in, but newspapers carried no obituaries of this singular human being. Indeed, only in *En-*

counter, which published an extract from his biography of de Tolly, was Josselson's memory publicly honoured – in a contributor's note, doubtless composed by Lasky, celebrating Josselson's moral and intellectual stature and exclaiming: 'This was a man.'

A more resilient, altogether less tormented personality, Lasky himself robustly survived the Congress/*Encounter* crisis of 1967. In the following years, he was to bring to fruition a voluminous, rabbinical study of utopianism and revolution, instalments of which had appeared in *Encounter* from time to time. With a succession of pliant English editors and a series of sponsors, he went on being *Encounter*'s editor-in-chief right up until the magazine's closure. During the 1970s and 80s, the magazine ceased to be much noticed, and few would dispute that by the time it stopped publication, its best days were long past, althought it was a rare issue of *Encounter* that was uniformly dull. Insistent to the last on exposing the iniquities of Soviet communism – those exemplary cold warriors, Ronald Reagan and Margaret Thatcher received its warmest support – *Encounter* grew ever more ideologically rigid. In the terminal phase of its existence, it was routinely given over to cold war-mongering, with many a dire warning against the perils of nuclear disarmament, with the result that Lasky's Review seemed bent on self-caricature. *Encounter*'s sudden death in January 1991 – bereft of backers, it became a casualty of the free market of which it had been such a champion – was hardly premature. Still, at a time when news of the Cold War's end was fresh, Lasky had reason to feel that he and his magazine had completed their work. The last two issues edited by him were full of contributions from fellow cold warriors celebrating *Encounter*'s part in the collapse of communism. Not that the close of Melvin Lasky's editing career otherwise occasioned much interest in Britain or anywhere else. Ferdinand Mount, the Tory editor of the *Times Literary Supplement*, wrote that Lasky was a 'prophet uniquely without honour in his adopted homeland'. Perhaps this New York *philosophe* of the Right was always too zealous for British taste. In any event, after the imbroglio of

1967, Lasky was to find himself shunned by much of literary London. Conor Cruise O'Brien thought of him as a 'Cold War conman', and many seemed only too ready to concur.

In the years since *Encounter*'s demise, Lasky has been resident mostly in Berlin. Familiar as a contributor to political discussions in the German media, he may be better known in Germany than in any other country. Like Josselson, he has been something of an intellectual nomad, something of a 'rootless cosmopolitan'. What seems curious about Lasky and Josselson alike is that they should have identified themselves so fervently with the USA after the Second World War, while evidently feeling more at home in Europe and certainly spending more time there than they ever did in America itself. What may also seem curious by this stage is how this pair of messianic Jewish ideologues ever came to be involved with the CIA, a body hardly known in recent years for its intellectualism. However, there was always more to the CIA than could be gathered from its latter-day delinquent image. The organisation's ranks have always included visionaries and salvationists, men for whom American power has been a thing of religious, or quasi-religious, significance. In concert with their KGB counterparts, such men could even be said to have revived something like the religious wars of old.

George Steiner, an admirer of Lasky's, proposed 'ill-met' as a pertinent title for a study of *Encounter*. The intellectual Review evoked by this long-standing *Encounter* contributor was a doomed union between tough-minded Jews and pusillanimous Anglo-Saxons. Steiner likes to recall how the fuming Kermode, in those days occupying a professorial chair at London University endowed by the tabloid-press baron, Lord Northcliffe, was rebuffed by Cecil King (who happened to be Northcliffe's nephew) with the stinging words: 'And I suppose your money smells good.' It is a good story – rather too good to waste, perhaps; though it must be said that Kermode himself dismisses it as a blatant fabrication, with not even the slenderest basis in fact.

Whether or not *Encounter*'s American and English editors were 'ill-met', both parties to the fracas of 1967 were to remain irreconcilably at odds. Ready, despite gloating over its collapse, to grant that *Encounter* had made a noble contribution to the fight against totalitarianism, Stephen Spender nevertheless felt an abiding sense of outrage over his American colleagues' conduct. 'What was unacceptable', he told the present writer in a conversation about *Encounter* three years before his death in 1995, 'was to find that you had been lending your name to a very large public deception – and to find yourself in a situation where all concerned were left looking like knaves and fools, with the knaves saying they had this terrible secret to keep in order to spare the feelings of the fools.' It is true that the more beady-eyed witnesses wondered how anybody so lengthily and so intimately involved in *Encounter* and the Congress for Cultural Freedom could credibly have remained so ill-informed. Did Spender know more than he cared to admit? Did he turn a blind eye to the truth? Or had he simply been displaying the naiveté for which he was widely known? With good reason has Frank Kermode remarked that his dealings with the Congress for Cultural Freedom will be a 'large knot' for Spender's biographer to untie.

After the grand rupture, both Spender and Kermode were loath so much as to glance at the magazine with which they had formerly been pleased to be identified. The latter, considering himself the victim of a 'velvet-glove' operation, was to conclude that he had been ill-advised ever to have had anything to do with editing *Encounter*, a publication about which disquieting rumours were circulating at the time when he stepped into Spender's co-editorial shoes. In his memoirs, in a section headed 'Errors', Kermode wryly recounted going to the Garrick Club at the height of the crisis of 1967 to meet Josselson, who assured him that he would 'no more lie to him than he would to his own son', a piece of bare-faced mendacity as it was soon to turn out. Rather more trenchant and dramatic in his verdict on the whole affair than either Spender or Kermode, Richard Wollheim believes that *Encounter* amounted to a 'very serious invasion of British cultural life, which bore responsibility for the complacency of the Labour Party and many British intellectuals over the Vietnam War.' This of course was much the line taken by Conor Cruise O'Brien – one, incidentally, that he subsequently found no reason to modify despite his later reputation for reactionary views.

Perhaps *Encounter* found its most cogent apologist in Malcolm Muggeridge. While controversy over the magazine was still raging, Muggeridge contributed some characteristically mordant thoughts on the matter of its sponsorship to the *New Statesman*. Quipping that cold war intellectuals were reverse versions of Goebbels, people who reached for their culture whenever they heard the word 'Gun', he confessed that he had never been able to discern more than a nuance between money subscribed by government agencies such as the Voice of America or the CIA, on the one hand, and money subscribed by charitable trusts such as the Ford Foundation, on the other. Was not the objective, in both instances, the same: to maintain the 'essential orthodoxy of liberal capitalist society' in face of the threat of Soviet/Chinese totalitarianism'? Moreover, were not *Encounter*'s liberal critics forgetting the menacing atmosphere in which the magazine was launched? The truth was, he averred, that at an earlier stage many such critics would have been on *Encounter*'s side – just as those who denounced the bombing of Dresden would have found *that* eminently acceptable in the context of 1945.

Still, the fact remains that *Encounter*'s American supporters proclaimed their commitment to truth and openness while themselves practising systematic lying and deception. John Gross, a contributing editor of *Encounter*, who went on to edit the *Times Literary Supplement*, came to suspect that 'nobody emerged from the *Encounter* affair with very much glory', and this seems a fair assessment. But how to explain the sheer fury, the lasting pique of Stephen Spender and company? Was this a case of high-minded British gentlemen nursing feelings of humiliation, of raw resentment at being manipulated by representatives of a country which their kind had long been accustomed to patronise? Curiously enough, the issue of the Anglo-American 'encounter', of the perceptions and sentiments that Britons and Americans have entertained about one another, was to become Spender's literary preoccupation. Following the breakdown of goodwill at *Encounter*, he completed a discursive study which has much to say about the volatile mixture of attraction and repulsion that has been the hallmark of Anglo-American intercourse. Published in 1974, *Love-Hate Relations* makes no mention of Spender's time at *Encounter*, but the English poet's ultimately painful entanglement with the American intellectuals could be read as a postscript to the story of mutual ambivalence that his book sets out to anatomise.

In many ways, the *Encounter* saga epitomised the shift in the balance of imperial power between Britain and the United States. At the end of the nineteenth century, Cecil Rhodes discussed with his friend, that most patriotic of English editors, W.T. Stead, the possibility of nurturing a secret society, a picked body of men to serve as champions of empire. This, it would seem, was never anything but madcap rhetoric. Fifty years later, however, *Encounter* was to provide the cover for just such a secret society – albeit one whose members were agents, not of the British, but of the American *imperium*, and whose mission was to usurp Britain's pan-continental cultural authority on behalf of the United States. A chapter in the history of the Cold War *Encounter* demonstrably was. But this epoch-making intellectual periodical was also an episode in British capitulation to American influence.

Karl Miller

9. The Restless Ringmaster

i. Northern Light

With his hunched shoulders and lank hair, his horn-rimmed glasses and sober suit and tie, Karl Miller might have passed for some hard-pressed government official but hardly for an empire-builder. Yet for more than thirty years, from the late 1950s till the beginning of the 1990s, this moody Scottish editor bestrode intellectual journalism in imperial style, with his most lasting achievement the creation of the *London Review of Books*, a paper with a politico-cultural thrust antithetical to that of *Encounter*. Ranging from Seamus Heaney to Clive James, from Frank Kermode to the late Angela Carter, from Edward Said to Martin Amis, the muster-roll of his contributors attests to Miller's status as a British intellectual *generalissimo*. Who else loomed half so large as a director of literary talent during the latter part of the twentieth century? Perhaps the most comparable of Miller's peers has been Robert Silvers, veteran editor of the *New York Review of Books*. However, by contrast with that invisible impresario of American letters, Miller has been not just a hyperactive editor but also a hyperactive writer, the author of much journalism, and of several notable, if eccentric, books.

Born near Edinburgh in 1931, Miller sprang from a culture peculiarly productive of editors and journalists. His secondary education took place at the Royal Edinburgh High School, the same establishment which those archetypal high-minded Scotch reviewers, Francis Jeffrey, Francis Horner and Henry Brougham, attended in the 1790s. As a teenager there in the 1940s, Miller used to stay up till daybreak putting together the school magazine with his English teacher, the celebrated Gaelic man of letters, Hector MacIvor, who was to urge him to follow the advice of George Bernard Shaw and commit himself to some 'mighty purpose'. At Cambridge in the early 1950s, he co-edited the university magazine *Granta* (a far cry then from the commercial publication which now bears that name) and published early verse by Ted Hughes and Thom Gunn. ('He matured my mind amazingly,' Gunn has recalled.) Thereafter, following short spells at the Treasury, and as a television producer, Miller struck out on a career during which he seemed determined to exhaust all the editing possibilities that British intellectual journalism had to offer. From 1957 to 1961, he was literary editor of the *Spectator*; from 1961 to 1967, he worked as literary editor of the *New Statesman*; and from 1967 to 1973, he edited the BBC's highbrow weekly, the *Listener*, where he perhaps made his biggest impact as an arbiter of public taste. Not for nothing would David Daiches dub Miller the 'restless ringmaster of London reviewers'.

In 1974, stuck for journalistic employment, Miller sought refuge in academe. At the age of forty-three, he was appointed Lord Northcliffe Professor of English at University College London – a post whose previous incumbents included Stephen Spender and Frank Kermode, in common with whom Miller found himself the intellectual beneficiary of an Edwardian press baron who made his fortune out of purveying trivia and sensationalism. The signs were that Miller's editing days were over. However, in the summer of 1979, he was given the chance to become founding editor of the *London Review of Books*. For the next thirteen years, during most of which time Britain was ruled by Margaret Thatcher, Miller busied himself as both editor and university teacher. In his own eyes, these were eminently compatible roles – though not everybody agreed. If captious academics dismissed him as a journalist, not a few journalists found him off-puttingly academic.

As a tyro contributor to the *Listener*, Clive James once found Miller in his office at Langham Place sheltering beneath an umbrella – to 'ward off my troubles'. Much-given to self-dramatisation, Miller played the part of embattled editor with relish – and often to hilarious effect. Yet his problems as a latter-day exponent of the 'higher journalism' were anything but theatrical. During his years as an editor, the brand of journalism for which he stood was fighting for survival, and perhaps the printed word itself forfeited something of its old lustre. Certainly the period witnessed the increasing dominance of television and ever greater diversification of the 'media'; and in the swaggering shape of Rupert Murdoch, editors of Miller's persuasion found themselves up against a uniquely powerful enemy, a media mogul dedicated to purveying mass culture as a matter of principle. Although they have endured, the *Spectator* and the *New Statesman* have become increasingly marginalised; yet they were not always thought to be flourishing when Miller worked for them forty-odd years ago. Less and less were they able to compete with well-resourced expansionist Sunday newspapers, aiming to offer something for everyone. It was efforts to make the *New Statesman* and the *Listener* more 'popular' that underlay Miller's reasons for quitting both those publications. Of course, much reflective journalism is nowadays to be found in the Sunday and daily broadsheets, but the kind of undilutedly intellectual paper epitomised by the *Listener* is a shrinking presence among today's public prints.

All this was to leave Miller looking ever more like a literary King Canute. For many reviewers, though, Miller's obduracy was the secret of his appeal. As committed as Francis Jeffrey ever was to 'instructing the public mind', Miller made his contributors feel that they were taking part in a great civilising mission and that slapdash work by them simply would not be tolerated. Often he summoned them to his office for what amounted to a private tutorial. Ian Hamilton, a contributor to the *Listener* and to the old *New Statesman*, remembered bumping into fellow reviewers – critics of repute among them – who were lining up outside Miller's door like guilty schoolboys waiting to see the headmaster. In his versified skit of the early 1970s, *Peregrine Prykke's Pilgrimage Through the London Literary World*, Clive James lampooned the then editor of the *Listener* as 'Klaus Mauler', a Führer of the reviewing scene who terrorised all who came into contact with him.

Cyril Connolly was evidently thinking of a figure such as Miller when he dreamed up 'Mr Vampire', the pitiless literary editor who features in Connolly's *Enemies of Promise* (1938) and who bamboozles the author's *alter ego*, the literary ingénu, Walter Savage Shelleyblake, into dissipating his energies writing reviews when really he ought to be husbanding his resources for the sake of some sustained creative endeavour. In Connolly's book, reviewing ranks as a pernicious distraction – though he himself came to practise it to the exclusion of everything else. Needless to say, the Mr Vampires of this world see matters from a different point of view. Possessed of a tyrannical will, Miller was an outstanding instance of the editor whose object is to goad writers into doing *his* work at the expense of their own; and because he not only chose contributors' subjects but often re-wrote their copy, while routinely punctuating it according to his own stringent standards, his personality pervaded the pages of the Reviews that he edited. 'I write writers', said the Edwardian editor, A.R. Orage. So, too, it may be said, did Karl Miller.

About Miller the editor – even though he declared himself an atheist – there was an element of the presbyter, just as there was perhaps a touch of the dominie. But what made this inky Scotsman so effective at what he did was that he was acutely conscious of human variety and inconsistency and something of a chameleon in his own person. Those familiar with the Miller who seemed made in the grim image of John Knox were also familiar with a Miller who was all charm, pawky humour and intellectual élan. Out of his own sense of being a riven individual, Miller developed a fascination with the literature of duality, writing much about James Hogg's *Confessions of a Justified Sinner* and Robert Louis Stevenson's *Jekyll and Hyde*, those grisly Scottish anatomies of the divided self. *Doubles*, the big book that he published in 1985, was an exhaustive treatment of the subject. Reviewers quipped that Miller seemed to be suffering from a bad case of double vision, and it is true that readers of this brain-cudgelling work can expect to find cases of double lives and of coincidence – a cognate authorial preoccupation – impinging on their attention as never before. What was the frisson experienced by Miller himself when – just as *Doubles* was about to come off the press – an antipodean writer named C.J. Kotch brought out a novel entitled the *The Doubleman*, with a character in it whose name was none other than Karl Miller.

With its knitting together of parts and striving after unity, editing seems to have had a magnetic attraction for divided Scotsmen. The Scots who have shone at editing are legion. It was after all that great Cham of Regency Edinburgh, Jeffrey, who first gave editing professional respectability. Another Scottish journalist it may be worth mentioning in this connection is John Rintoul, who, a year before Jeffrey's retirement from editing in 1829, became founding editor of the *Spectator*, a weekly which now ranks as Britain's oldest surviving intellectual periodical. Unlike Jeffrey, Rintoul decamped to London, becoming a signal example of the Scottish literary migrant ambitious to conquer the metropolis. Over a century later, with his several editorships – one of them the literary editorship of the *Spectator* itself – Miller was keeping up an old tradition.

Karl Miller may be seen as the culmination of a long line, as a kind of omnibus edition of an old national type. If Jeffrey and Rintoul were among his precursors, so were sundry other bygone Scotch literati, including the redoubtable Aberdonian bookman, David Masson, who prefigured him as a Scottish professor of English literature at University College London, teaching there in the early 1850s. Another forerunner, in whom Miller himself took a keen interest, was his mid-Victorian namesake, Hugh Miller. In *Rebecca's Vest*, the memoir he published in 1994, he evoked in empathetic terms this fey, manic-depressive stonemason who had set up as a crusading editor. In an expanded version of the same book, Miller also advertised his sense of kinship with the paradoxical James Boswell – with his gloom and high spirits, his vanity and guilt, and his compulsion for living his life on paper. How strange that he never wrote more extensively about his judgemental compatriot, Thomas Carlyle. In common with Carlyle, he was to reside for much of his professional life in Chelsea. Like his great nineteenth-century predecessor, moreover, he was to nurse a horror of idleness, a sense of the heroic virtue of literary endeavour, and a penchant for composing prose of maddening sinuosity.

▼▲▼

As clever as he was industrious, Karl Miller attended Downing College, Cambridge, from 1952 till 1955, studying English literature under F.R. Leavis. In the early 1950s – an era stamped by the Labour Party's historic victory in the General Election of 1945 and the founding in Britain of the Welfare State – Leavis was at the height of his controversial fame. A Puritan of compelling personality, his shirt kept open at the neck, he projected himself as an enemy of the British establishment and the prophet of a 'meritocratic' new order. The truth was that, in concert with his wife, Q.D. Leavis, Leavis was bent on creating a counter-establishment, a body of discriminating 'Leavisites', united in their reverence for the work of D.H. Lawrence and in their rejection of what, with propagandist insistence, he termed 'technologico-Benthamite civilisation'. There was much about Leavis that appealed to Miller, the hard-working, pontifical young Scotsman; equally did he find favour with Miller's Cambridge contemporary, Norman Podhoretz, the furiously dogmatizing New Yorker who went on to lay down the intellectual law as editor of *Commentary*. Yet Miller was never a diehard 'Leavisite' for whom Leavis's writings had the status of holy writ: if he respected his tutor's cult of rigour, he baulked at his dogmatic sectarianism, at his blanket condemnation of most of modern literature and all of modern life. Before leaving Cambridge he would suffer the fate that befell so many of Leavis's students whose fealty proved less than absolute: he was blacklisted.

On some, the impact of being rejected by Leavis was psychologically devasting. But it was otherwise with Miller. Made of sterner stuff, he was already staking his own claim to critical leadership. During his statutory two post-school years as a national serviceman, he had enjoyed the opportunity to specialise in broadcasting, and as a Cambridge student he was soon travelling down to London every fortnight to chair cultural discussions for the BBC's 'young persons network'. His Cantabrigian contemporaries were duly impressed. A profile of him contributed to the university newspaper, *Varsity,* by his friend and rival, Nicholas Tomalin – with whom he edited *Granta* – drew envious attention to this radio work and to the practised microphone manner which had apparently convinced one listener that he was 'at least forty years old, tall, distinguished, with an Anthony Eden hat, a greying moustache and a walking stick.'

Entitled 'Northern Light', Tomalin's piece evoked the twenty-year old Miller as an individualist who affected 'slightly strange clothes: black and grey workmen's shirts, with coloured shoes, brogues with great bizarre decorated tongues, narrow tartan ties and bright Fair Isle jerseys.' Fellow students were apparently struck by Miller's 'impulsive gregariousness', by the relish with which he both made and broke friendships. On Sunday afternoons, everyone gathered in his room at Downing College to drink tea out of china mugs painted with the names of favourite poets. As host, Miller presided over the conversation like the famous BBC broadcaster Richard Dimbleby, quizzing newcomers with aplomb – yet liable to appear uneasy when directly addressed himself. At other times, the future London editor sat in the front row of Leavis's lectures and made the occasional judicious note, or strode about Cambridge with a big briefcase and the 'air of something very exciting and interesting to do'.

Students from privileged backgrounds, such as his Cambridge coeval, the ex-Etonian, Neal Ascherson, were in awe of this mature and purposeful Scotsman. Rough of dress and pugnacious in argument, Miller cultivated the image of the sans-culotte, anticipating the proletarian chic of the 1960s. At the same time, he adopted the habit of addressing female students, among them the young Joan Bakewell – destined for a career in broadcasting – with ungentlemanly candour. Not that there was anything very unusual in 1950s Cambridge about manifestations of masculine arrogance. A seat of learning where, from time immemorial, women had been a patronised minority, the Cambridge of Miller's day remained a citadel of male supremacy, a fastness of patriarchal thinking and traditions. It was in keeping with this background that – with conspicuous exceptions, and despite his enduring marriage to the feminist academic and writer, Jane Miller – Miller's circle of reviewers was to be dominated by his own sex.

If Miller was impatient with punctilio, it is also true that he had no objection to being enrolled as a member of that select Cambridge circle of male symposiasts, the Apostles (his exclusion from which had so galled that earlier Cambridge-educated Review editor, Kingsley Martin). Once ornamented by Tennyson, and later by divers participants of the Bloomsbury Group, the Apostles' clandestine ranks had more recently embraced Guy Burgess and Anthony Blunt, English public school boys who took to spying for the Soviet Union and who also happened to be homosexuals. In many ways, Miller's generation of Apostles, which included Neal Ascherson and Jonathan Miller, stood apart from their 'marxisant' forerunners of the 1930s, with their romantic image of the Soviet Union. Imbued with the 'scientific' spirit which informed the work of Leavis and his fellow Cambridge critics, I.A. Richards and William Empson, they regarded themselves as a sober new breed, at once sceptical and civic-minded. Where they resembled their predecessors was in the ease with which they went on to occupy prestigious positions in British cultural life. Those inclined to suspect that the Apostles amounted to a kind of intellectual freemasonry were bound to note that when Miller was appointed Professor of English at University College London, the selection committee for the post included Noel (otherwise 'Lord') Annan, an Apostle who was active not just in the academic world but in the literary and political worlds as well.

Miller's membership of this antique Cambridge clique was part of his progress. As an Apostle, he could be said to have been initiated into Britain's intellectual élite, with which the country's 'higher journalism' had long enjoyed such an intimate connection. All the same, Miller would continue to pride himself on being a working-class Scotsman who supported the Labour Party and who professed a passion for football, deeming it the British working-class's prime contribution to modern civilisation. The novelist and reviewer, Colin MacInnes, thought of him as a somehow colonial figure. The son of the well-bred English novelist, Angela Thirkell, MacInnes himself received a rugged upbringing in Australia prior to settling in London in the 1950s, and was to be dubbed by his biographer an 'inside-outsider'. The same description could be applied to Miller. It was surely no accident that this Scottish editor came to enjoy a special affinity with writers in English from outside England, finding common ground not just with MacInnes but also with the Sydney-born Clive James, with the Kimberley-born Dan Jacobson, and with the Trinidad-born V.S. Naipaul.

As a literary editor, Miller was to have no difficulty in surrounding himself with like-minded contributors, for the generation over which he set out to hold sway was a notably homogenous one. This was the sanguine, able, well-favoured generation that was to be satirised – and romanticised – by Frederic Raphael in his televised novel, *The Glittering Prizes* (1975). It was a generation that had undergone the levelling experiences of National

Service and of post-World War Two rationing, and which warmed to the nose-thumbing antics of Kingsley Amis's 'Lucky Jim', with his contempt for British class-consciousness and snobbery. It was also a British generation much impressed by the USA, a country newly enjoying superpower status, and that seemed to be everything Britain was not: dynamic, progressive, egalitarian. Meaning to make a study of American Puritanism, Miller went to Harvard, where he began graduate work under the supervision of the noted authority on the subject, Perry Miller.

The strange thing is how traditional Miller and his Cambridge circle now seem. Save for Jonathan Miller – in whom the savant endlessly vied with the showman – here was a coterie largely indifferent to the burgeoning new medium of television. Neal Ascherson, latterly a columnist on the *Independent on Sunday* and the *Observer*, first achieved prominence as a foreign correspondent; the late Peter Jenkins made his name writing about domestic politics, chiefly for the *Guardian;* and – until he was killed, while covering the Arab-Israeli War of 1967 – Nicholas Tomalin was a well-known reporter on the *Sunday Times*. Miller's friend, Mark Boxer, meanwhile, a dandy who might have stepped from the pages of Max Beerbohm, worked as a fashion magazine editor, before becoming celebrated as the cartoonist 'Marc'. It was 'Marc' who – at Miller's sly suggestion – drew the waspish *Listener* cartoon strip of the late 1960s, the 'String-alongs', which, with captions supplied by Alan Bennett, pilloried Tomalin and his wife, Claire, as a faddish media couple.

Despite working briefly in television, Miller himself far preferred the world of print and gravitated inexorably towards the London weeklies, fancying them to be the instruments of influence. Rejecting Leavis's conviction that such organs were synonymous with cliquism and charlatanry, he also spurned his erstwhile tutor's belief that the gap between 'mass civilisation' and 'minority culture' was unbridgeable. As ambitious as he was determined, Miller intended to publish mentally strenuous Reviews that appeared on news-stands, challenging public attention along with the rest of the press.

ii. A Touch of Really Disastrous Difficulty

When Miller became literary editor of the *Spectator* in 1957, the paper's proprietor was the Tory Lord and man of letters, Ian Gilmour, with whom, years later, he was to make common cause in anathematising the monetarist zealotry of Margaret Thatcher. At the hands of this landed Scottish gentleman, Miller could be said to have enjoyed a contemporary species of literary patronage. The two men had been brought together by a mutual friend, Miller's Cambridge contemporary, the upper-class Scottish painter, Rory McKewan, whose family estate adjoined that of the Gilmours. Born in a nearby mining village, Miller sometimes fantasised an alternative existence for himself in which his lot was to scrape a living as one of Lord Gilmour's peasants. As it was, he became Lord Gilmour's literary editor: the intellectual meritocrat was 'taken up' by the intellectual aristocrat, thereby continuing an old British story. In a manner not so dissimilar had Francis Jeffrey become the favourite of the Whig grandee, Lord Holland.

Tinged with romantic radicalism and positively subversive by comparison with its current incarnation, the *Spectator* that Miller went to work for foreshadowed the 1960s reaction against ingrained British stuffiness and snobbery – qualities which, in an age thrilling to the novelty of rock and roll, were being thrown into ever starker relief. It was in the *Spectator* that the bibulous columnist, Henry Fairlie, kindled controversy about the machinations of the British Establishment. And it was largely thanks to the same weekly that Kingsley Amis, Philip Larkin, John Wain and others gained recognition as the blunt new literary generation collectively known as the 'Movement'. One of the paper's sprightliest performers in the late 1950s was the young Bernard Levin, alias 'Taper', a columnist who pioneered the customarily derisive treatment of public figures – 'our elders and betters' – that was to become the stock-in-trade of 60s satirists such as Peter Cook. Prominent, too, among the paper's contributors were its Irish editor, Brian Inglis, an early champion of 'alternative medicine', and Ian Gilmour himself, who inveighed against capital punishment while embarking on what was to prove a life-time's campaigning on behalf of displaced Palestinians.

In those days, the *Spectator*'s offices were at 99 Gower Street, a slender Georgian terraced house – formerly an Edwardian brothel – in the middle of Bloomsbury, a metropolitan enclave long synonymous with literary highbrowism. Huddled in a book-cluttered cubicle, the *Spectator*'s new literary editor found himself marking up the copperplate copy of Evelyn Waugh, an old and highly irascible, if not half-mad, *Spectator* contributor, who had taken to accusing literary editors of making off with his manuscripts and selling them for private profit. With fewer complications, he also edited the weekly journalism of Amis and Larkin. No more than anyone else could Miller have anticipated that these *Spectator* writers of the 1950s, then seen by the likes of Evelyn Waugh as uncouth iconoclasts, would one day emerge as Waugh-like curmudgeons in their own right. Other contributors to his pages were his Cambridge friends, Neal Ascherson, Ronald Bryden and Thom Gunn; the literary academic and fashionable critic-in-the-making, Frank Kermode; the poet/critics and 'Movementeers', D.J. Enright and Donald Davie; the aforementioned novelist and social commentator, Colin MacInnes; the philosophers A.J. Ayer and Richard Wollheim; the Labour Party ideologue, Anthony Crosland; and a fiercely intelligent Irish diplomat who, for diplomatic reasons, was styling himself Donat O'Donnell, but whose real name was Conor Cruise O'Brien. Such was the regiment of reviewers with which the young Miller set out to establish himself as Britain's arbiter-in-chief of literary taste.

Much influenced by Donald Davie's seminal text, *Purity of*

Diction in English Verse (1952), Miller liked eighteenth-century plain-speaking and thought of himself as a literary democrat. Two of his favourite writers were to be Dan Jacobson and V.S. Naipaul, and, chafing at British culture's class-bound exclusivity, he pursued an agenda that routinely took in not just English literature but Scottish and American and 'Commonwealth' literature as well. At the same time, he took pains to publicise developments in sociology (an embryonic field of enquiry in those days) while lending support to what he regarded as the 'rational', middle-of-the-road Leftism of Anthony Crosland. What was missing from this purportedly wide-ranging agenda was much discussion of science. It was, as it happened, during Miller's incumbency as the *Spectator*'s literary editor that C.P. Snow brought out his historic tract, *The Two Cultures* (1959), with its much-quoted misgivings about the apparently deepening mutual incomprehension of the literary and scientific communities. Miller's old Cambridge tutor, Leavis, had no hesitation in condemning Snow as a symptom of cultural crisis in his own right: in a vituperative public lecture, he insisted that Snow's success as a novelist and status as a British sage themselves bore witness to the decay of cultural standards. (Published in the *Spectator*, Leavis's *ad hominem* tirade led to much national agonising over the 'two cultures' question – testimony to the public impact which weekly journalism could still make in those days.) Much readier to grant Snow a fair hearing, Miller himself stopped short of acquiescing in this damning verdict. Indeed, in common with Kingsley Martin, he was to remain beset by the sense that when it came to tackling so patently vital an area of modern knowledge as science, his record as an editor was less than adequate.

Still, if Miller's reach tended to exceed his grasp, many were struck by the calibre of his work, by its scope and penetration. Before long, he had established himself as a powerful figure, who, exploiting reviewers' mental energies on behalf of his own mission of public enlightenment, sought to publish writing that was at once learned and readable, stylish and incisive. According to the literary scholar, Claude Rawson, Miller's achievement was to blood a vibrant new school of reviewers, sharp performers trained to address the world in an idiom 'free of specialist narrowness but high in expertise'. That Miller had been a national serviceman was perhaps not irrelevant to the way he approached his literary work: early and late, his editorial endeavours resembled well-planned military operations.

One of those alert to Miller's efforts at the *Spectator* was the Guardsman turned political journalist, John Freeman. Soon after becoming editor of the *New Statesman* in 1961, Freeman persuaded Miller to join him as literary and arts editor of what was then, by a wide margin, Britain's pre-eminent intellectual weekly. Miller's confident expectation was that reviewers he had employed on the *Spectator* would instantly transfer their allegiance to the back half of the *New Statesman*, and that was what virtually all of them did. Full of reformist fervour – elderly *New Statesman* hands like J.B. Priestley resented him as a literature-loathing 'Leavisite' – Miller arrived at Great Turnstile fairly trumpeting his determination to impart fresh rigour to the paper's review pages. It is true that Janet Adam Smith, literary editor of the *New Statesman* throughout much of the 1950s, and likewise of Edinburgh background, had hardly been known for her laxity; indeed, a don *manqué* and something of a *grande dame*, she used to dispatch letters to unsatisfactory contributors, pulling them up over their literary shortcomings. In the fullness of time, she would be recalled by her headstrong successor as a fellow Scotch reviewer and kindred spirit.

Among the reviewers published by Adam Smith had been 'moon-lighting' academics; but under Miller's new dispensation, the academic aspect of the *New Statesman*'s literary section grew more pronounced. Keen to commission the work of a new generation of university critics – writers such as Frank Kermode and Christopher Ricks – Miller wondered initially whether he really had any use for the *New Statesman*'s veteran chief reviewer, the self-made man of letters, V.S. Pritchett. Thinking of himself as a tough-minded professional, he was inclined to view Pritchett as a superannuated amateur, a mere bellettrist. What especially irritated him was the difficulty of extracting a judgement – that key Leavisite desideratum – from Pritchett's burnished sentences. However, the more he was exposed to Pritchett's work, the more he found himself yielding to its enigmatic charms. In an elliptical *New Statesman* article written at Miller's behest and entitled 'Settlement or Symposium', Pritchett was to muse on the paper's tradition of conversational criticism, and on the 'marital quarrel' which had long gone on between its front and back halves – suiting, he maintained, the times and the facts of life alike. Miller's own mature opinion was to be that there are 'many modes of literary apprehension, many ways of rewarding the attention.' For all his academic sabre-rattling, he was an editor of catholic temper who – like Cyril Connolly in his days as editor of *Horizon* – could be said to have believed in 'God the either, God the Or and God the Holy Both'.

Much about Miller's outlook was peculiarly Scottish. Witness his championing of the Scottish historian George Davie's polemical study, *The Democratic Intellect* (1961). Naturally sympathetic to the historian's arguments, Miller arranged for the book to be discussed by C.P. Snow, who shared Davie's objections to the narrowness of Oxbridge education, together with his preference for the broader curriculum and wider social access which had traditionally been exemplified by the Scottish university system. Failure to 'democratise' and modernise higher education in Britain, Snow prophesied, was going to deepen the baleful 'Venetian shadow' lying across British culture. Miller's own commitment to a more democratic culture was much bound up with his dislike of the snobbery pervading metropolitan intellectual life, not least the pages of the *New Statesman*. Too often, it seemed to him, the *New Statesman*'s gentlemen contributors had acted on the patronising assumption that it was their role to 'raise up the huddled masses', as though the masses lacked all culture of their own. Anxious to do justice to aspects of British society hitherto slighted by Britain's leading socialist organ, Miller was quick to direct attention to the work of Alan Sillitoe and Richard Hoggart, writers felt to be shedding fresh light on working-class life. By the same token, he exposed the *New Statesman*'s readership to football, the 'people's game', with regular articles on the subject by Danny Blanchflower, a great soccer celebrity in those days.

Miller's regime was not entirely respectfully evoked by Edward Hyams in his history of the *New Statesman*, published to mark the paper's fiftieth anniversary. In Hyams's chronicle, Miller figures as a rather insular alumnus of Leavis's Cambridge English School, sadly innocent of that Bloomsbury fervour for all things French and classical that had distinguished Raymond Mortimer's literary editorship of the paper in the 1930s and 40s. Where Miller differed most significantly from his Great Turnstile forerunners was in his routine readiness to appraise the literature of the United States. He recognised that the world had moved on since the *New Statesman*'s destiny lay in the hands of Kingsley Martin and Raymond Mortimer, British editors who had found it easy to affect indifference to American culture. If American political power had become impossible to ignore, so too had American literary power. Rapidly assuming Victorian dimensions, the *œuvres* of writers like Norman Mailer and Saul Bellow compelled critical attention.

Yet at this stage, few doubted Britain's – or to be exact, London's – historic pre-eminence in the field of the 'higher journalism'. When Robert Silvers was in the process of setting up the *New York Review of Books* in the early 1960s, it was to the editorial example set by Karl Miller that he turned – even to the extent of making blatant overtures to many of the latter's favourite contributors. Miller's leading reviewers were to receive flattering communiqués from this transatlantic intellectual entrepreneur entreating them to write for his new paper and offering to pay them at rates unheard of in literary London. Despite issuing a *Schreibverboten*, Miller was obliged to get used to seeing *New*

Statesman reviewing stars such as Kermode plying their trade in Silvers's columns as well as his own. Running his eye over familiar by-lines in an early number of the *New York Review*, he wryly observed: 'This is the best Review that I ever edited.' Or so legend has it. Years later, in 1979, with his support for Miller's efforts to launch the *London Review of Books*, Silvers was in some sort honouring an old debt.

A Scottish editor with Irish blood, Miller published the early verse of Seamus Heaney during his years at the *New Statesman*, directed the polemical talents of the Anglo-Irish feminist, Brigid Brophy, and did much to promote the critical journalism of Conor Cruise O'Brien. When Hyams brought out his 'official' history of the paper in 1963, Miller invited O'Brien to discuss the book, confident that this least sentimental of reviewers would hardly let emotion cloud his judgement of the paper's record. The Irish writer's clinical dissection of Kingsley Martin's editorial shilly-shallying over the fate of Czechoslovakia on the eve of the Second World War – it made Martin himself wince – was keenly read. 1963 was also the year in which – at Miller's instigation – O'Brien perpetrated his remarkable critique of *Encounter*, impugning the claims of that magazine's editors that they had no 'line' to promote, and depicting them as disingenuous servants of Washington. Proof of O'Brien's formidable incisiveness, these historic contributions to the back half of the *New Statesman* were also indicative of Miller's sense of journalistic occasion, of his flair for staging attention-grabbing intellectual dramas.

As editor of the *Listener* from 1967 till 1973, Miller went on employing O'Brien, but by the time he began editing the *London Review of Books* in 1979, relations between him and a writer onto whom he once 'fastened with talons of steel' had foundered. By many on the Left, O'Brien was felt to have become a right-wing reactionary. Latterly, he had emerged as a champion of Israel, unsympathetic to the Palestinian cause. Miller, on the other hand, had grown increasingly pro-Palestinian. Indeed, the *London Review* was to afford one of the few platforms in the West for pro-Palestinian writers like Edward Said and Ian Gilmour – in the process scandalising much Jewish intellectual opinion, not least in the United States. When, in 1986, O'Brien brought out his pro-Israeli polemic, *The Siege*, Miller published a review of the book by Gilmour's son, David, which cast a cold eye on O'Brien's Zionist fervour – the kind of cold eye for which O'Brien himself had long been noted. The headline on the issue of the *London Review* that carried Gilmour's piece – a withering jibe at O'Brien's new-found zeal – ran: 'Conor Cruise O'Zion'.

Kingsley Martin's long-serving assistant, Norman MacKenzie, felt that the growing vogue in the 1960s for investigative reporting did much to undermine the old-style 'journal of opinion'. However, he also came to believe that if anyone could have preserved the world-wide kudos and authority which the *New Statesman* had attained under Martin, it was Miller. Certainly, Martin and Miller had much in common as editors for whom intellectual journalism was a consuming preoccupation. As events were to unfold, though, Miller's connection with the *New Statesman* came to an abrupt end early in 1967. In the course of the previous year, the paper had acquired a new editor in the person of Paul Johnson. Except that they were both pugnacious personalities, Johnson, an English public school Catholic, and Miller, a Scot of working-class background and an atheist, were very different individuals. Regarding him as a snob, Miller took exception to a *New Statesman* diatribe by Johnson belittling the music of the Beatles and making the group's female fans out to be ill-bred morons. Johnson, for his part, considered that Miller's books pages were altogether too rarefied for weekly journalism. When Miller persisted in publishing brain-teasing reviews by William Empson, Johnson dashed off a testy memorandum recording his conviction that the overwhelming majority of readers were likely to find Empson's work 'incomprehensible'. Miller was outraged, as perhaps he was meant to be, and promptly handed in his resignation.

Ruminating on the falling-out between himself and Johnson

in a collection of essays dedicated to Empson, Miller was to argue that a Review which fights shy of publishing 'difficult' contributors – in the hope of projecting the reassuring impression that all subjects are equally accessible – runs the risk of seeming untrustworthy. Believing that a 'properly conducted weekly need yield nothing in point of authority to any academic periodical', he declared that there is scarcely anything more wholesome about a set of books pages than a 'touch of really disastrous difficulty'. Such touches were to mark out Miller's work on the *Listener* and the *London Review of Books*, and many readers were grateful for them – dwindling minority though, in Britain at least, that 'many' appeared to be. Meanwhile, despite enjoying something of an Indian summer in the 1970s under the editorship of Anthony Howard – when its contributors included such rising stars as Martin Amis, Julian Barnes and Christopher Hitchens – the *New Statesman* was destined to turn into a crisis-stricken weekly labouring beneath the burden of its legendary past; only recently, robustly sceptical once more about the virtues of the American *imperium*, has the paper recaptured something of its old pungency and sense of purpose.

It may be that the Miller/Johnson fracas was a portent of the paper's historic downfall. Seldom given to admissions of fallibility, Johnson himself was to confess that robbing the *New Statesman* of Miller's services had been the biggest blunder of his journalistic life.

iii. Miller's Millennium

When he was working for *Encounter* in the mid-1950s, the American journalist Dwight Macdonald found himself charmed by two things: the city's well-kept parks and its wealth of highbrow weeklies. The *New Statesman*, the *Spectator*, the *Economist*, the *Listener, Time* and *Tide*, the *Times Literary Supplement* – what repositories of wide-ranging mental stimulus such publications were. The journalistic scene in the United States – Macdonald bemoaned the 'gravitational pull' of mass culture – seemed barren by comparison. A veteran of the American Left crossed with a fastidious English gentleman, Macdonald was partial to the *Listener*, whose owner was the BBC. For Macdonald, the *Listener* epitomised the close-knit, family atmosphere of literary life in London. Here learned uncles discussed Kant and Josephus round the tea table; cousins in parliament reported on affairs of state; and kinfolk of curious information dilated on the migration patterns of the herring. Other family members, meanwhile, found much to say about books and art and cookery. In this New York Anglophile's eyes, the *Listener* was quintessentially British: polished, post-prandial discourse by cultivated amateurs who treated their readers as intellectual equals.

Founded in 1929, by the 1960s the *Listener* had become a sedate institution, satirised for its genteel highbrowism. When Karl Miller became its fourth editor, in mid-1967, he was anxious to make the *Listener* new, to enhance its contemporary appeal. Dismayed by Johnson's choleric *New Statesman* attack on the Beatles and their fans, he aimed, among other things, to demonstrate that weekly journalism could take a rational interest in the Beatles' work – as in other aspects of popular culture. With a cover featuring a photograph of America's versifying hippy guru, the hirsute Allen Ginsberg, Miller's début issue of the *Listener* led off with an article on the 'new music' by his Cambridge friend, the poet, Thom Gunn, who had settled in California. Pausing to pooh-pooh the controversy raging in Britain over pot-smoking – two of the Rolling Stones had recently come close to serving prison sentences for possessing cannabis – Gunn acclaimed the artistry of Beatles lyrics such as 'Eleanor Rigby'. At best, he maintained, pop songs were like the border ballads of old – demotic compositions of lasting power.

Echoing Gunn's sentiments in an inaugural editorial, Miller argued that, like the border ballads, some of the better pop lyrics were expressive of the 'flight from convention which any society must find room for if it is not to go stale'. Thus was Johnson royally rebuked. The same editorial gave notice that henceforth the *Listener* was to be a 'communications weekly', a paper that would pay rather more attention to the output of television – commercial television included – than had previously been the case. This was the heyday of Marshall McLuhan, the oracular Canadian academic who insisted that television was turning the world into an 'electronic village'. With McLuhan's views in mind, Miller saw a role for the *Listener* as a new kind of 'parish magazine'. Not, he added, that the *Listener* – whose books pages had been made famous by J.R. Ackerley – was about to join McLuhan in prophesying the 'death of literature'. After all, he insisted, written down and read, was not the *Listener* a form of literature in its own right? And indeed, for all his efforts to bring it up to date, Miller's weekly, sparsely illustrated and dense with print, now has a curiously antiquated look – the look of an old-style literary Review gamely contending with the novel challenges of the media age.

Quartered hard by Broadcasting House, in a grand Victorian pile formerly famous as the Langham Hotel, the *Listener* under Miller did what it had always done – which was to publish the texts of noteworthy BBC broadcasts, many of them donnish talks given on the Third Programme. But thanks to the paper's founding editor, R.S. Lambert, his successors were entitled to commission material of their own, so long as it seemed pertinent to some current television or radio programme. Eager to set himself up as an interpreter of the times, Miller exercised this right to the hilt. Student unrest, women's liberation, black power, futurology, the 'alternative society', the expansion of the media, the Vietnam War – all of these leading themes of the Sixties were to be much discussed in the *Listener*'s pages. In his pursuit of that great desideratum of the period, 'relevance', the paper's new editor could scarcely have been more zealous.

Many of his contributors were reviewers with whom Miller had worked before, among them Kermode, Wollheim, Ricks, O'Brien and Davie; in due course, they would also include a pair of thrusting new reviewers: Clive James and John Carey. One of the most busily employed of his colleagues on the *Listener* was D.A.N. Jones, who had worked with him on the *New Statesman*. A wizard at solving the *Listener*'s mind-bending crossword puzzles, 'Trooper' Jones – in common with his editor, an ex-national serviceman – became a Stakhanovite reviewer of books and plays, a roving reporter, and an erudite habitué of Marylebone public houses. Like the paper's long-serving literary editor, Derwent May, he was to stay at the *Listener* after Miller's frowning departure from the BBC in 1973, a witness to the paper's fading fortunes. Other regular writers for the paper at this point were Ian Hamilton, a poet and critic with a passion for football, and the logic-chopping Viennese musicologist, Hans Keller, who was likewise a highbrow football fan. A less regular but by no means infrequent contributor was Jonathan Miller. It was in the *Listener* that the celebrated theatrical sage rehearsed his penetrating critique of 'McLuhanism'.

A sixth-former at a Liverpool grammar school in the late 1960s, the present writer became an avid reader of Miller's eclectic weekly. To many older readers, however, much, if not everything, about his revamped version of the *Listener* proved offensive. From rectories the length and breadth of Britain – country parsons were among the *Listener*'s oldest and staunchest devotees – cancelled subscriptions poured in. There were even those who judged that Miller was guilty of vandalising a precious national heirloom. 'You are the man who *ruined* the *Listener,*' snapped W.H. Auden – in whose background clergymen were prominent – on being introduced to him at a London literary gathering. When Miller demurred, venturing to assert that this was a matter of opinion, the touchy poet instantly retorted: 'Yes, it's *my* opinion.'

It was not long before Miller fell foul of two other opinionated

English literati – the right-wing historian of the Soviet Union, Robert Conquest, and his increasingly reactionary novelist friend, Kingsley Amis, sometime members of the 'Movement', on whose side he had once thought himself to be. Rabid anti-communists with a histrionic horror of 'trendy Leftism', Conquest and Amis appear to have suspected that Miller was editing the *Listener* in subversive spirit – thereby breaching the terms of his contract as the employee of a public corporation. When a photograph of the Latin American revolutionary, Che Guevara, appeared in the *Listener*, with the interrogative caption, 'Man of the Year?' appended to it, Amis experienced a spasm of abdominal alarm. Or so – maybe not altogether jokingly – he reported to Robert Conquest. A quarter of a century later, reviewing his editorship of the *Listener*, Miller pointed out that not long after printing the offending picture of Guevara, he published an article by Conquest himself on the problems of 'coping with communism'. During the same period, he also published an interview with the ageing British fascist, Oswald Mosley, whose photograph appeared on the *Listener*'s cover. Miller liked to think that such gestures in the direction of editorial balance had done something to settle the novelist's irritable bowels.

The years when Amis and Conquest were finding fault with Miller's conduct of the *Listener* were a time when the BBC as a whole was subject to concerted attack from many angles. Among the Corporation's most persistent critics in the late 1960s was the Labour Prime Minister, Harold Wilson, who believed himself to be the victim of systematic media misrepresentation. Perhaps the least likely, but hardly the least voluble, of the BBC's detractors was a prim Kidderminster housewife named Mary Whitehouse. This unsleeping media watchdog endlessly reiterated her conviction that the BBC and commercial television alike were agents of moral decline, creators of that decadent phenomenon, the permissive society. Strange bedfellows, Wilson and Whitehouse were united in their distaste for the BBC's iconoclastic

Director General, Hugh Greene. To all this Miller could not be indifferent – especially since he himself held Greene in high regard. Following the latter's not altogether voluntary retirement in 1969, Miller set to work on a voluminous judicial assessment of his contribution to broadcasting, bringing high seriousness to bear on the question of the media's role during a period of dramatic social change.

In a lecture entitled 'Dissent, Disobedience and the Mass Media', originally delivered at the University of East Anglia and later published in the *Listener*, Miller applauded Greene's efforts in making the BBC more 'democratic', in disavowing the élitist ethos associated with the Corporation's didactic Scotch founder, the Presbyterian Lord Reith (who now seems in many ways more of a nineteenth- than a twentieth-century figure). According to Miller, the retiring Director General had always acted on the assumption that the BBC owed an obligation to society at large – to 'young people, poor people, agnostics, the frivolous, the unruly, as well as to the middle income range and the eminent'. What was more, Greene had licensed the BBC to 'speak out', to be irreverent – in the process pointing up his faith that fighting shy of risk is a dubious virtue, serving only, in the words of E.M. Forster, to 'confirm thousands in the uncongenial habit of avoiding unwelcome truths'. Greene's example, Miller believed, had made for a rich phase at the BBC, an era of Athenian enlightenment and creativity. Those who claimed that the BBC of the 1930s – the BBC of John Reith – represented paradise lost, were wrong. Greene's BBC, on the other hand, Miller seemed to fear, already had the makings of the real thing, of a *bona fide* vanishing golden age.

Miller was much exercised in his lecture by media coverage of the burgeoning Sixties youth culture. Among Britain's middle classes – beset by mounting evidence of national decline, and endlessly bombarded by television images of youthful rebelliousness – anxiety was rampant. Among the young, meanwhile, distrust of the entire media seemed to be growing apace. To Miller, believing that the sentiments of disaffected youth could hardly be ignored, it followed that customary journalistic approaches – not least in his own corner of the communications industry – were bankrupt. The traditional defect of the 'higher journalism' – he instanced the treatment meted out to the Beatles by the *New Statesman* – had been snobbery. The need now was to set journalism free from old attitudes, to jettison that Establishment style of address which had long presumed the working classes to be alien and which had latterly taken to presuming the young to be alien too. Miller was equally keen to take issue with Establishment figures who – when it came, for example, to student unrest – had a mind to muzzle the media. Was it not countries with muzzled media that had witnessed student unrest's more extreme manifestations? The irony was that Miller's plea for openness was not always easy to follow. Indeed, couched in high mandarin rhetoric and demanding the reader's patient attention, 'Dissent, Disobedience and the Mass Media' could have been the pontification of some verbose Victorian sage – albeit a Victorian sage with a frank enthusiasm for Johnny Speight's comic television creation, the foul-mouthed, taboo-flouting, working-class bigot, Alf Garnett. It is hard to imagine any of today's media pages finding room for such a dense deliberation.

Clive James, a *new-style* sage, was tickled by Miller's conscientious convolutions. Was this the editor so expert at untying the knots in his contributors' copy? It was, as it happened, during the period when Miller was agonising over youth and the media that James made his *Listener* début. A flamboyant graduate of Sydney University voracious for culture of every kind – latterly he had been a mature student at Cambridge, serving as president of the Cambridge Footlights – James was deputed by Miller to review radio broadcasts. The medium was not his favourite; however, it was not long before he got the chance to write about television, the medium that was to become the lucrative passion, if not obsession, of his existence.

As one of Miller's by no means well-paid contributors, James became part of a team of *Listener* television critics, along with Hamilton, Carey, Stuart Hood and Raymond Williams – writers taken by Miller to be fellow intellectual democrats, fellow foes of Establishment stuffiness, as committed as he was to what T.S. Eliot, and after him, Leavis, termed the 'common pursuit of true judgement'. What set the future host of the *Clive James Show* apart from most of his colleagues on the *Listener* was the well-wrought, self-advertising *sprezzatura* of his prose. Here was an Australian who wrote like a hard-boiled American: Philip Marlowe, the wise-cracking shamus of Raymond Chandler's detective novels, seemed to have turned into an learned television reviewer. James's was a style for the media times, befitting an age when the work of McLuhan was making mass culture intellectually fashionable. It was a style – soon to be all too widely imitated – which enabled James to flaunt his enjoyment of television good and bad while always seeming smart and knowing. Who before had ever thought to describe a crass piece of programme-making as the 'complete carbon-fibre, twin-shafted RB211 bummer'? Sparkling like catherine wheels, James's television reviews – like his book reviews – were dazzling performances, criticism as show business. 'And I suppose', Miller drily observed when the rising star delivered his copy, 'you've done another of your cabaret turns.'

When James announced that he was leaving the *Listener* to join the *Observer*, which in those days was as much a stylish weekend Review as a newspaper, Miller made no attempt to conceal his displeasure. For several years, he and his sometime television reviewer were barely on speaking terms. In 1979, however, as Miller got into his stride as editor of the *London Review of Books*, the journalistic relationship between the two men was to be rekindled. For a period, James – by this stage a risen star with a face familiar to millions in Britain who had never heard of

Karl Miller or his paper – reviewed regularly for the *London Review*. Bringing out ever more publications of his own, he was also to be regularly reviewed in it – mostly, though not always, in flattering terms. Miller himself wrote an effusive review of James's playful first volume of autobiography, *Unreliable Memoirs* (1983). The sketch it drew, of James as a forlorn youth who became a crowd-pleasing man of masks, reappeared in the closing pages of *Doubles*, the book that he was bringing to fruition at this time. Not long afterwards, committing flagrant literary incest, James composed an encomiastic assessment of a *London Review of Books* anthology, and published it in – the *London Review of Books*. At a later date still, James would contribute to the *Spectator* a review of Miller's memoir, *Rebecca's Vest* (1994), amongst other things acclaiming his old editor as a 'key figure' in the transformation of the British arts scene that had taken place since the Second World War. Who could have guessed that this pair of ardent mutual admirers had ever been at odds with one another?

Frantically busy intellectual careerists – both of whom grew up bereft of fathers – Miller and James were in many ways kindred spirits. Yet in one fundamental respect, they could hardly have been less alike. Much though he protested his concern with modern communications when he became editor of the *Listener*, Miller was perhaps only grudgingly reconciled to the media age. Indeed – like their common literary friend, Ian Hamilton, who published much writing by Clive James in his magazine, the *New Review* – Miller was an old-fashioned man of letters, neither willing nor able to follow his *Listener* protégé in the pursuit of mass appeal. As a contributor to the *Listener* and the *London Review of Books*, James was pleased – not to say honoured – to take part in what was tantamount to the *Karl Miller Show*; but a reciprocal appearance by Miller on the *Clive James Show* would have been the summit of improbability. Stung by suggestions that there was any incompatibility between his work in the field of the 'higher journalism' and his career as a joshing television personality, James liked to think that he could straddle different worlds without compromising his intellectual integrity. His intellectual peers – even when they could not stop chortling at his rapid-fire jokes – were apt to think that he was deluding himself.

If the careers of Miller and James present a curious, and perhaps instructive, contrast, so do those of Miller and John Carey. An industrious Oxford English don, who developed a parallel career as a reviewer, Carey made a name for himself as a terse scourge of cant and sloppy thinking. Even in his days as a contributor to Miller's *Listener*, Carey's loathing of vainglorious intellectuals was sufficiently apparent. What could hardly have been foreseen then was that by the 1980s, this intellectual-baiting intellectual would have become, in effect, Rupert Murdoch's chief British book reviewer, writing regularly for the *Sunday Times*, a newspaper which, under the brash editorship of Murdoch's sometime senior adjutant, Andrew Neil, championed the free market and heaped endless abuse on the so-called 'chattering classes' – on, in a word, intellectuals. It may be that Carey did not always, or even often, see eye to eye with his right-wing employers, but the manifest populism of his Sunday journalism was well calculated to appeal to their robust prejudices. In 1992, Carey was to publish a caustic work of polemic called *The Intellectuals and the Masses*, which excoriated intellectuals as obscurity-mongering snobs and all but branded them enemies of the people. A fan of the unpretentious, readily intelligible book reviews that the novelist Arnold Bennett once contributed to the London *Evening Standard*, Carey came to rejoice in the soubriquet, the 'people's don'. While Carey was addressing the mass readership of the *Sunday Times*, Miller was editing the *London Review of Books*, a minority organ which was often said to be difficult, and which certainly devoted much space to the cruelly difficult subject of literary theory. No one seems to have thought of dubbing him the 'people's editor'.

In the days when they were involved with the *Listener*, Miller,

James and Carey could be said to have shared much the same attitudes and values. Linking this trio of highbrow journalists was a dislike of paternalism and snobbery, a desire to say a definitive goodbye to the stiff, quasi-Victorian ethos epitomised by the BBC of Lord Reith. What they coveted was a new, inclusive British culture, purged of oppressive old élitist attitudes: in a way, their journalistic careers were branches of the same tree. Yet, notwithstanding his own keen sense of the desirability of 'inclusiveness', Miller was to end up seeming a very different sort of intellectual democrat from his erstwhile *Listener* coadjutors. Was he after all so very unlike John Reith – that craggy old fellow Scot, with his Calvinist conscience and zealous determination to subject people to what he believed was best for them? Perhaps it is not altogether fanciful to think of Miller as the Reith of the reviewing world.

▼▲▼

Roughly coinciding with the demise of that fabled vehicle of Reithian edification, the Third Programme, Miller's editorship of the *Listener* belonged to a dying era at the BBC, if not to a dying era in British culture. Impressed by the quality of his work, Richard Crossman thought that Miller had turned the *Listener* into the leading British weekly, eclipsing his rivals on the *New Statesman* and the *Spectator*. But if many were ready to agree with Crossman, few of them were to be found among the executive echelons of the BBC. Though its circulation of approximately 40,000 was far from abject, Miller's paper was eyed with disquiet by BBC managers increasingly anxious about the popular appeal of the Corporation's wares. To them, Miller was a nuisance, a turbulent priest. What gratification Miller's detractors must have experienced when a consumer report commissioned by the BBC in 1973 on the *Listener*'s prospects arrived at the blunt conclusion that there was really 'very little market' for such a publication. This was the background against which Miller arrived at the conclusion that his time at the BBC was up.

Miller's problems as editor of the *Listener* were not altogether unprecedented. There was friction between the BBC and the paper's founding editor, R.S. Lambert, for whom the Corporation was an authoritarian institution rife with fear. In his plangent memoir, *Ariel and All His Quality* (1940) – a book which anticipates current anxieties about the creeping totalitarianism of big business – Lambert intimated that the *Listener*'s editor could scarcely avoid suffering much frustration. The trouble was that the BBC, while purportedly keen to recruit creative individualists, was loath to let such types flourish. All the same, Lambert had to confess – as Miller did thirty years later – that, in spite of everything, he had been able to shape the *Listener* according to his own ends. The son of a freethinking Liberal MP, soaked in the public service ethic of the British upper-middle-class – he taught for the Workers' Education Association and helped to found the British Film Institute – Lambert was a cultural missionary who liked to measure himself against sturdily independent British editors of the past such as Stead and Massingham. It was by virtue of his high-minded endeavours that the *Listener* acquired its legendary status, its faintly medicinal reputation as a weekly medium of the best that had been thought and known.

Lambert's misfortune was to become embroiled in a farcical law-suit. Keen, like Stead, on psychical research, he had been to the Isle of Man with a writer on the occult, a friend named Harry Price, to investigate the rumoured existence of a talking mongoose called 'Gef'. In due course, Lambert happened to describe his outing to Sir Cecil Levita, a seemingly agreeable old gentleman known to Lambert through the British Film Institute. It soon transpired, however, that over lunch at his club with a senior BBC figure, the half-deaf Levita had insinuated that Lambert was unfit to occupy a position of professional responsibility, only too ready, as he seemed to be, to credit the incredible. Lambert wasted no time in bringing a libel action against his calumniator, and in the closing months of 1936, he and his talking mongoose made the headlines, provoking much public mirth, while visiting acute embarrassment on Lambert himself and on the BBC – the ultimate success of his action notwithstanding. The episode became enshrined in *Listener* folklore. The travails of the paper's founding editor were still a source of entertainment to Miller and his colleagues in the late 1960s.

For all his self-belief, Miller perhaps took himself marginally less seriously than R.S. Lambert, whose own account of the talking mongoose affair is a tissue of solemnity. Nevertheless, he and his forerunner – paragons of high-mindedness prepared to fight for the soul of the *Listener* – did have something important in common. Once, in a *Listener* column that made reference to Lambert's *contretemps*, Miller described his predecessor as 'contumacious'. Here was an adjective that the BBC's more literate managers might have thought applied every bit as strongly to Miller himself. Was it the lack of contumacy among the *Listener*'s later editors which slowly but inexorably robbed the paper of meaning? At any rate, the years following Miller's departure from the paper in 1973 were hardly the most memorable of the *Listener*'s career. In the course of the 1980s, the BBC weekly that had enjoyed international cachet became a middlebrow media magazine, as inoffensive as it was expendable. So far as could be judged, the *Listener*'s sudden, unheralded closure in January 1991 was a matter of minimal public interest.

iv. Miller Agonistes

In the late 1960s, affronted by the discovery that *Encounter* had been sponsored by the CIA, Miller's confrère, Frank Kermode, mooted a 'counter-*Encounter*', a liberal British Review that would be free from suspicion of American manipulation. Miller was among those with whom Kermode discussed his proposal, along with sundry eminences of Britain's intellectual establishment, such latter-day Whigs as Isaiah Berlin, Stuart Hampshire and Noel Annan. Launched in 1979, with Miller as its editor (and published at first as a supplement of the *New York Review of Books*), the fortnightly *London Review of Books* was in a way the tardy realisation of this counter-*Encounter* project. It is true that by this stage the days when Kermode and his friends could feel that *Encounter* was urgently needing to be countered were past: the magazine was nothing like the powerful influence that it had once been. But then, by 1979 scarcely anything to do with Britain or British culture seemed what it had once been. Editing a special issue of *Encounter* in 1963, Arthur Koestler had posed the question: was Britain committing suicide? A decade and a half later, the belief that Britain had no future was no longer peculiar to anguished intellectuals like Koestler. Occasioning endless hand-wringing, the 'British disease' was now a standard topic.

Miller began editing the *London Review of Books* soon after Margaret Thatcher's rise to power in the wake of the 'winter of discontent', the period of convulsive industrial unrest which convinced many that Britain was ungovernable. Compared with uncollected refuse and unburied bodies – features of the winter of discontent that became grisly items of British folklore – the crisis facing Britain's 'higher journalism' was perhaps of little moment. Still, the crisis in question was real enough. Dogged by striking print workers, the *Times Literary Supplement* – like the *Times* itself – had had to suspend publication, and it was this which presented Miller with the opportunity to launch a rival attraction. Meanwhile the *New Review*, the plush literary magazine edited by Miller's old friend, Ian Hamilton – with which he himself had been associated – had fallen prey to bankruptcy. As for the *New Statesman* – caught up in the ideological maelstrom of the time, the paper was metamorphosing into an abrasive left-wing scandal-sheet with limited appeal to many of its older readers; indeed, before long the British weekly that had been revered all over the world was to find itself being outstripped by its antique rival, the pro-Thatcher *Spectator*. What a contrast all this made with the spectacular success of Rupert Murdoch's tabloid 'newspaper', the *Sun*. Purveying sport, strident 'Thatcherite' jingoism and bare-breasted 'Page 3' girls, the *Sun* was increasingly setting the tone of the British press, if not of British society in general. Never before had journalists of Miller's ilk looked so beleaguered.

Like Mrs Thatcher, the editor of the *London Review of Books* set to work as though time was short. Single-minded, hard-working Puritans, Miller and Britain's first female Prime Minister were kindred personality-types – though what united them was hardly equal to what divided them. If Miller had a mission, it was to make people think – while demonstrating that literature, and for that matter, literary journalism, could thrive irrespective of the state of the nation. Mrs Thatcher's message, by contrast, was 'enrich yourselves': private enterprise was her remedy for all Britain's ills. The fact was that the right-wing, 'deregulated', Americanised Britain championed by Mrs Thatcher and her fellow free-marketeers represented the antithesis of much, if not all, that Miller valued; in this sharp but philistine British leader, the 'higher journalism' could be said to have faced its Nemesis. Small wonder that the view of her taken by the *London Review* was unflattering. Candid contempt for the whole phenomenon of 'Thatcherism' was, to be sure, the hallmark of a Review that Clive James was to describe as the 'house magazine of the British intellectual élite'.

As editor of the *London Review*, Miller became much concerned to re-state the case for the Welfare State, to the creation of which such previous exponents of the 'higher journalism' as Knowles and Martin had made important contributions. It must be said that Miller and his colleagues on the paper were not without a vested interest in crying up the virtues of state provision.

For if the private money of Miller's editorial colleague (and eventual successor) Mary-Kay Wilmers, was to play its part in keeping the *London Review* going, so was the sponsorship of the Arts Council, that monument to the high-minded paternalism of John Maynard Keynes (who had set so much store by the old *New Statesman* as a vehicle of British civilisation). Why Mrs Thatcher, with her vengeful instincts, did not seek to challenge the subsidy of a journal so consistently scornful of her whole philosophy remains something of a mystery. Admittedly, it is hard to imagine this self-styled 'conviction politician' brooding over the contents of an intellectual periodical like the *London Review*. Besides, this was not the era of the *Fortnightly Review*, and what reason had she to mind the hostility of a journal with a circulation of barely more than 15,000 when she was able to bask in the favour of the leading British newspapers owned by her powerful antipodean ally, Rupert Murdoch – newspapers which included not just the *Sun* but the *Times* and *Sunday Times* too. Every day, thanks to Murdoch, who had also become proprietor of the *Times Literary Supplement*, the blessings of 'Thatcherism', of ubiquitous privatisation, were being communicated to a readership of many millions, made up of people from all sections of society.

Though uneasy about social inequality, Miller was perhaps no more a radical, let alone a revolutionary, than the establishment-minded Knowles had been. In the 1980s, it was the Social Democrats – the centrist party formed by Roy Jenkins and other defectors from the Labour Party – who found most favour with the *London Review*'s self-consciously judicial editor. Yet so far to the Right did the British centre of political gravity shift under Mrs Thatcher that this habitual moderate was to end up seeming something like a left-wing dissident. What began this improbable process were the dramatic events of Mrs Thatcher's first term of office – events for which liberal opinion in Britain proved but little prepared. In the summer of 1981, as unemployment in Britain rose to a level not seen since the 1930s, the streets of south London and Liverpool witnessed black youths fighting pitched battles with the police. Presaging a decade of civil disturbances, the riots of 1981 were portrayed in the *London Review* as a complex phenomenon, one which may have been triggered by communal feelings of alienation but which defied instant analysis. So measured a reaction was far removed from that of the Prime Minister who was becoming known as the 'Iron Lady'. In Mrs Thatcher's view, the only thing to be said about the rioters was that they were criminals who needed to be arrested and punished.

Less than twelve months later, as domestic discontent deepened, the same Prime Minister was dispatching much of the British army and navy to the South Atlantic with a view to liberating the Falkland Islands – one of Britain's last remaining imperial possessions – from Argentine invaders. Politicians of the Right and of the Left thrilled to Mrs Thatcher's parliamentary bellicosity – as did nearly the entire British press. One of the few British editors to challenge the general bias of British public opinion, Miller was to turn the *London Review* into a rare forum for dissenting views on the Falklands War. It was Miller's paper which afforded the Scottish Labour MP, Tam Dalyell, the opportunity to develop his case that Mrs Thatcher deliberately escalated the war for her own political purposes. Dalyell's central contention was that the Prime Minister cynically ordered the sinking of the Argentinian battleship Belgrano at the very point when the vessel was sailing away from the combat zone and when peace talks were making excellent progress. Not that many seemed to care very much about the substance of Dalyell's indictment. Following the example of Mrs Thatcher's cheerleader-in-chief, Paul Johnson, right-wing columnists took to describing the MP as the 'Belgrano bore'.

Prior to the Falklands War, Mrs Thatcher's standing in opinion polls was sinking fast. By the time that the war was over, however, her political prospects had been hugely enhanced. Returned to power with an increased majority in the post-Falklands War General Election of 1983, the triumphant Tory Prime Minister henceforth made short work of her chronically divided opponents. While the leader of the Labour Party, Neil Kinnock, persisted in the futile belief that he could beat Mrs Thatcher by himself, the leader of the Liberal Party, David Steele, and the leader of the Social Democrats, David Owen, formed an alliance which – before it broke down in mutual acrimony – served largely to split the anti-Tory vote and to perpetuate the Thatcherite hegemony. Much of a piece with all this was the behaviour of Mrs Thatcher's critics inside the Tory Party, the most notable of whom, Miller's patrician friend, Sir Ian Gilmour, took to damning the dogmas of 'Thatcherism' in the pages of the *London Review*. Loath to join any other party, Gilmour and his fellow Tory 'wets' condemned themselves to political impotence.

The remainder of the 1980s were to see the inexorable implementation of Mrs Thatcher's project of 'privatisation'. Having dealt with the Argentinians, the Prime Minister set about imposing her will on the servants of the Welfare State, subjecting them to authoritarian new management structures and to a seemingly endless round of spending cuts. Employees of local government began to feel despised and demoralised – and so did teachers in schools and universities, together with doctors and nurses and social workers, and all those involved in the so-called 'caring' professions.

To Miller, nostalgic for the days when the 'politics of consensus' held sway and the rationale underlying the Welfare State was seldom impugned, Britain seemed to be labouring under a curse. Early in 1985, he wrote a grim diary column for the *London Review* in which he looked back over the previous year and declared that it had lived up to its Orwellian name. During that year, thousands of the country's miners had embarked on a protracted and bloody strike against pit closures under the militant left-wing leadership of Arthur Scargill. Objecting to Scargill at least as much as he objected to Thatcher, Miller had felt no compunction in publishing a leading article by the economist, Michael Stewart, which attacked the miners' leader as a self-serving demagogue with a contempt for democracy. Among the *London Review*'s readership, as it turned out, there was much sympathy for the miners. Indeed, many deplored the 'line' on the strike taken by Miller and his paper, suspecting that it was tantamount to acquiescence in Mrs Thatcher's efforts to eradicate all resistance to her ideological programme. Miller's critics included some of his own colleagues. On the *London Review* – as in the rest of Britain – dissension raged.

In a fulminating introduction to a *London Review* anthology published in 1985, Miller struck the attitude of a latter-day Thomas Carlyle, judging Britain to be 'full of anxiety and ill-feeling and the sense of a dishonoured public life'. Nevertheless, he acknowledged that bad times – times of crisis and foreboding – generally made for excellent copy. He could have added that the same was true of a leader like Margaret Thatcher, who excited more extreme reactions than any other British politician of recent times. Viewed by Miller (as by great numbers of others) as a mad ogre, a vandal menacing the cultural life of the nation and much else, the 'Iron Lady' was in a way the *London Review*'s chief inspiration, the source of its intellectual drama, and in its pages – which naturally embraced many other subjects besides British domestic politics – the forces of light appeared locked in mortal combat with the forces of Thatcherite darkness.

Of course by no means all intellectuals in Britain were at odds with Mrs Thatcher. Pundits of the Right such as Paul Johnson and the philosopher Roger Scruton were among her favourite courtiers. But intellectuals jealous of the Prime Minister's good opinion were perhaps all the more conspicuous for being comparatively few. Figuring in Thatcherite demonology as enemies of enterprise, the kind of people to whom the *London Review* was appealing yearned for her downfall. British intellectuals of liberal leanings were simply not accustomed to receiving short shrift from the powers-that-be: think of the prestige vis-à-vis the country's governing class enjoyed by Kingsley Martin and his fellow new statesmen before and after the Second World War. Hence it was that in 1985 a majority of Oxford dons voted against awarding the Prime Minister an honorary degree – a calculated snub that made the supporters of Mrs Thatcher boil with rage. In a leading *London Review* article, the Oxford Professor of Politics and Public Administration, Peter Pulzer, argued that the Prime Minister's friends were invoking an ideal of consensus which their own heroine had herself done much to discredit. Belatedly, Britain was acquiring what had long been familiar in other parts of Europe: an alienated intelligentsia.

R.W. Johnson, another dissident don who wrote for the *London Review*, was to liken the Britain of Mrs Thatcher to the distempered France that emerged in the wake of the Franco-Prussian War of 1870. In an article for Miller's paper entitled 'Their Affair and Our Affair' (April 1987), Johnson remarked that the idea that Britain had made a graceful retreat from empire was turning out to be a smug illusion. In common with the France of yore, Britain was a nation burdened by a traumatic sense of psychological defeat. Was not the country over which Mrs Thatcher presided comparable to the France that had persecuted the Jewish army captain Alfred Dreyfus as a German spy? Did not Britain likewise have its spy mania, its obsession with the 'enemy within'? And it was true that in Britain during the 1980s there was much talk of subversion, and that 'spy mania' was stimulated afresh by the discovery that the eminent art historian (and former Apostle), Anthony Blunt, had served as a Soviet agent. What, according to Johnson, was under attack in Mrs Thatcher's Britain was the 'world of Keynes, of intellectuals in general, of anyone who ever sympathised with the Spanish Republic or was a premature anti-fascist, even the wettish Tory gentry of the Macmillan era who are now reviled for leading us into national decline'.

Wearying of Britain, Johnson would in due course return to his native South Africa, though not before using the columns of the *London Review* to bid a long and mordant goodbye to the country that had been his home for thirty years. When not attacking British political culture as a secrecy-ridden anachronism, Johnson was treating Mrs Thatcher's claim to have turned Britain into a modern and efficient nation as so much bombastic hyperbole. Reviewing Hugo Young's biography of her in 1989 – and incidentally suggesting that Britain's first female Prime Minister was the nearest that the country had come to spawning a fascist dictator – the prescient Johnson argued that so far from making Britain great again, Mrs Thatcher was reducing the country to a shambles. Where, he demanded to know, was the evidence to justify the Thatcherite boast that Britain was at last enjoying 'successful management'? Thanks to Mrs Thatcher, transport disasters in Britain had become commonplace; thanks to her, a failing education system was yielding an increasingly ill-trained and uncompetitive work-force; thanks to her, the country's currency was hugely and damagingly over-valued. And this was meant to be 'successful management'!

A writer of bare-knuckled trenchancy, R.W. Johnson put Miller in mind of his namesake, the rugged polemicist, Paul Johnson. In a *London Review* critique of the latter's book, *Intellectuals* (1989) – a venomous attack on its subjects' mental and moral credentials – Miller ventured a serio-comic comparison between the two Johnsons, one of them convinced that Mrs Thatcher was reversing British decline, the other no less certain that she was speeding it up. Here, remarked Miller, was a pair of exceptionally forceful journalistic denouncers, both of whom happened to have been formed by Oxford University and the Catholic Church, both of whom also happened to be red-headed. Idiosyncratic drollery aside, Miller's review of Johnson's book added up to a sardonic meditation on the redundancy of intellectuals in Mrs Thatcher's

Britain. As it seemed to him, Johnson's blanket condemnation of intellectuals as mountebanks given to hoodwinking ordinary people epitomised the mental atmosphere of the Thatcher era. Granting that its strictures on the dubious morals of certain notable thinkers were not without justification, he nevertheless rated his old adversary's book a 'sinister performance', the product of a time when it was fashionable to sneer at talk of the commonweal and at the contribution which intellectuals could make to it. There was, protested Miller, more to Britain's heritage than the value system of Margaret Thatcher; Britain, he insisted, had other traditions – however much maligned they might currently be.

In many ways, the Review edited by Karl Miller during the 1980s was an attempt to defend liberal Britain's embattled traditions – to speak up for what R.W. Johnson called the 'world of Keynes', or what could equally well have been called the 'world of Kingsley Martin'. Miller was hardly an evangelical socialist after the fashion of Martin (just as it is true that his paper's miscellaneous format bore no direct resemblance to Martin's *New Statesman*, with its political front and literary rear). Still, he had more than a little in common with his forerunner. Like Martin, he shrank from the prospect of a world dominated by the free market and championed the cause of welfare and social planning; and, like Martin, he behaved as though politics and letters were phenomena of rival significance, while practising the principle that 'influence is style'. Especially, however, did he resemble Martin in his belief that exponents of the 'higher journalism' are engaged in a crucial pursuit, the most vital of cultural activities.

▼▲▼

Like Martin – like all the great intellectual editors – Miller pursued the more or less self-conscious goal of publishing a Review that no self-respecting intellectual could afford to be without. But what, as the twentieth century drew to a close, constituted a self-respecting intellectual? The existence of that famous figure, the informed general reader – to whom the 'higher journalism' had long been principally addressed – seemed increasingly chimerical. The headlong pace of scientific and technological progress, the endless expansion of the media, the mushrooming growth of popular culture – all this posed a welter of problems for a Review editor wedded to the old formula of politics and letters. How often did the *London Review of Books* embrace material likely to interest the scientifically-minded? What did it have to say to the teeming devotees of film, television and the music industry, or to the swelling numbers of 'computer nerds' and 'net surfers'? Rather more than in earlier times, the kind of Review which purports to purvey a common intellectual culture is nowadays liable to seem like nothing other than one specialised taste among many.

It is of course well to remember that, in one way or another, talk of Reviews and reviewing no longer being what they were is a hoary old theme. Writing in the January 2002 centenary issue of the *Times Literary Supplement*, the cultural historian, Stefan Collini, brought a salutary scepticism to the discussion of such claims. Among other things, 'The Golden Age That Never Was' suggested that behind present-day lamentation for the great Reviews of the past lies frustrated paternalism, a 'wish to belong to a dominant intellectual élite whose tastes could hold sway'. But notwithstanding his scholarly scepticism, his propensity to cry 'Plus ça change, plus c'est la même chose', Collini was bound to to acknowledge that Reviews now occupy a diminished place in a public culture which is altogether more diverse than it used to be.

What Miller, in spite of everything, may be said to have demonstrated during the 1980s, is that the 'higher journalism' is a field where old-fashioned intellectual fervour plus editorial flair and purposefulness can still pay dividends. By the time of its tenth anniversary, in 1989, the *London Review of Books* was a familiar piece of cultural furniture, a British journal of international standing whose contributors added up to a cornucopia of contemporary literary and intellectual talent. They included many old associates of Miller's, among them Frank Kermode, Ian Hamilton, John Bayley, Christopher Ricks, Neal Ascherson, Peter Jenkins, Hans Keller, D.A.N. Jones, Dan Jacobson and Donald Davie. They also embraced many new literary luminaries, such as the novelists Martin Amis, Julian Barnes, Angela Carter and Salman Rushdie, the politico-cultural commentator, Christopher Hitchens, the historians, Linda Colley and David Cannadine, the critic and cultural commentator, Edward Said, the poet and disputatious media pundit, Tom Paulin, and notable literary academics like John Sutherland and Marilyn Butler. Nor were politicians entirely absent from the *London Review*'s ranks. In 1987, a rising but then little-known Labour MP contributed a Diary piece to the paper predicting the forthcoming 'failure of the market' and projecting the emergence of a new-style Labour Party which nevertheless remained true to its founding socialist principles. His name was Tony Blair. However, the connection between the world of politics and the world of intellectual Reviews had become increasingly tenuous, and of the British political class, Miller contemptuously observed: 'They no longer write. They no longer think.'

Yet even as the *London Review* evolved into an established concern, Miller's relationship with the paper was becoming impossible to sustain. In October 1992, two years after Margaret Thatcher fell from power, Miller fell from power too. At the time, he was in the throes of preparing a commissioned article for the *Guardian* on the conduct of Britain's tabloid press, then in the midst of an orgy of scandal-mongering and personality-assassination. Headlined the 'Age of Spite' and accompanied by a photograph of the author looking wrathful, Miller's piece accused tabloid editors of no longer having any purpose in life save the commercial exploitation of ill-will. But for all the cogency of his case, this high-minded scourge of low-minded journalism had other reasons for being preoccupied with ill-will, caught up as he was in a professional partnership with his old colleague and protégée, Mary-Kay Wilmers, that had turned sour. Fearing – groundlessly, as it proved – that he himself was about to become an object of media tittle-tattle, Miller closed his *Guardian* polemic with the announcement that he was leaving the paper that he had edited for the previous thirteen years.

His distinguished career as an intellectual editor appeared to be over. And it was.

"THE OVER-ALL PICTURE"

SPECTATOR

FRIDAY, JULY 3, 1942

CONTENTS

UNCONVINCING ASSURANCES

Church and State in Germany

The Listener

Thursday 4 May 1972 Volume 87 No 2249 9p

'Everyman' rebuked. Mary-Kay Wilmers: Everymum 573, 580
Roy Bradford: Ulster. Desmond O'Malley: the IRA 575, 592
Cosmology Now: Hermann Bondi's model of the universe 581
Marxism Now: Hampshire, Kolakowski, Charles Taylor 583
Frank Kermode: the worship of the good Lord Goodman 591

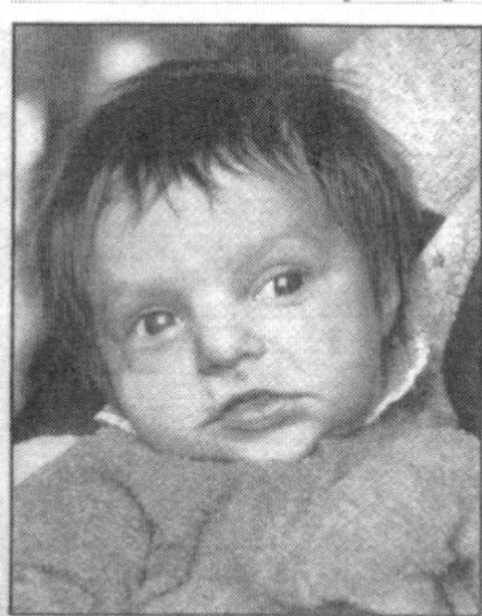

John Carey on Radio 4's 'Long March of Everyman'

RANDOLPH QUIRK: NEWSPEAK
London Review
OF BOOKS
VOLUME 6 NUMBER 3 16 FEBRUARY TO 29 FEBRUARY 1984 70P
EDWARD SAID:
MIDDLE EASTSPEAK

Postscript

Interviewed not long before his untimely death in 2001, Miller's co-conspirator, Ian Hamilton, looked back in wonder at the high seriousness of the 1950s, a time when bookish Britons like himself were espousing the gospel according to F.R. Leavis, the belief that the advance of American-style mass culture and consumerism boded ill for the life of the mind. 'Join the resistance now,' was the Leavisite cry. 'Your civilisation needs you.'

It was as a reconstructed Leavisite concerned for the integrity of British intellectual life that Miller edited the *London Review of Books*. But the march of events was scarcely favourable to this critical *Kulturkampf*. For some years now, the triumph in Britain of the philo-American, privatising ideology of Margaret Thatcher's Tory Party has been an accomplished fact. The upshot, among other things, is a market-driven literary culture stripped of its historic autonomy and progressively less hospitable to writing that fails to chime with the imperatives of mass merchandising. It is not necessarily that challenging books are being robbed of review space – of which Britain, with its swollen weekend broadsheets, is far from short (even if much of that space is nowadays swallowed up by that suspect feature, the celebrity interview). The problem is that such books have an increasingly hard job to get published in the first place.

Lamenting, amid much else, the absorption into conglomerate ownership of London's formerly many-sided publishing scene, the New York publisher, André Schiffrin, argues in *The Business of Books* (2000) that the prevailing market mania has been accompanied by what is tantamount to literary censorship. The thrust of Schiffrin's important polemic is that unyielding corporate insistence on the commercial viability of every single published title is making for a world where books in general are scarcely more than bland adjuncts of the mass media. Already, Schiffrin believes, control of the circulation of ideas is 'stricter than anyone would have thought possible in a free society.' It especially dismays him to think that the emasculated publishing culture of the present time is the only one that younger people have known; for them, it is perfectly normal.

That, despite all this, and without compromising its highbrow credentials, the *London Review of Books* has grown in circulation since Miller parted company with it – rising from 15,000 to a reported figure of nearly 39,000 – constitutes a remarkable publishing phenomenon. Its success, however, has possibly sprung rather less from setting its face against the market economy and US cultural hegemony than from entering into a canny rapprochement with them. Giving up as a lost cause Miller's resolute defence of the quondam British public service ethic, and relying more on private subscriptions than direct sales, Mary-Kay Wilmers, the *London Review*'s editor for the past ten years, has fashioned a paper – or perhaps it would be more accurate to say 'product' – with an ethos that is more mid-Atlantic than British (and which certainly contrasts sharply with that of the *Times Literary Supplement*, a publication stamped indelibly, for all its attention to the American scene, with the official imprimatur of the British establishment). Her efforts seem designed to appeal to an Anglo-American 'niche market' of leftist intellectuals with a taste for expansive articles; prominent among her contributors are such pre-eminently Anglo-American figures as James Wood, Michael Wood and Christopher Hitchens, British critics resident in the United States whose by-lines are much in evidence on both sides of the Atlantic. Of a piece with this pitch has been the paper's tendency in recent years to appear *au dessus de la mêlée,* with its very covers (decorative water colours in place of the topical photographs favoured during the 1980s) suggesting detachment. Detachment – not say say complacency – seems implicit, too, in the *London Review*'s promotional profile of itself as an 'oasis of reason in a difficult world'.

Not that the paper was guilty of a non-committal response to the events of September 11th, 2001. By publishing, in the wake of those events, frank criticism of US geo-political attitudes, the *London Review* became embroiled in an intellectual furore of extraordinary virulence and found itself irreconcilably at odds with a section of its American readers. A number of them hastened to cancel their subscriptions; one even threatened to visit the Review's office and 'shove' the 'loony leftist faces' of its staff into 'some dog shit'. The episode was to earn the paper what was almost certainly an unprecented degree of publicity.

It may be that the future of intellectual journalism lies in niche marketing – together with the exploitation of new tools of communication. In a period when society has become at once globalised and privatised, much mental activity is even now being sustained by the Internet, by more or less specialised Websites. The latest twist in the career of the London reviewer-cum-media personality, Clive James, is perhaps worth considering in this connection. Increasingly impatient with the mass marketing dictates that have come to govern mainstream broadcasting, James has been quick to sense the Internet's possibilities for giving expression to the free play of intelligence. In the high-tech seclusion of his London home, he has set up as a dot.com symposiast, orchestrating low-cost, on-line discussions with writers and intellectuals – discussions which, once filmed, can in principle be 'accessed' in any place at any time. Many newspapers and periodicals are likewise now on-line, of course, the *London Review of Books* among them. It could seem that the 'democratic intellect' was never so well catered for, with talk, images and print available in potentially enriching abundance from the same piece of computerised domestic technology.

James's worry is that in practice the niche marketing of culture will turn out to be a recipe for highbrows addressing fellow highbrows. As a media man, he is nostalgic for the days before populist communications moguls like Rupert Murdoch assumed their present overwhelming ascendancy – for the long period following World War Two when cultural broadcasters were free to address large audiences in elevated terms, and when those audiences were routinely confronted by unfamiliar subjects and worldviews, with sometimes life-enhancing results. Ready to allow that Murdoch is 'half right' to regard the old public service approach to propagating culture as patronising, he has nonetheless come to the conclusion that he prefers the 'other half' – the one, that is, which attaches virtue to the business of widening people's intellectual horizons. Inside James the showman, a *philosophe* dedicated to the educative mission of the 'higher journalism' was always struggling to break out.

So much has changed in the thirty years since this inordinately versatile Australian wordsmith was writing for Miller's *Listener*, thrilled to be in a position to style himself 'the metropolitan critic'. Born in 1939, he belonged to what was probably the last colonial generation capable of thinking of London as the centre of the intellectual universe, and of experiencing coming to Britain as a journey towards the light. As an aspirant man of letters, he may well have been predisposed to believe that the British capital's long-nurtured periodical press was just what it traditionally purported to be – the stuff of civilisation – and that those in charge of it were persons of exalted stature. Certainly, he was to hold in the highest esteem both Miller and Hamilton, the two Review editors with whom he had most to do during his rise to fame; to this day, he is prone to speak of them as leading luminaries of their age, great civilising influences. What distinguished these metropolitan literati in James's eyes was the fact that they were accomplished writers in their own right, with more qualifications for their work than were strictly necessary. With characteristic rhetorical bravura, he likens them to the philosophers in Plato's *Republic*, who, out of a sense of civic duty, set aside their own endeavours in order to guide the efforts of others.

This, admittedly, is pious stuff. But I have little doubt myself that, for all their ambition and professional worldliness, loyalty to literature and the commonweal were indeed what actuated the editors in question. Miller and Hamilton were, after all, products of an historic moment in the middle of the twentieth century when Britain was renouncing its *laisser-faire* past and institutionalising the claims of community. Having done their bit as military national servicemen, they became, one might say, *literary* national servicemen. If British literary journalism is not what it was, it is arguably because the ardent, tutelary example set by James's old mentors – and once set by many others – is being set no longer. Still, what scope is there in a commercialised, privatised, atomised culture for public spirit, for old-style high-mindedness – literary or otherwise?

▼▲▼

His editing career over, Miller made no secret of how much he missed commissioning copy and brandishing his blue pencil. Being without a Review to edit, however, was not going to stop him from indulging his legislative instincts. Soaked in the literary form of the Protestant work ethic, he busied himself with criticism, undertaking much reviewing – and becoming practically acquainted with a circumstance of which beforehand he was perhaps but theoretically aware: that freelance reviewing in contemporary Britain is much like it was in eighteenth-century Grub Street, a woefully ill-rewarded activity. (See on this subject the rancorous introduction to her posthumous collection of literary pieces, *Pandora's Handbag* [2002], by the refreshingly undiplomatic Elizabeth Young, a latter-day Scotch reviewer whose finishing school was the Punk scene of the late 1970s.)

Miller also poured his energies into completing two volumes of memoirs. The first, *Rebecca's Vest* (1993), which evokes his

Edinburgh youth, was well received, but with the publication of the second, *Dark Horses* (1998), a detailed résumé of his journalistic career, the editor who had been known for his astringency was to find out what it feels like to be the biter bit. The *Times Literary Supplement*'s reviewer, David Sexton, portrayed him as a literary egomaniac who, for all his celebrated skills as an editor, had composed a turgid, ill-structured, more or less unreadable book. Sexton's excoriating critique was well calculated to make its victim smart, and smart Miller did.

Unable to let the matter lie, he published – in the American academic quarterly, *Raritan* – a meditation on 'Bad Reviews' in which he deliberated on the ethics of literary disparagement, animadverting as he did so on the extraordinary licence to abuse that has long been enjoyed by reviewers in Britain (and which, to be sure, is hardly paralleled in any other sphere of public life.) Nor did he fail to allude to his own ordeal at the hands of a reviewer who – as he felt – had reacted to *Dark Horses* rather as a sanitary inspector might to a public health hazard. Identifying him as an officious representative of the New Right, Miller described his assailant as a 'clever brute' who conformed to an old literary type: the critic who specialises in 'serial detraction'. It was perhaps surprising – given his taste for quirky observations – that he made no comment on the fact that 'sexton' used to be the popular term for 'gravedigger'. But then, Miller was declining to mention Sexton by name.

Missing from 'Bad Reviews' was much attempt to engage with Sexton's specific criticisms of *Dark Horses*. But the essay was less an exercise in self-vindication than a cry of 'Mea culpa,' an outpouring of contrition on the part of a retired editor who repented the part that he himself had played in promoting what Hans Keller had once labelled 'remunerated destructive disrespect'. Reviewing his own record, Miller confessed that he had been 'insufficiently sensitive to the pain of the reviewed', and concluded his remarks with the extraordinary assertion that British reviewing, in contrast to American, had always been, 'to the point of strangeness, excessively hostile'. The irony was that even as he condemned excessive critical severity, Miller was being his usual hypercritical self. Yet if judgemental as ever, the season when he loomed large as a high-minded public arbiter, an intellectual *Pontifex Maximus*, was increasingly remote. His polymathic brother-in-law and coincidental namesake, Jonathan Miller, thought of him as an 'old snow leopard', a figure of 'frosted nobility' amid the cultural dross and down-market vulgarity of post-Thatcherite Britain.

One day, while writing these pages, I bearded the old snow leopard and quizzed him about the state of things. Our talk took in the commodity-fetishising life-style magazines which have become such a gaudy feature of present-day news-stands. It seemed that an English literature graduate known to him was cutting a dash in this priapic new world – the sort of educated young man who might once have dreamed of writing for the *New Statesman*. Miller, however, was in no mood to luxuriate in cultural pessimism. It was, he exclaimed, only too easy for an 'elderly party' like himself – somebody whose bones were aching and who could barely get out of his chair – to start discerning signs of decline and decay everywhere, and he mocked me for being a 'catastrophist'. He also warned me to mind that I did not turn into that facile figure, the *laudator temporis acti*, the praiser of the past.

Keeping people on their toes had been the business of Karl Miller's existence, and he was not finished yet.

N.B.
Stoke Newington, London,
June, 2002

Select Bibliography

1. Jeffrey and *The Edinburgh Review*

Bagehot, Walter, *Estimates of Some Englishmen and Scotsmen*, Chapman & Hall, London, 1858.

Bell, Alan, *Sydney Smith: A Biography*, Oxford University Press, Oxford, 1980.

Berry, Neil, 'The *Edinburgh Review* under Jeffrey', London University Ph.D thesis, 1985.

Burrow, J., S. Collini, D. Winch, eds., *That Noble Science of Politics*, Cambridge University Press, Cambridge, 1983.

Butler, Marilyn, *Romantics, Rebels and Reactionaries*, Oxford University Press, Oxford, 1981.

Carlyle, Thomas, *Reminiscences*, edited by E.E. Norton, Macmillan, London, 1887.

Clive, John, '*The Edinburgh Review*: The Life and Death of a periodical', in *Essays in the History of Publishing*, edited by A. Briggs, Longman, London, 1974.

Clive, John, *Scotch Reviewers: The Edinburgh Review 1802-1815*, Faber & Faber, London, 1957.

Cockburn, Henry, *Life of Lord Jeffrey, with a Selection of His Correspondence*, Adam & Charles Black, Edinburgh, 1852.

Cockburn, Henry, *Memorials of His Time*, new edition, with an introduction by Henry A. Cockburn, Foulis, Edinburgh, 1909.

Grierson, Sir Herbert, *Letters of Sir Walter Scott*, 12 Volumes, Constable, London, 1932-1937.

Howe, P.P., *The Life of William Hazlitt*, Hamish Hamilton, London, 1947 (revised edition).

Jeffrey, Francis, *Contributions*, 4 volumes, Longman, London, 1844.

Lockhart, J.G., *Peter's Letters to His Kinsfolk*, Blackwood, Edinburgh, 1819.

Miller, Karl, *Cockburn's Millennium*, Duckworth, London, 1975.

Mitchell, Leslie, *Holland House*, Duckworth, London, 1980.

Roper, Derek, *Reviewing Before the Edinburgh*, Methuen, London, 1978.

Stephen, Leslie, *Hours in a Library* (3rd Series), Smith, Elder & Co., London, 1879.

Stuart, Robert, *Henry Brougham: His Public Career 1778-1868*, The Bodley Head, London, 1985.

2. John Morley

Churchill, Winston, S., *Great Contemporaries*, Thomas Butterworth, London, 1937.

Everett, Edwin M., *The Party of Humanity: The Fortnightly Review & Its Contributors 1865-1874*, University of North Carolina Press, Chapel Hill/Oxford University Press, Oxford, 1939.

Gardiner, A.G., *Prophets, Priests and Kings*, Alston Rivers, London, 1908.

Hamer, D.A., *John Morley*, Oxford, 1968.

Hirst, F.W., *Early Life & Letters of John Morley*, Macmillan, London, 1927.

Howe, Mar DeWolfe, ed., *Holmes-Laski Letters: The Correspondence of Mr Justice Holmes and Harold J. Laski*, Geoffrey Cumberedge, London/Oxford University Press, Oxford, 1953.

Jones, Kennedy, *Fleet Street and Downing Street*, Hutchinson, London, 1920.

Koss, Stephen, *John Morley at the India Office*, Yale University Press, New Haven, 1969.

Koss, Stephen, *The Rise & Fall of the Political Press in Britain*, Hamish Hamilton, London, 1981.

Morgan, J.H., *John Morley: An Appreciation and Some Reminiscences*, John Murray, London, 1924.

Morley, John, *Diderot and the Encyclopaedists*, Chapman & Hall, London, 1878.

– *Critical Miscellanies*, 3 volumes, Macmillan, London, 1886.

– *Studies in Literature*, Macmillan, London, 1890.

– *Recollections*, 2 volumes, Macmillan, London, 1917.

Stead, W.T., 'Character Sketch of John Morley', *Review of Reviews*, 2, November 1890: 424-437.

3. W.T. Stead

Arnold, Matthew, 'Up to Easter', in *The Nineteenth Century*, 21, May 1887: 638-639.

Eckley, Grace, ed., *NewsStead: A Journal of History and Literature*, Golden, Colorado, 1992-.

Gardiner, A.G., 'Book of the Month' [a review of Estelle Stead's *My Father*], in *Review of Reviews*, 48, October 1913: 305-307.

Harper, Edith, *Stead The Man*, W. Rider & Son, London, 1914.

Jones, Victor, Pierce, Saint or Sensationalist? *The Story of W.T. Stead*, Gooday Publishers, East Wittering, West Sussex, 1988.

Kent, William, *John Burns: Labour's Lost leader: A Biography*, Williams & Norgate, London, 1953.

Kingsmill, Hugh, *After Puritanism*, Duckworth, London, 1929.

Massingham, H.W., *HWM: A Selection from His Writings*, edited by H.J. Massingham, Cape, London, 1925.

Robertson Scott, T.W., *Life and Death of a Newspaper*, Methuen, London, 1952.

Schults, Raymond, L., *Crusader in Babylon: W.T. Stead and the Pall Mall Gazette*, University of Nebraska Press, Lincoln, 1972.

Shannan, R.T., *Gladstone and the Bulgarian Question*, Nelson, London, 1963.

Stead, Estelle, *My Father*, Heinemann, London, 1913.

Stead, W.T., 'Government by Journalism', in *Contemporary Review*, 49, May 1886: 653-674.

Whyte, M.T., *Life of John Stead*, 2 volumes, Jonathan Cape, London, 1925.

4. James Knowles

'James Knowles: A Tribute from Some Friends', in *The Nineteenth Century*, 63, April 1908: 683-696.

'Our Fiftieth Anniversary', in *The Nineteenth Century*, 101, March 1927: 289-329.

Brown, A.W., *The Metaphysical Society: Victorian Minds in Crisis, 1869-1890*, Oxford University Press, Oxford, 1947.

Desmond, Adrian, *Huxley: From Devil's Disciple to Evolution's High*

Priest, Michael Joseph, London, 1994.
Goodwin, Michael, ed., *Nineteenth Century Opinion: An Anthology of Extracts from the First Fifty Volumes of* The Nineteenth Century, 1877-1901, Penguin, London, 1951.
Harrison, Frederic, *Autobiographic Memoirs*, 2 volumes, Macmillan, London, 1911.
Hutton, R.H., 'The Metaphysical Society: A Reminiscence', *The Nineteenth Century*, 18, August 1885: 177-196.
Marriott, Sir John, 'Our Father That Begat Us', *The Nineteenth Century*, 122, August 1937: 179-188.
Metcalf, Priscilla, *James Knowles: Victorian Editor and Architect*, Clarendon Press, Oxford, 1980.

5. Kingsley Martin and the *New Statesman*

Cole, Margaret, ed., *The Webbs and Their Work*, Frederick Miller, London, 1949.
Crossman, R.H.S., *The Charm of Politics*, Hamish Hamilton, London, 1958.
Hyams, Edward, *New Statesmanship: An Anthology Selected by Edward Hyams*, Longman, London, 1963.
– The *New Statesman: The History of the First 50 Years*, Longman, London, 1963.
Jones, Mervyn, ed., *Kingsley Martin: Portrait and Self-Portrait*, Barrie & Jenkins, London, 1969.
Kingsley Martin Papers: University of Sussex, The Library, Special Collections.
Leavis, F.R., *Scrutiny: A Retrospect*, Cambridge University Press, Cambridge, 1963.
MacKenzie, Norman, *The Diary of Beatrice Webb*, 4 volumes, Virago, London, 1982-1985.
Mairet, P., *A.R. Orage*, Dent, London, 1936.
Martin, Kingsley, *Critic's London Diary*, Secker & Warburg, London, 1960.
– *Editor*, Hutchinson, London, 1968.
– *Father Figures*, Hutchinson, London, 1966.
– *The Crown and the Establishment*, Hutchinson, London, 1962.

Muggeridge, Malcolm, *Chronicles of Wasted Time*, Part I, Collins, London, 1972.

Rolph, C.H., *Kingsley: The Life, Letters and Diaries of Kingsley Martin*, Gollancz, London, 1973.

Skidelsky, Robert, *John Maynard Keynes*, Volume 1: *Hopes Betrayed, 1883-1920*; Volume 2: *The Economist as Saviour, 1921-1937*; Volume 3: *Fighting for Britain, 1937-1946*, Macmillan, London, 1992, 1994, 2000.

Smith, Adrian, *The New Statesman: Portrait of a Political Weekly, 1913-31*, Frank Cass, London, 1996.

Spotts, Frederick, ed., *Letters of Leonard Woolf*, Weidenfeld, London, 1990.

6. *Encounter*

Coleman, Peter, *The Liberal Conspiracy: The Congress for Cultural Freedom and the Struggle for the Mind of Postwar Europe*, The Free Press, New York, 1989.

Crossman, R.H.S., ed., *The God That Failed: Six Studies in Communism*, Hamish Hamilton, London, 1950.

Epstein, Jason, 'The CIA and the Intellectuals', *New York Review of Books*, April 20th 1967.

Fiedler, Leslie, *The End of Innocence*, Beacon Press, Boston, 1955.

Galantière, Lewis, ed., *America and the Mind of Europe*, Hamish Hamilton, London, 1951.

Kermode, Frank, *Not Entitled: A Memoir*, Harper Collins, London, 1996.

Koestler, Arthur, *The Yogi and the Commissar*, Jonathan Cape, London, 1945.

– *The Trail of the Dinosaur*, Collins, London, 1955.

Kristol, Irving, *Neo-Conservatism: The Autobiography of an Idea: Selected Essays, 1949-55*, The Free Press, New York, 1995.

Leeming, David, *Stephen Spender: A Life in Modernism*, Duckworth, London, 1999.

O'Brien, Conor Cruise, *Writers and Politics*, Chatto & Windus, London, 1965.

Podhoretz, Norman, *Making It*, Jonathan Cape, London, 1968.

Saunders, Frances Stonor, *Who Paid the Piper? The CIA and the Cultural Cold War*, Granta, London, 1999.
Shils, Edward, 'Remembering the Congress for Cultural Freedom', *Encounter*, 75, September 1990: 53-65.
Spender, Stephen, Irving Kristol, Melvin Lasky, eds., *Encounters: An Anthology from the First Ten Years of* Encounter, with an Introduction by D.W. Brogan, Weidenfeld, London, 1963.
Spender, Stephen, *Journals*, edited by John Goldsmith, Faber & Faber, London, 1985.
Worsthorne, Peregrine, *Tricks of Memory*, Weidenfeld, London, 1993.
Wreszin, Michael, *A Rebel in Defence of Tradition: The Life and Politics of Dwight Macdonald*, Basic Books, New York, 1994.

7. Karl Miller

Annan, Noel, *Our Age*, Weidenfeld, London, 1990.
Calder, Angus, *Revolving Culture: Notes from the Scottish Republic*, I.B. Tauris, London/New York, 1994.
Davie, Donald, *Purity of Diction in English Verse*, Chatto, London, 1952.
Gill, Roma, ed., *William Empson: The Man and His Work*, Routledge and Kegan Paul, London, 1974.
James, Clive, *Even As We Speak*, Picador, London, 2001.
Johnson, B.S., *All Bull*, Allison & Busby, London, 1973.
Lambert, R.S., *Ariel and All His Quality: An Impression of the BBC from Within*, Gollancz, London, 1940.
McKillop, Ian, *F.R. Leavis: A Life in Criticism*, Allen Lane, London, 1995.
Miller, Karl, ed., *Writing in England Today: The Last 15 Years*, Penguin, London, 1968.
– ed., *Memoirs of a Modern Scotland*, Faber & Faber, London, London, 1970.
– ed., *A Listener Anthology*, August 1967-June 1970, BBC, London, 1970.
– ed., *A Second Listener Anthology*, June 1970-May 1972, BBC, London, 1973.
– *Cockburn's Millennium*, Duckworth, London, 1975.

– ed., *London Review of Books Anthology 1*, Junction Books, London, 1981.
– ed., *London Review of Books Anthology 2*, Junction Books, London, 1982.
– ed., *London Reviews*, Chatto and Windus, London, 1985.
– *Doubles*, Oxford University Press, Oxford, 1985.
– *Authors*, Oxford University Press, Oxford, 1989.
– *Rebecca's Vest*, Hamish Hamilton, London, 1993.
– *Dark Horses: An Experience of Literary Journalism*, Picador, London, 1998.
– 'Bad Reviews', *Raritan,* XVIII: 3, Winter 1999: 38-48.

8. General

Brogan, D.W., 'The Intellectual Review', *Encounter*, XXI, 5, November 1963: 7-15; reprinted as the introduction to *Encounters* (op. cit.).

Collini, Stefan, 'The Golden Age That Never Was', *Times Literary Supplement*, 18 January 2002: 17-19.

Curtis, Anthony, *Lit. Ed.*, Carcanet Press, Manchester, 1998.

Graham, W.S., *English Literary Periodicals*, Thomas Nelson & Son, New York, 1930.

Gross, John, *The Rise and Fall of the Man of Letters*, Weidenfeld & Nicolson, London, 1969.

Treglown, J., and B. Bennett., eds., *Grub Street and the Ivory Tower: Literary Journalism and Literary Scholarship from Fielding to the Internet*, Clarendon Press, Oxford, 1998.

Index

Index

Index

Index

Index

Other Titles from Waywiser

Very far North
poems by
Timothy Murphy

Advent
poems by
Daniel Rifenburgh

New & Selected Poems
by
Al Alvarez

One Another
a sonnet sequence by
Peter Dale

Forthcoming

The Darkness and the Light
poems by
Anthony Hecht

The Art of the Lathe
poems by
B.H. Fairchild

One Unblinking Eye
poems by
Norman Williams

The Size of Happiness
poems by
Deborah Warren

Jigsaw
poems by
Clive Watkins